Modernism on File

Modernism on File

Writers, Artists, and the FBI, 1920–1950

Edited by

Claire A. Culleton and Karen Leick

palgrave
macmillan

MODERNISM ON FILE

First published in 2008 by
PALGRAVE MACMILLAN™
175 Fifth Avenue, New York, N.Y. 10010 and
Houndmills, Basingstoke, Hampshire, England RG21 6XS
Companies and representatives throughout the world.

PALGRAVE MACMILLAN is the global academic imprint of the Palgrave Macmillan division of St. Martin's Press, LLC and of Palgrave Macmillan Ltd. Macmillan® is a registered trademark in the United States, United Kingdom and other countries. Palgrave is a registered trademark in the European Union and other countries.

ISBN-13: 978–0–230–60135–2
ISBN-10: 0–230–60135–9

Library of Congress Cataloging-in-Publication Data

Modernism on file : writers, artists, and the FBI, 1920–1950 / edited by Claire A. Culleton and Karen Leick.
p. cm.
Includes bibliographical references.
ISBN 0–230–60135–9
1. American literature—20th century—History and criticism. 2. Politics and literature—United States—History—20th century. 3. Literature and state—United States—History—20th century. 4. Art and state—United States—History—20th century. 5. United States. Federal Bureau of Investigation—History—20th century. 6. Freedom of speech—United States—History—20th century. 7. Anti-communist movements—United States—History—20th century. 8. Modernism (Literature)—United States. 9. Modernism (Art)—United States. I. Culleton, Claire A. II. Leick, Karen.

PS228.P6M57 2008
810.9′112—dc22 2007027102

A catalogue record for this book is available from the British Library.

Design by Newgen Imaging Systems (P) Ltd., Chennai, India.

First edition: February 2008

10 9 8 7 6 5 4 3 2 1

Printed in the United States of America.

CONTENTS

Part II The FBI and the Arts

Acknowledgments

The editors wish to acknowledge generous support from the Kent State University Research Council and The Ohio State University—Lima Research and Special Projects Committee. Kent State undergraduates Derek Bailey, Alison Guerin, Douglas Hite, Emily Dale Mitchell, Kurt Voss-Hoynes, and Anastasa Williams apprenticed on this project and worked diligently as proofreaders and indexers. Professor Culleton acknowledges their support and intellectual exuberance.

We are grateful for permission to quote from the following copyrighted materials: excerpts from *Redemption: The Life of Henry* Roth by Steven G. Kellman used by permission of W.W. Norton and Company, Inc.; a version of Christoper Faulkner's essay originally appeared in the *Canadian Journal of Communication*, vol. 26, nos. 2–3 (2001): 191–209, and is reprinted by permission; a version of Andrea Weiss's essay originally appeared in *GLQ: A Journal of Gay and Lesbian Studies* 7.3 (2001): 459–481, and is reprinted by permission; Alexander Stephan's essay originally appeared in *neue deutsche literature*, vol. 51, no. 549 (2003): 123–144, and is reprinted with the author's permission.

INTRODUCTION

SILENCE, ACQUIESCENCE, AND DREAD

CLAIRE A. CULLETON AND KAREN LEICK

INSTITUTIONAL SURVEILLANCE SEEMS COMMONPLACE TO AMERICANS IN AN age where everyone can be tracked via credit card purchases and E-Z-Pass registries, watched via satellite, and monitored by the National Security Agency (NSA) and its collaborative partners. In our post-9/11 world, where perfectly ordinary, everyday settings and events in the lives and activities of world citizens are cast with criminal suspicion, we are easily reminded of the authority wielded by agencies and institutions of power. As happens, measures and practices designed to protect citizens during national emergencies tend to inhibit the span of their freedom, reduce the richness of their opportunities, and limit the boundaries of their worlds as well as their imaginations. Such was the case for hundreds of thousands of people during J. Edgar Hoover's reign as director of the Federal Bureau of Investigation. As the 12 chapters in this book show, for nearly 50 years Hoover's investigative practices had considerable effect on the lives and creative activities of writers and artists working during his directorship, and as often as his efforts curtailed their work and artistic license, their counterefforts to stave off or circumvent government interventions shaped and affected the burgeoning modern arts movement consequently making it a self-conscious movement fed on and not starved by the twentieth-century federal gaze.

Analyzing, classifying, and scrutinizing the work and lives of modernist writers and artists has long been a preoccupation of scholars, and the debate over which characteristics make the work of a writer or artist authentically modernist shows no signs of waning, and has in fact "become something of an academic obsession" (Rainey xx). Hoover's obsession with modernism's leading figures caused him to expend considerable energy investigating the activities of some of the movement's most prominent modernists. Not interested in fine distinctions among the aesthetic choices of these artists, the FBI focused on an array of criteria: one's political views and activities, his or her engagement with the political culture of the day, and his or her standing as a leading figure poised to inspire significant changes in domestic and international thinking by their publications, lectures, readings, international travels, and celebrity status.

Still startling, the massive surveillance of private lives during J. Edgar Hoover's reign at the FBI clipped short the civil liberties of creative artists as well as other American citizens and immigrants in an effort to maintain the security of the nation; those who trusted the government to monitor only the lives of the most dangerous among these were disheartened to learn how wide a net Hoover cast during the modernist period, and the thousands and thousands of bureau files that chronicle particular aspects of modernist discourse still staggers the American imagination. Individuals who belonged to the Communist Party, participated in radical demonstrations, or criticized the U.S. government became targets of FBI investigations and surveillance. Incongruently, modernists who avoided political activism or whose politics obviously leaned to the right could arouse the suspicions of the FBI, as well. After a reference to T.S. Eliot appeared in a 1949 issue of the *Daily Worker*, the bureau opened a file on the expatriate, although he had famously defined himself two decades earlier as "an Anglo-Catholic in religion, a classicist in literature, and a royalist in politics" (Robins 424; Eliot 7). Equally absurd and indicative of the bureau's undiscerning shrimp net, American poet Marianne Moore came under suspicion in 1935 after the FBI received an unmarked envelope containing a list of communist writers that included Moore (Robins 435).

Like Eliot, the apolitical expatriate Gertrude Stein attracted bureau attention. Her tenuous association with *Partisan Review*, a publication already flagged by the FBI as "radical," garnered the bureau's suspicion. Though the name of the journal remains redacted in her file, it was likely Stein's response to the 1939 *Partisan Review* symposium, "The Situation in American Writing," that prompted the bureau to open her file, even though her responses to the interviewer's questions would have allayed bureau fears about her loyalty: when asked "How would you describe the political tendency of American writing as a whole since 1930?" Stein replied, "Writers only think that they are interested in politics, they are not really it gives them a chance to talk and writers like to talk but really no real writer is really interested in politics" (40–41). Sometimes offhand remarks made by friends or acquaintances to bureau Special Agents in Charge (SAC) came to fuel the investigations and to steer their conclusions. For example, when one subject whose name is redacted in Stein's file (probably Francis Rose's friend, Carley Mills) commented to an agent in 1945 that Stein "had resided in Europe so many years, her sympathies were not very strongly with America else she would not have stayed abroad so long" and that "he considered her as not having been strongly in favor of any political theory, although he knew her to be very anti-Roosevelt," pages were swiftly added to the file.

No wonder the acceleration: J. Edgar Hoover was nicknamed "Speed" as a boy, after the swiftness with which he would deliver groceries. Raised in a family of mapmakers, something William Beverly proposes had a "suggestive influence upon the man and administrator he would become" (Beverly 30), Hoover spent his career mapping out the contours of degenerative ideologies such as anti-Americanism and Communism, and locating communities of anarchy and sedition, to name a few. After working from 1913 to mid-1917 in the Library of Congress, Hoover began his career with the Justice Department working in the Aliens Registration office, where he developed knowledge of and cultivated information about political radicalism that would prove useful to him in the future (Jeffreys 55). "Hoover's first months in the Justice Department put him in the middle of . . . hysteria over traitors, spies, and saboteurs," Richard Gid Powers notes (47). Later that year, Hoover would be responsible for organizing the haphazard files of the Justice Department, and would organize them obsessively, "out of a great personal and political need to control the flow of information in America" (Robins 33). Though a functionary in the Aliens Registrations office, Hoover's reputation as a Red-baiter matured when at the height of the Red Scare in 1919, he successfully deported hundreds of alien radicals and foreign-born agitators following November and December raids. The hysterical search for anarchists and radicals that would eventually be called the Red Scare began in mid-1919, when, as Christopher Finan explains,

> eight bombs exploded outside the homes of prominent men, including the mayor of Cleveland and judges in New York City, Boston, and Pittsburgh. . . . The June bombings convinced many that the United States must be ruthless if it was going to meet the threat of Communist revolution. A Montana senator introduced a bill making it a crime to advocate violent revolution. [Attorney General A. Mitchell] Palmer appointed a new chief of the Justice Department's Bureau of Investigation to take charge of the search for the bombers and created a new assistant attorney general to help. Congress gave the federal Red hunters $500 million to speed their work. (127)

Palmer's home targeted, he encouraged Hoover and the bureau to open and maintain files on subversives and anarchists likely responsible for planning and carrying out the multiple explosions. As a result, Sanford Ungar reports in *FBI*, "during its first three and a half months in existence, the GID [General Intelligence Division] compiled personal histories of some sixty thousand individuals thought to be radicals; before long the special indices grew to include more than two hundred thousand names" (43).

With such efficiency, it was not long before the United States relied on the Bureau to monitor group and civilian activity. In August, 1936, for example, President Franklin D. Roosevelt asked for Hoover's help in determining the role of Communist and Fascist organizations in the United States. As a result, Hoover sent one of his personal and confidential memos to SACs on September 5, which read, "The Bureau desires to obtain from all possible sources information concerning subversive activities being conducted in the United States by Communists, Fascists, and representatives or advocates of other organizations or groups advocating the overthrow or replacement of the Government of the United States by illegal methods" (Whitehead 158–59). Not many years later, during World War II, Hoover expanded these criteria to include "persons of German, Italian, and Communist sympathies," whether citizens or alien residents, and others whose "interest may be directed primarily to the interest of some other nation than the United States." Hoover listed suspicious individuals on the Custodial Detention index, and as Athan G. Theoharis observes, "The controlling criteria for these listings was not conduct but *anticipated* conduct" (20).

Though Hoover worked hard to maintain the image of his bureau as a tightly run organization, and often gained publicity and popular notoriety from its dissemination,[1] evidence uncovered in the FBI files of figures the 12 authors discuss in this book demonstrate that the "fact"-finding missions of Hoover's agents yielded files that were fraught with inconsistency, rampant with misinformation, and burgeoning with ignorance. These files contain not only errors but reports that contradict one another. Despite these truculent contradictions, despite what evidence the files belie, none of the opposing reports is investigated further, no misrepresentations get clarified, and no piece of evidence cancels out another piece. In effect, bureau files morph over the years into hodgepodge and ragbag assortments of unqualified and often unreliable information. Reading and studying these archival files astonishes: they appear not to have been carefully read through or prudently analyzed from one report to the next (except when one writer parrots "facts" from earlier SAC reports); and the multiple narratives in each file are rarely organized into a coherent bureau "take" on an individual. In fact, that a subject *had* a file seemed reason enough to continue it. Jeffrey Meyers observes that the files are often "unintentionally funny" (17), but because pieces of information could be pulled out of files and used as evidence against individuals under bureau suspicion, the inconsistencies and inaccuracies canalized the very real dangers associated with being under bureau investigation.

MODERNISM AND THE FBI

Until recently, the words "modernism" and "modernist" classified literary and artistic works created between 1900 and 1945, and were terms that came to characterize creative art produced in that period. Today, these terms define a variety of cultural products and artistic manifestations that are not necessarily bound to the first half of the twentieth century but connected by a set of roughly shared aesthetics. We now think of modernism not so much as one movement confined to the first half of the twentieth century but as a bunch of literary movements inspired by and in reaction to a series of events occurring throughout the twentieth century. (Some critics and scholars even prefer the term modernism*s*, since it captures the multiplicity of the movement.) Modernism was a literary movement full of contradictions and diversities. "Make it new," the dictum of American writer Ezra Pound whose FBI file numbers 1,512 pages, resounded throughout the movement as writers and other artists tried to formulate new kinds of responses to industrialization, to changes in technology, to world wars, to depersonalization, alienation, machination, popular culture, and to the new theories of psychoanalysis and mass human behavior, such as those developed by Freud. Modernism was a movement known for (among other things) its experimentation with forms, styles, and voices; its efforts to articulate crises of authority, anxiety, and frustration with mass culture; its exploration of sexuality, eroticism, and the libidinal currents that give shape to the subjects and styles of the movement; its frank examination of sexual energies and its openness to treat as literary subjects "errant" or "deviant" sexualities; and its investigations into identity, subjectivity, and psychology. Also characterized by the apparent willingness of writers and artists to confront and challenge the structures of capitalism and to enter into political debate about its failures and its degeneracy, modernism flourished, for example, when writers and artists aligned themselves with the Communist Party USA (CPUSA), awake and well aware of the evolution of communist aesthetic policies.

American author Erskine Caldwell, for example, long hounded by Hoover and other public notables engaged in social purity campaigns focused on American literature, noted that "by 1931, almost every writer he had admired in the 'little magazines' in the late twenties was moving leftward. Many were dedicated Communists" (Miller 155). Granville Hicks explained the movement in similar terms when interviewed in July 1934 by *International Literature*; the article features prominently in Hicks's FBI file. When asked what problems interested him the most at this time, Hicks replied:

> At present, the most significant development in the United States, it seems to me, is the beginning of an alignment of intellectuals on a more or less consciously Fascist basis. Three or four years ago the most important tendency

> was that toward Communism. Today many of the intellectuals who were then only slightly interested in Communism have become strong supporters; others have been unable to affiliate themselves in practice with the revolutionary movement, but remain sympathetic. These writers, together with the younger men who are growing up in the revolutionary movement, represent a strong and important literary tendency. But, on the other hand, a certain number of other writers, who three years ago seemed too bewildered to take any stand, are now openly anti-Communist and a few of them are supporting avowedly Fascist movements. I think this movement toward Fascism is bound to continue because it is becoming increasingly difficult for any intellectuals to remain neutral and many intellectuals are, for one reason or another, unable to accept Communism. This situation obviously offers a challenge, both of a literary and of a political nature, to those writers who are on the revolutionary side. (Hicks FBI File, August 14, 1945)

Little magazines, magazines, and political newspapers such as the *Masses* and *Partisan Review* were largely responsible for this intellectual shift. Irving Howe explained:

> For a brief time, roughly between 1912 and 1918, *The Masses* became the rallying center—and sometimes also a combination of circus, nursery, and boxing ring—for almost everything that was then alive and irreverent in American culture. . . . *Partisan Review*, published in the late thirties, brought together anti-Stalinist Marxism and avant-garde culture with a boldness that for a time made it a significant innovating force. . . . Both *The Masses* and the *Partisan Review* did, however, succeed in accomplishing what every magazine expounding a point of view hopes to accomplish: they affected the intellectual temper of their day. (5–6)

By the end of the 1920s, then, as members of the popular John Reed Clubs were brandishing the CPUSA slogan "Art is a Class Weapon," and already likening the potency of journalism and literature to "paper bullets," Hoover was growing uneasy about the changing relationship between art and politics, and worked to beleaguer writers, artists, and intellectual leaders during his tenure as director of the bureau, frustrating, as best he could, their insurgent cultural practices with a special watchdog division. While Hoover and his henchmen knew little, if anything, about art or literature per se, because so much of it (it seemed) had begun to transgress the boundaries between art and obscenity, or art and political insurgency, it was identified as a legitimate area of exploration for the bureau.

Modern artists such as Picasso, Lautrec, Degas, and writers such as Joyce, Rhys, Steinbeck, Wright, Brecht, Hughes, and Porter insisted on introducing new types and classes of characters into their works—poor characters, for example, with equally impoverished personalities. These were not the strong moral heroes of previous works but were weak, insane, infirm, alcoholic, abusive, self-abusive, and diabolical. Modernists captured these traits in their subjects, offering them up as heroes because of their ability to survive the nightmares of the modern condition. Their efforts to "make it new" led writers to experiment with narrative forms, narrative styles, narrators, and narrative arrangements. To this end, narratives of modern literature seemed increasingly afflicted by the highly personal and largely introspective musings of modern characters who contemplated with alarming frequency the privacies of the toilet, the bedroom, and the body. In this sense, then, unbridled streams of consciousness and unfettered interior monologues came to typify modern storytelling. To an institution such as the FBI, a growing and deliberately unrestrained movement in the arts seemed threatening indeed. The popular success among the masses of the modernist project called attention to its own depravity, detractors agreed, and Hoover and his G-Men worked to curb its appeal and clip its rise.

The period was shaped as much by novels and plays, by poems and autobiographies, cultural documents, and aesthetic manifestoes as it was by controversial events such as the 1913 Armory Show in New York City, or the Paterson Pageant of that same year, by international suffrage rallies, by anti-lynching marches and crusades, by free-speech and obscenity trials, by courtroom high dramas, by the rise in the number of class disputes and general workers' strikes, by discoveries about the human mind and its motivation, by world wars, revolutions, and international causes célèbre. Also shaping the period was the cold climate Hoover's bureau created for activists involved in writing and/or inciting these twentieth-century commotions.

Hounded for years by Hoover and Special Agents in his bureau, many of the writers and artists associated with modernism eventually were bullied into silence, acquiescence, and dread. Recent books by scholars such as Mike Keen, David Price, Claire Culleton, Herbert Mitgang, and Natalie Robins who have worked with declassified Freedom of Information Act (FOIA) documents, effectively demonstrate that the FBI rigorously pursued American intellectuals, anthropologists, sociologists, writers, publishers, and editors at Hoover's insistence, and that the intensity of the bureau's persistent harassment not only affected the development of the disciplines but constrained the intensity and limited the participation of its most essential and creative figures. We are left only to imagine how intellectuals under surveillance and artists under scrutiny might have allowed their disciplines and movements to advance without regular interference and constant meddling from the bureau, that brute force of institutional chauvinism.

The 12 chapters included in this collection analyze the ways writers and artists working between the years of 1920–1950 were affected by J. Edgar Hoover's repressive policies, and seek to articulate the consequences, often dangerous, of governmental surveillance and of law enforcement strategies founded on the politics and extremities of fear. FBI files released to scholars under the FOIA reveal that the bureau aggressively targeted individuals whose political views threatened the strictly defined limits of postwar "Americanism," for example, and that under Hoover's 50-year directorship, the bureau grew to control, manipulate, and shape American experience. The chapters also show that the harassment compromised the militancy of modernism.

MODERN WRITERS UNDER ATTACK: MODERN ARTISTS UNDER SIEGE

Modernist writers and artists who aligned themselves with issues affecting workers, or whose writing championed the cause of labor, sentimentalized the working class, highlighted their invisibility and growing powerlessness, or issued calls for solidarity and/or action were yoked together in bureau files with other radicals who advocated, just as dangerously, for social change in other aspects of American life. Central to their commitment was their anti-war stance, and many modernist writers and artists protested America's growing involvement in World War I. For these and other such "disloyalties," Hoover placed many of the twentieth century's most original and imposing writers and artists in Group A on the bureau's Custodial Detention list, a list of people to arrest first in the event of a national emergency; some of them even made it onto the bureau's infamous Public Enemy list. At a time when modernist projects in literature and in art were not only poised to flourish and mature, but were about to penetrate the thick intellectual stuporous haze of American nationalism, the bureau made prosecuting artists and writers one of its priorities, and worked to bully artists and limit the dissemination of their work. For many modern writers and artists, this meant they had to shop their creative projects around more, and suffer frequent, inexplicable rejections. One writer tells of his book manuscript being returned from several different publishers, rejected but still unopened, after an ideological run-in with the bureau.

One might well wonder what it was that the bureau found so threatening about modern literature and art. Modern art exacerbated Hoover's degenerist anxieties; he feared that its practitioners were orienting the public toward illicit or dangerous subject matter, the very stuff that could destabilize America, he frequently argued. Hoover's contempt ran dangerously, and his distaste for modern writers and artists, especially his desire to limit the dissemination of their work through censorship, bullying, and courtroom dramas, came to define the bureau's attitude toward modernism. With so many writers and artists squarely engaged in revolutionary climates (Bertolt

Brecht, John Reed), their attitudes shaped by cataclysmic war (Pablo Picasso, Ernest Hemingway), political and social turmoil (Richard Wright, John Steinbeck, Claude McKay, Thomas, Erika, and Klaus Mann, Edna St. Vincent Millay, Langston Hughes), or caught up in witnessing and reporting from some of the century's most heartbreaking worksite disasters or massacres (Theodore Dreiser, Muriel Rukeyser, Mary Heaton Vorse), modernists saw fit to capture the spirit of the age by marking their steadfast alignment with politics. The artists involved in the movement were bent on translating into different media the vicissitudes of twentieth-century life, and as such, were likely to sway public understanding and effect dramatic change. Because of this, Hoover labeled many writers and artists as radical insurgents, and ordered bureau agents in field offices across the country to shadow them and to investigate their histories. When applicable, he made a point of indicating in bureau files which writers were sexual "deviants," since he felt these "types" hastened America's sexual degeneration and threatened the strength and purity of the American family.

To be sure, bureau harassment and surveillance directly affected many writers and artists. Richard Wright, who realized he was the target of an FBI investigation, subsequently wrote obsessively about the bureau's shadowing and was plagued by paranoia in the later part of his career; Henry Roth's fear of the FBI contributed to his debilitating writer's block; and Muriel Rukeyser, who with countless other modernist writers articulated her anger over the unjust execution of workers Sacco and Vanzetti, remained a bureau suspect most of her life. Ernest Hemingway, too, was aware of the FBI's interest in him: certain that he was being shadowed by bureau SACs, Hemingway alarmed his doctor at the Mayo Clinic with seemingly fantastic tales of constant surveillance. His doctor dismissed these fears as delusional, but Hemingway's FBI file confirms his very real suspicions. Edna St. Vincent Millay grew so frustrated by bureau surveillance that she developed the practice of leaving calling cards wherever she visited just to taunt FBI agents curious about her day-to-day routines. Even more extreme, Claude McKay suffered political exile for 14 years as a result of the FBI's anxiety over his political views, his affiliations with the Industrial Workers of the World (IWW), and his homosexuality. Langston Hughes, another Harlem Renaissance poet, suffered the bureau's attention as much for his communist writings as for his race, sexual orientation, political affections, and international travel.

Not only dealing with writers but curbing "communist" infiltration of the movie and book industries in Hollywood and New York also was vitally significant to Hoover and the bureau. To this end, the bureau manipulated screenwriters as well as musical composers, publishers as well as copy editors, international stars of the stage and screen as well as lesser-known performers.

Bertolt Brecht's telephone conversations, for example, grew to equal in significance Hanns Eisler's musical scores, Tess Slesinger's screenplays, or Jean Renoir's film work. Josephine Baker's efforts to boycott racist clubs, for example, were yoked together with the political examples of Paul Robeson's cheek and Charlie Chaplin's lust. The FBI file on publisher Henry Holt demonstrates the bureau's deep involvement with American publishing for more than three decades. What effect the bizarre and troubling business arrangement between Holt & Co. and the FBI had on the book industry is only now becoming clear and is part of an unknown chapter in the history of Hoover's war on the freedom of expression. Erika and Klaus Mann, writers and performers who were the eldest children of the naturalized American writer Thomas Mann, felt the bureau's wrath in the late 1930s after they were accused of supporting fascism. While these are all individual stories of bureau persecution and manipulation, when gathered together they demonstrate the cultural strong-arming of American arts in the early twentieth century.

Recent scholarly work by Saunders and others has shown that government institutions such as Hoover's FBI and Michael Josselson's CIA pressured modernist writers and artists to produce less politically charged, radical work in order to stifle the aesthetic and political contours of the movement, often through bribery or intimidation. Hoover silenced, censored, or otherwise intimidated writers and publishers who created works that critiqued the U.S. government, for example, showed sympathy for Communism, the labor movement, racial equality, or any other ideological organization identified by the paranoiac Hoover as "radical." Celia Marshik notes in her 2006 book on modernism and censorship that much of what she writes about "may seem a historical curiosity, with . . . prosecutions of individual writers, and specific social purity campaigns appearing to be distant artifacts of a naïve and repressive culture resistant to modernity. And yet, the history of censorship across the breadth of the twentieth century indicates that the questions over which social purists, government officials, and modernist writers tussled still preoccupy us" (13). Indeed they do. Expanding the important work recently published by literary critics and social and cultural historians, *Modernism on File* provides more detailed evidence and discussion of Hoover's malevolent and often illegal practices. The analyses here examine only a select number of FBI files and are by no means exhaustive; but each reveals a pattern of surveillance and intimidation that significantly contributes to our understanding of the means by which modernist artists were beleaguered and the movement hectored by the FBI.

The FBI and Modern Writers

The Chapters by William J. Maxwell on the FBI and Afro-modernism, Andrew Strombeck on Richard Wright's *Savage Holiday*, and Josh Gosciak on

Claude McKay's spectral hauntings demonstrate that these writers were special targets of the FBI, as were numerous African American writers in this period. Influential figures such as Hughes, McKay, DuBois, and Wright greatly interested Hoover, who sought to repress the power of political agitators who might successfully bring about potential crises, such as a widespread and violent demand among African-Americans for civil rights. Those figures who expressed interest in the Communist movement were thought to be deliberately educating themselves about ways to bring about a revolution on American soil. The FBI feared that strategies learned from the Soviets might be used by intellectuals in the United States to expose and disrupt racist practices throughout the country—practices that Hoover was strongly invested in preserving, as several chapters in this book show.

In "Ghostreaders and Diaspora-Writers: Four Theses on the FBI and African American Modernism," William J. Maxwell shows that the FBI's ghostreaders and spy-critics confessed a worried admiration of Afro-modernist writing, but kept close watch on the writing and international travel of writers such as Langston Hughes, Claude McKay, and Richard Wright. Under the FBI's spyglass, Afro-modernists learned to grapple with their own image, some of them politically domesticated by bureau prying. The tight surveillance reinforced the bureau's role as censor and border guard, and its intrusions affected the best twentieth-century African American writers. As bureau encroachment grew more frequent, Maxwell argues, it delayed or deferred important literary consummations and forced or sidetracked intellectual travels. Equally important, Hoover's ghostreaders, working day and night reading and reviewing Afro-modernist work in the FBI's Book Review Division, grew to become powerful literary critics who shared the bureau's sense of literature's sway, and worked to become the final critical authorities on African American modernism.

The FBI's paranoia about writers associated with leftist politics can be seen in the files of Henry Roth, Muriel Rukeyser, and Ernest Hemingway. None of these writers could be accurately described as a Communist revolutionary, yet the FBI dedicated enormous amounts of time and money to record the activities of each. Hemingway's activities on behalf of the Loyalist cause in Spain during the 1930s, for example, provided enough proof of his radicalism to justify the bureau's efforts to track him for the rest of his life. Although field officers and SACs filing reports in Hemingway's file explicitly state that the writer was not considered a major threat, Hoover was personally irritated by Hemingway's public criticism of the FBI, and aggressively harassed the writer. The Director's personal grievances, in fact, frequently fueled the bureau's pursuit of artistic subjects. With zeal, Hoover could easily cloak his animosity with the bureau's general concern with radical subversives.

Steven G. Kellman shows in his essay "Raising Muscovite Ducks and Government Suspicions: Henry Roth and the FBI" that in 1934, shortly after completing work on his first novel, *Call it Sleep*, Roth joined the Communist Party in the United States. He attended meetings of the John Reed Club in Manhattan, signed petitions for candidates supported by the CPUSA, and publicly endorsed the Moscow show trials. Though he was never a never major figure within the party, and he withdrew from urban intellectual life becoming a duck farmer in Maine for most of two decades until his rediscovery in 1964, Roth was under sporadic bureau surveillance from the 1930s until the 1950s. Roth claimed political repression was one of the causes for his legendary writer's block (he did not publish his second novel until 1994, 60 years after his first), and he believed that he was ostracized by his neighbors in Maine and lost a job at a local high school because FBI agents came snooping around and spread the word about his leftist background. Kellman's essay presents an example of the unrelenting pressure writers felt from the FBI by one writer whose career was diminished and whose life was constantly troubled by their persistence.

Debra A. Moddelmog's "Telling Stories from Hemingway's FBI File: Conspiracy, Paranoia, and Masculinity" analyzes the writer's FBI file and explores the ways Hemingway's file has contributed to his masculine myth and, in particular, the ways the story of his FBI investigation have been used in popular culture. In fact, Hoover's preoccupation with his own masculine image seems to have fueled his animosity toward Hemingway. Ironically, that the FBI perceived Hemingway to be dangerous to the United States actually added to his virile persona. Indeed, his much-publicized FBI file has been discussed by numerous scholars and fans who continue to investigate and assess his writing, lifestyle, and political views; Hemingway's file is even central to the plots of several works of fiction that celebrate his heroic response to his investigation by the FBI.

In "Most Wanted: Claude McKay and the 'Black Specter' of African American Poetry in the 1920s" Josh Gosciak discusses Claude McKay's file opened by bureau SACs after he published in the red summer of 1919 the call-to-arms poem "If We Must Die." McKay then traveled abroad to England (1920), where his first two years in Europe were meticulously tracked and ciphered by the U.S. Justice Department's Bureau of Investigation. After traveling to Moscow in 1922, McKay was prevented from returning to the United States, and he found himself in an unusual political exile. The U.S. Justice Department circulated a sketch of McKay and suggested that he was dangerous not only because of his sympathies for the IWW, but because he was homosexual. McKay became a "specter," and this not only bolstered his own shadowy literary-political reputation, but helped to perpetuate tremendous amounts of misinformation as well. A topic of concern for

McKay, he wrote about his treatment in an essay titled "He Who Gets Slapped." The Jamaican-born poet and novelist finally returned to the United States in 1934 and became a U.S. citizen in 1940. He died eight years later, impoverished and derided by critics. Gosciak shows how McKay's life and career were changed and abused by the government and its sanctioned censors, whose anxiety was related to his politically charged work and his dangerous homosexuality.

The case of Ezra Pound is unlike that of other writers discussed here in that he was not interested in leftist politics but, like the other writers discussed in this collection, he was clearly interested in creating dissent among Americans during World War II. In anticipation of Pound's trial for treason, the FBI collected and subsequently provided evidence against Pound. Karen Leick shows in "Madness, Paranoia, and Ezra Pound's FBI File" that much of Ezra Pound's extensive bureau dossier consists of interviews with individuals who knew or had met Pound, since the bureau was searching for individuals who could identify Pound's voice in recordings of his pro-Mussolini broadcasts over Rome Radio and appear as witnesses against him. Pound's notorious insanity plea, an assumed strategy to avoid execution if convicted, allowed him to be found unfit for trial and he was subsequently incarcerated in Washington D.C.'s St. Elizabeths hospital for almost 13 years. FBI files, however, suggest that most of Pound's friends and enemies uniformly believed him to be unstable at best; at worst, they told bureau investigators, he was unquestionably insane. In her essay, Leick asks that we accept the notion that Pound was mentally unstable, and she ponders the implications of his paranoid delusions. In particular, Pound thought he was being watched and persecuted by Jews, a belief that psychiatrists thought to be delusional; but as constant surveillance was a new part of everyday life in the modernist period, Pound's symptoms more than likely reflect and reinforce the culture of paranoia promoted by the FBI who closely watched the American writer and expatriate. Like Wright, Hemingway, and other modernist writers, Pound's suspicions that he was pursued by the U.S. government proved true.

In "Figuring Hoover in Richard Wright's *Savage Holiday*," Andrew Strombeck argues that Richard Wright and the FBI exhibited paranoia toward one another: the FBI was paranoid about Richard Wright's Communist affiliations and thus created a 169-page file on him, while Richard Wright was paranoid that he was being watched by the FBI. Wright expressed his concerns to family, friends, and colleagues, fueling rumors at his death that with a mysterious injection, the government had killed him. The constant threat Wright perceived from the FBI dramatically shaped his later work, which Strombeck shows regularly explored what Wright saw as the harmful effects of an investigative gaze. Wright's poem entitled "The FB Eye Blues" and his unsuccessful novel *Savage Holiday*, further explore the subject of surveillance and paranoia. Another writer affected by the bureau's scrutiny, Wright reveals the FBIs obsession with surveillance and moral guardianship in these two works, considered subversive and threatening to Hoover and his henchmen.

As with Roth, McKay, Hemingway, Pound, Wright, and others, Muriel Rukeyser also was scrupulously monitored by the FBI, who provided in dozens of field reports a thorough accounting of the newspapers she wrote for, the speeches she gave, the classes she taught, and the company she kept. Seemingly mundane details—such as the fact that Rukeyser obtained a library card at the University of California, Berkeley, on February 7, 1945—indicate the extent of their research into her everyday, ordinary activities, and in this case lead us to suppose that bureau SACs kept fastidious track, as well, of what Rukeyser read and checked out from the UC library. After public accusations of a Communist presence in the Office of War Information (OWI) in 1943, two thousand OWI employees were investigated by its director, Elmer Davis, who announced that only six Communists had been found. Not satisfied with this result and leery of the modest number that Davis reported, the FBI undertook its own enthusiastic investigation of the OWI. The activities of Muriel Rukeyser, hired to work in the propaganda office's Domestic Division, were thrown into relief. Quickly, the New York *Times* reported, "Poetess in OWI Here Probed by U.S. as Red" (May 7, 1943). Now flagged, Rukeyser became the subject of the bureau's concentrated investigation in 1950 after Louis Budenz included her in his infamous list of "400 concealed Communists." Although the FBI never found any evidence that she was a party member, its investigation of Rukeyser and others in the OWI indicated that each had suspected ties to "international Jewery" as were "aliens, radicals, and subversives." Jean Perreault's essay, "'Poetess Probed as Red': Muriel Rukeyser and the FBI" shows how startlingly but readily the bureau conflated antifascism with anti-Americanism.

THE FBI AND THE ARTS

Chapters in this section explore the reach of Hoover's gaze into other artistic venues. Christopher Faulkner, Alexander Stephan, and James Wierzbicki, for example, consider artists whose activities in Hollywood were scrutinized by the FBI. Acquainted with one another, Bertolt Brecht, Jean Renoir, and Hanns Eisler were marked and followed by bureau agents.

As Faulkner observes, "Brecht, whom Renoir had known since the early 1930s and with whom he socialized in Hollywood, was the 'eleventh' of the Hollywood ten, and fled the day after his HUAC hearing on October 30, 1947. The composer, Hanns Eisler, who wrote the music for Renoir's *The Woman on the Beach* (1947), was denounced by his sister, Ruth Fischer, and after a year-long investigation 'voluntarily' deported to East Germany in February 1948" (201–02). Faulkner's "An Archive of the (Political) Unconscious: Jean Renoir at the FBI" considers the FBI as a paradigm of all archives and, in that light, examines the meaning of bureau notes in the FBI files of Jean Renoir, the French filmmaker who directed some 40 films over the course of 45 years in France, the United States, Italy, and India. His files provide evidence of a heretofore ignored political activism on Renoir's part in the United States during the 1940s that must lead us to rethink critical and historical assumptions about his film work during his American period and immediately thereafter. In this new light, for example, *This Land Is Mine* can be seen as a film that engages with the ethics of naming names before the activity became a fact and perennial condition of American life in the 1940s. Concerned with a right-wing assault against the working class, against women, and against Jews, the film was implicated as subversive in the files of the FBI along with other pro-labor, antifascist resistance films from 1943 such as Fritz Lang's *Hangmen Also Die*, written by John Wexley from a script by Bertolt Brecht. Faulkner's essay provocatively argues that *This Land Is Mine* belongs to a minor genre of films from the early 1940s that engaged a number of left-wing film personnel in a body of related subject matter and that this is the political and cinematic context within which Renoir's work should be situated and understood.

Alexander Stephan's chapter, "New Information from the FBI, CNDI LA-BB-1: The Phone Surveillance of Bertolt Brecht in Los Angeles," looks at the valuable information gained by Brecht scholars about his political, cultural, and personal views in the 1940s by examining telephone conversations recorded by FBI agents in Los Angeles between 1944 and 1945. The writer came to California in 1941 as an exile looking for work in Hollywood. His "ill-fated efforts to write for the movies, the 'dream factories,' as he called them, would begin and end with Lang's *Hangmen Also Die* (1943). Little did Brecht know, however, that during his six years in American exile—and he was quite adamant about thinking of it as 'exile' rather than as permanent migration—he was the subject of intense scrutiny by FBI agents" (Isenberg 36). Alexander Stephan traces that intense scrutiny in his essay that details some of the 2,250 bureau-recorded telephone calls. In particular, Brecht's discussions of Nazism, fascism, and the politics of postwar Germany, with people such as fellow exile author Lion Feuchtwanger, will be of interest to scholars. The FBI was also interested in all of the minutiae of the Brecht's lives, such as Brecht's affair with Ruth Berlau, the cooking techniques of his wife Helene Weigel, and Weigel's addiction to sun tanning. Although the byzantine nature of FBI documentation is disturbing, the positive side to Brecht's file is that we learn much about the relationship between everyday life and politics in the Hollywood exile community.

James Wierzbicki's chapter, "Sour Notes: Hanns Eisler and the FBI," looks at bureau dossier material on German composer Hanns Eisler, who lived in the United States from 1937 to 1948, wrote a handful of scores for Hollywood films, and collaborated with Frankfurt School philosopher and social critic Theodor Adorno on *Composing for the Films*, 1947, a book focused on theories of film scoring. Wierzbicki argues that although American audiences have not taken Eisler seriously as a musician, the FBI took him seriously as a suspected enemy agent. Eisler's 686-page file documents a long series of wiretaps, surveillance tails, and break-ins engineered for the purpose of securing potentially damaging information. Eisler was admittedly a sympathizer with the Communist cause, but he was always anti-Nazi and never joined the Communist Party. Nonetheless, for six years he was subjected to intense investigation and his questioning in 1947 by the House Committee on Un-American Activities (HUAC)—in effect, the start of HUAC's purge of the motion picture industry—was unusually prolonged and harsh. Wierzbicki's essay explores why Eisler was singled out for such relentless scrutiny, and argues that Eisler's peculiarly accessible modern music was suspected of being dangerously influential in ways that the FBI could not hope to understand.

Andrea Weiss, in "Communism, Perversion, and Other Crimes against the State: The FBI Files of Klaus and Erika Mann," shows that the Mann siblings, two of the strongest and most dedicated advocates for the American democratic system, were stridently harassed by the FBI while fascism swept across Europe in the late 1930s. The eldest children of Thomas Mann, Erika and Klaus were openly gay, antifascist authors and performers who emigrated from Germany immediately after Hitler came to power. The FBI was unable to link either Erika or Klaus to the Communist Party, but because of what they called their "premature antifascism" as well as their candid admission of their bi- and homosexuality, the FBI continued to treat them as dangerous subjects. This essay explores the effects of the FBI investigation on the lives of this brother-sister pair, and details an investigation that did not let up until Klaus died and Erika collapsed under the pressure and was forced to leave her adopted homeland for good.

Claire Culleton's chapter, "Extorting Henry Holt & Co.: J. Edgar Hoover and the Publishing Industry," shows that the bureau director went to great lengths to effect decisions made by editors working at the Henry Holt & Co. firm. In addition to harassing writers, Hoover strong-armed men in powerful positions in the trade. In 1950, Hoover began to "develop" informants who were higher-ups in the industry—Random House's Bennett Cerf, and Ed Rigg, president of Henry Holt & Co., for example. Evidence in Henry Holt's FBI file reveals that over the course of at least 36 years, roughly from 1936 until J. Edgar Hoover's death in 1972, the FBI director held considerable sway over the firm, and reviewed sets of advanced galleys and approved the publication of any and all books dealing with the FBI or with political subject matter. As his and the bureau's relationship with Holt & Co. developed, Hoover tightened the reins, and by the 1950s, remarkably, he was micromanaging the firm, gouging its marketing and production resources, and extorting thousands of dollars from the company by ordering hundreds (and hundreds) of copies at a time of his books *Masters of Deceit* (1958) and *A Study of Communism* (1962) at a generous 46 percent author's discount. Moreover, he was especially vigilant about the editing, production, and marketing of his books. Culleton explores Hoover's influential relationships with twentieth-century American publishers and editors, and traces the weight of his and his bureau's authority on American print culture.

It is impossible, of course, to determine precisely how censorship and its counterpart auto-censorship affected the work of modern writers and artists who feared Hoover's oppressive policies. Evidence overwhelmingly suggests that the FBI was not subtle when gathering information, deliberately keeping artists aware that they were under investigation. Bureau files maintained on writers and artists effectively prevented or curtailed their activities, their creative productivity, their collaborations, and their coactions. *Modernism on File: Modern Writers, Artists, and the FBI, 1920–1950* brings together important new scholarship focused on J. Edgar Hoover's FBI and its institutional presence in shaping and directing American print, film, and art culture. Writers and artists discussed in this collection were tagged, tracked, and in some cases trapped by Hoover and his bureau workers who, from Harlem to Hollywood, were bent on decontaminating America's creative productivity. As a collection, *Modernism on File, 1920–1950* details the threatening aspects of political power, and critiques the very historiography of modernism, acknowledging that modernism was on trial during these years. Without bureau prying, without the bureau's ponderous reliance on tactics, strategies, policies, and institutional brawn (not to mention Hoover's own obsessive preoccupation with modern and avant-garde writers and artists), creative work produced in America from 1920s through the 1950s could certainly have developed differently, harnessing the masses and producing the kind of revolutionary social action the bureau feared. It is important to remember that the bureau's oppressive measures and its continuous surveillance were part and parcel of writers' and artists' everyday lives during these years. As such, the culture of American modernism was irrevocably charged with paranoia, censorship, and equivocation during these years, as writers and artists were forced either to brave the elements of Hoover's tempestuous political storms or to surrender to them via silence, acquiescence, or dread. These 12 chapters expose the startling effects of bureau interventions on creative activity in the United States at this time.

Note

1. Whether at the movies watching a newsreel, at home, or in the shops listening to the radio, whether reading the newspaper or a popular magazine, whether reading one of Hoover's prologues or prefaces in the new True Crime genre, whether reading any of Hoover's own books (ghostwritten, we now know), or a G-Man comic book, one could not easily escape the Hoover media blitz. He even conscripted some of the nation's hottest pulp fiction writers into his army. Their books championed Hoover and his role in "cleaning up" law enforcement. Richard Gid Powers has done remarkable work uncovering this particular aspect of Hoover's mania.

Works Cited

Beverly, William. *On the Lam: Narratives of Flight in J. Edgar Hoover's America.* Jackson: U of Mississippi P, 2003.

Culleton, Claire A. *Joyce and the G-Men: J. Edgar Hoover and the Manipulation of Modernism.* New York: Palgrave Macmillan, 2004.

Eliot, T.S. *For Lancelot Andrewes: Essays on Style and Order.* New York: Doubleday, Doran and Co., 1929.

Faulkner, Christopher. "An Archive of the (Political) Unconscious," *Canadian Journal of Communication* 26 (2001): 191–209.

Finan, Christopher M. *Alfred E. Smith: The Happy Warrior.* New York: Hill and Wang, 2002.

Hicks, Granville. FBI file. 1 Section. Approximately 220 pages.

Isenberg, Noah. "Double Enmity," *The Nation* 272, 1 (January 1, 2001): 35–37.

Jeffreys, Diarmuid. *The Bureau: Inside the Modern FBI.* Boston: Houghton Mifflin, 1995.

Keen, Mike Forrest. *Stalking Sociologists: J. Edgar Hoover's FBI Surveillance of American Sociology.* New Brunswick: Transaction Publishers, 2003.

Marshik, Celia. *British Modernism and Censorship.* Cambridge: Cambridge U P, 2006.

Meyers, Jeffrey. "Wanted by the FBI!" *New York Review of Books* 30 (March 31,1983): 17–20.

Miller, Dan B. *Erskine Caldwell: The Journey From Tobacco Road.* New York: Knopf, 1995.

Mitgang, Herbert. *Dangerous Dossiers: Exposing the Secret War against America's Greatest Authors.* New York: Donald I. Fine, Inc., 1988.

Powers, Richard Gid. *Secrecy and Power: The Life of J. Edgar Hoover.* New York: The Free Press, 1987.

Price, David H. *Threatening Anthropology: McCarthyism and the FBI's Surveillance of Activist Anthropologists.* Durham: Duke U P, 2004.

Rainey, Lawrence. Ed. *Modernism: An Anthology.* Malden, MA: Blackwell Publishing, 2005.

Robins, Natalie. *Alien Ink: The FBI's War on Freedom of Expression.* New York: William Morrow and Company, Inc., 1992.

Saunders, Frances Stonor. *The Cultural Cold War: The CIA and the World of Arts and Letters.* New York: New Press, 2001.

Theoharis, Athan G. Ed. with Tony G. Poveda, Susan Rosenfeld, Richard Gid Powers. *The FBI: A Comprehensive Reference Guide*. Phoenix, AZ: The Oryx Press, 1999.

"The Situation in American Writing: Seven Questions," *Partisan Review* 6 (Summer 1939): 25–51.

Ungar, Sanford J. *FBI*. Boston: Little, Brown and Company, 1975.

Whitehead, Don. *The FBI Story: A Report to the People*. New York: Random House, 1956.

PART I

THE FBI AND MODERN WRITERS

CHAPTER 1

Ghostreaders and Diaspora-Writers: Four Theses on the FBI and African American Modernism

William J. Maxwell

Since the winter of 2004, a parade of leaks and reluctant document dumps has sparked unease and controversy over revived political spying by the U.S. government. Disclosures of Pentagon eavesdropping on domestic peace groups have been followed by news of warrantless wiretapping by the National Security Agency (NSA) and the FBI's use of tens of thousands of "national security letters" to monitor the private communications of American citizens since the passage of the 2001 PATRIOT Act (ACLU Says). The present thus qualifies as a dramatically appropriate moment in which to inspect the historical links between American state sleuthing and African American speech. Even so, concern with the effects of federal surveillance on African American expression is hardly a unique product of the short, edgy twenty-first century. Well before the Freedom of Information Act (FOIA) allowed access to scores of formerly secret FBI files on Afro-modernist writers, these writers themselves contemplated how J. Edgar Hoover's Federal Bureau of Investigation surveyed and stirred up their work.

Imagine, if you can, a world in which a federal police force aims to decipher and recast the best of African American writing; a world in which the repressive state apparatus moonlights as a racially expressive apparatus, not only monitoring African American criticism, but also composing its own variety. For his part, Richard Wright, author of the classic naturalist novel *Native Son* (1940), could readily imagine such a world, since he often trusted he was living in one beginning in 1942. In that hair-trigger year, FBI Director Hoover, agitated by Wright's WPA-style photo-history *12 Million Black Voices* (1941), ordered the bureau's New York field office to review his collected works for signs of sedition. "If your inquiry develops information of an affirmative nature," Hoover directed, "you should of course cause an investigation to be undertaken as to the subject's background, inclinations, and current activities" (U.S., Wright file, December 8, 1942). Unsurprisingly, information of an affirmative nature was developed, and an investigation undertaken, leaving Wright hyperconscious of the bureau agents who seemed to track every turn of his literary and romantic lives (Rowley 276). Wright's expatriation to Paris and the world, launched in 1947 with encouragement from Hoover's spy-readers, delivered some of the analytical advantages of statelessness, but could not outrun the impression that FBI snoops lurked around the next alien corner.

Consider Wright's voyage to Buenos Aires aboard the SS *Uruguay* in the fall of 1949. Snapshots taken on deck show him trying on the Hemingway uniform, working bare-chested on a punching bag in hopes of slimming down enough to play his own character, Bigger Thomas, in the Argentinean film version of *Native Son*. Wright boxed conscientiously during the three-week journey and dropped from 170 to 145, losing a pound for every year he had on the teenaged Bigger (Rowley 383). But he felt compelled to interrupt his rejuvenation in international waters long enough to complete a poem whose satirical take on U.S. espionage incompletely masked its anxiety. In "The FB Eye Blues," Wright turned the tables on bureau note-taking, filling blues stanzas with wry digs at the intimacy of spy-sight. Living under bureau scrutiny, Wright joked, was uncomfortably close to sleeping—and writing—with the enemy:

> That old FB eye
> Tied a bell to my bed stall
> Said old FB eye
> Tied a bell to my bed stall
> Each time I love my baby, gover'ment knows it all.
>
> Woke up this morning
> FB eye under my bed
> Said I woke up this morning
> FB eye under my bed
> Told me all I dreamed last night, every word I said.
>
> (ll. 1–10)

Wright's compulsion to box with Hoover's shadow even while steaming toward foreign film stardom reveals his judgment that the FB eye was just as able as he to board a chronotope of Black Atlantic mobility and sail outside the limits of the nation-state. More important, however, this compulsion also unveils one of the most typical impulses in the literary modernism born with the Harlem Renaissance. Wright's unusually explicit wrestling with the long arm of the bureau, I believe, is representative of a larger Afro-modernism compelled to reckon with its image in the FBI's spyglass. To an extent that even Wright could not imagine, the Federal Bureau of Investigation, the best-publicized agent and symbol of the modern U.S. security state, shaped the leading edge of twentieth-century African American writing. From the safety of what he modestly called the "Seat of Government," the bureau's Washington headquarters, J. Edgar Hoover, the original G-Man and nemesis of Martin Luther King Jr., fostered a slyly intimate relationship between FBI scrutiny and African American literary experiment from the birth of the Harlem Renaissance in 1919 to the height of the Black Arts movement in 1972, the years of Hoover's protracted tenure as the bureau's critic-in-chief. Targeting black modernists as memorable as James Baldwin, W.E.B. Du Bois, and Langston Hughes, Hoover's FBI acted as a concealed censor and border guard, distorting or deferring publications and forcing or sidetracking international travels. At the same time, bureau spycraft could be received by its writer-targets as a stimulating new school for aesthetic research, inspiring the African American prose genre of the "counterfile" and an inventive modern poetics of double agency. And this spycraft spurred the FBI to become a pioneering scholar of black transnationalism, tracing the New Negro's intellectual connections across the Black Atlantic and into the Bolshevized Black Sea. Through both poles of its influence, the restrictive and the inspirational, the bureau helped to mold a worldly but state-hunted, sometimes state-haunted, tradition of the new. As scholars from sociology to comparative politics declare the "return of the state" as both a central prop and a desirable alternative to the dynamics of neoliberal globalization; and as the cosmopolitan dreams of transnational studies are tested by the raw divisions of the global War on Terror, the time thus seems right for a set of speculative, easy theses—four, to be exact—addressing how the FBI's ghostreaders surveyed and stirred up black literary modernism.

Thesis One: The Development of African American Literary Modernism Is Coterminous with the Development of the Modern FBI

The FBI's 50-year war on African American protest is no longer a state secret. Armed with a FOIA (temporarily) given teeth in 1986, historians have confirmed that the bureau's plot to shame Martin Luther King, Jr. into suicide was only the tip of the iceberg. J. Edgar Hoover's arrival at the FBI during the Red Summer of 1919 kicked off half a century of harassment of black political life, culminating in the bloody COINTELPRO program aimed at so-called "Black Nationalist-Hate Groups" ranging from the Black Panthers to the non-nationalist, nonviolent Southern Christian Leadership Conference. Born the son of a Washington, D.C. mapmaker at the height of Jim Crow in 1895, a conventional public racist troubled by rumors of his own black ancestry, Hoover entered the bureau with the conviction that New Negro discontent was triggered by equal desires for Marx and miscegenation (Hack 28–29). When not coauthoring the antiradical Palmer Raids, Hoover was thus poring over the *Negro World* and the Harlem *Messenger* and personally hatching a scheme to prosecute Marcus Garvey for mail fraud. In a 1919 message to a bureau underling, he complained that the provisions of the wartime Alien Act lagged behind his campaign to capsize the radicalizing traffic of the Black Atlantic. "Unfortunately," Hoover protested, Garvey "has not as yet violated any federal law whereby he could be proceeded against on the grounds of being an undesirable alien, from the point of view of deportation" (U.S., Garvey file, October 11, 1919).

Hoover eventually got his man, succeeding in extraditing Garvey to his native Jamaica. But I don't think we've yet gotten the news that the bureau's long offensive against black political leadership was always married to an excited dread of black literature. From the late teens through the early 1970s, Hoover's hard-line bureaucracy also qualified as a major if inconspicuous consumer of African American texts, a half-buried interpretive empire with aboveground effects on the creation of Afro-modernism. Practically alone among publicly funded institutions of literary study, Hoover's FBI never treated African American writing as an ineffectual fad and never forgot its heavy traffic with the twentieth-century left. Classic Harlem Renaissance scholarship by Nathan Huggins and David Levering Lewis insinuates that the bureau, acting in concert with Attorney General A. Mitchell Palmer, accidentally nurtured the New Negro literary awakening. The first American Red Scare, Huggins argued, sparked "a channeling of energy from political and social criticism into poetry . . . [and] fiction" (9), or what Lewis, adopting the psychoanalytical vocabulary, later labeled "the cultural sublimation of civil rights" (xxiv). More convincing than the theory that New Negro militants went strategically artsy is the case for the bureau's own cultural turn. Mountains of released FBI files indicate that the bureau discerned the simultaneous emergence of the Harlem Renaissance and the modern U.S. security state, each built in the wake of World War I. In the radical byways of the Harlem movement, the FBI first rehearsed several of the techniques of literary meddling that Claire Culleton dubs Hoover's "manipulation of modernism" (17). A year prior to the publication of *The Weary Blues* in 1925,

Langston Hughes's membership in the All-American Anti-Imperialist League had thus earned him a bureau file of his own. Seasoned proletarian poems such as "Goodbye Christ" (1932) did nothing to relieve mistrust, receiving national circulation through a pamphlet written by Hoover himself and winning Hughes the bureau tag of "Negro pornographic poet" (Robins 63). Even before it was looking for Langston, the FBI was tailing globetrotter Claude McKay, painstakingly reproducing his "violent sonnets" and directing customs officials to retain the poet and his effects at every U.S. port of entry. As early as 1921, the State Department seconded the FBI's opinion that McKay was the single strongest link between Harlem's growing race capital and Moscow's Vatican of global Communism. Beginning that December, both federal agencies began stuffing an FBI file whose initial page tells of its subject's faith in the Communist Party and guilt over tardy dues to the Industrial Workers of the World (IWW) (U.S., McKay file, December 16, 1921).

The list of post-Harlem Renaissance authors who inherited the Harlem movement's bad reputation at bureau headquarters is long and distinguished, and is not confined to close affiliates of the Communist Party. Richard Wright passed his FB eye blues down to defiant pupil James Baldwin, shadowed by a gang of confidential FBI sources who intercepted his mail and photographed his daily rounds, not just in Harlem and France, but in Istanbul, where he began plotting retaliation through a never-completed anti-bureau treatise (Campbell, "I Heard" 153–67). The works and days of W.E.B. Du Bois clinched his high place on the bureau's Security Index of imminently arrestable leftists from 1950 until his death in Ghana in 1963 (Keen 15). Chester Himes did not make the Index, but his Harlem detective fiction was foreshadowed by FBI gumshoes who began investigating his prison time and anticolonial outlook in 1944, with the results itemized in a personal file marked "Internal Security-Sedition" (Walters 6–7). Alice Childress's involvement with an alphabet soup of committees on the 1950s left attracted what her FBI file describes as "a discreet surveillance"; so did Lorraine Hansberry's early work as a roving labor journalist for Paul Robeson's paper *Freedom* (Washington 185–94). Paule Marshall and Ishmael Reed escaped with relatively slim files for the high crime of petition-signing, while Amiri Baraka's wide swath beyond the home base he rechristened "New Ark," New Jersey, was sufficient to generate over 2,000 bureau-authored pages of grapevine noise and reconnaissance beginning in 1960 (Robins 411, 349–52). Years earlier, a bureau memo had wondered if fellow Jerseyite William Carlos Williams's "very queer or possibly mental" poetry concealed revolutionary cryptograms (qtd. in Robins 293). Given the FBI's equally intense concern for the highlights of African American modernism, we may eventually discover that it judged Jean Toomer's *Cane* a work of both elusive Imagism and secret Bolshevik code.

This drawn-out roll call of literary suspects, stretching from the Harlem Renaissance to the Black Arts movement's Renaissance II, betrays an unshakable suspicion that authoring African American modernism and menacing national security were one and the same. In the elephant's memory of the FBI, black letters shattered the historical bonds of the slave narrative without breaking with the need to enter the literary under the sign of criminality. For Hoover's ghostreaders, the state of exception that removed normal legal checks on executive power during World War I was thus never completely rescinded. The Treaty of Versailles officially sealed the conclusion of the global conflict philosopher Giorgio Agamben describes as a general laboratory for testing the "abolition of the distinction among legislative, executive, and judicial" branches (7). Yet the formally abandoned Sedition Act of 1918 retained its practical criminalizing power at bureau headquarters, able to illegitimate the publication of what the Act dubbed "disloyal, profane, scurrilous, or abusive language about the form of government of the United States," providing that language came with an African American accent (qtd. in Agamben 21). From 1919 until Hoover's death in 1972—or from McKay's "If We Must Die" to Baraka's *Spirit Reach*—the Bureau probed the leading edge of black expression for crimes against the state, growing in institutional authority with the aid of investigative procedures partly honed in collecting literary transgressions. If the most sensational public history of Anglo-modernism can be found in the transcripts of federal censorship trials over *Ulysses* and *Lady Chatterly's Lover*, the most dramatic private history of Afro-modernism can be located in FBI memos planning to suppress Hughes's *Fine Clothes to the Jew* and Baldwin's *Another Country*.

Thesis Two: The FBI Is Perhaps the Most Dedicated and Powerful Forgotten Critic of Twentieth-Century African-American Writing

Hoover's self-lacerating panic over unconcealed homosexuality once led him to ask an assistant "Isn't Baldwin a well-known pervert?," and to assign the bureau's General Crimes section to comb *Another Country* (1962) for traces of obscenity (Campbell, "I Heard" 170). He must have been disappointed with the book report that followed: an open-minded FBI reviewer discovered a novel of genuine "literary merit . . . [that] may be of value to students of psychology and social behavior" (Robins 347). Appreciative, blurb-worthy evaluations of this kind are not the norm in the FBI's many files on African American writers, but the gravity of the response, its tendency to overspill the immediate need to detect, discipline, and punish, is emblematic of the bureau's generous sense of literature's sway. The publicity-savvy Hoover cultivated an inflated fear and respect for the power of authors to act as "thought-control relay stations" (qtd. in Robins 50); he shared the modernist avant-garde's extravagant estimation of literature's ability to order minds in a fallen world, though never the avant-garde's faith in its own intellectual novelty. Thick studies by Herbert Mitgang, Natalie Robins, and, most recently, Claire Culleton, document the repressive effects of the bureau's excessive alarm over literary dissidence. Hundreds of American authors, they disclose, had their publications scanned by an FBI division actually named the Book Review Section; the most "anti-American" or "anti-FBI" among them had their phones tapped, their letters opened, and their lecture tours stalled; publishers as influential as Henry Holt and Bennett Cerf were pressed to become FBI informants; and in-house sources supplied bureau agents with notes from editorial board meetings at *Time* and *Life*, *Reader's Digest* and the *Daily Worker*.

For all the emphasis on *sub rosa*, prepublication surveillance, bureau files analyzing African American modernists cannot always refrain from hinting at the pleasure of the enemy couplet or sentence. McKay's file, packed with memoranda carefully transcribing his poetry and journalism, contains one of the most careful anthologies of his American sonnets to be found outside of James Weldon Johnson's *Book of American Negro Poetry* (1922) and McKay's own *Harlem Shadows* (1922). Chester Himes's file offers capsule interpretations of every early story he placed in *Esquire*. The direct object of these readings was to unearth sedition, but their anonymous FBI author could not help from noting Himes's richly woven "descriptive material" (U.S., Himes file, August 1, 1945). It is not too much to propose that such bureau files should be considered as revealing works of literary criticism, as state-sponsored, collectively authored compilations of textual analysis privately bidding for interpretive dominance. The compatibility of the author and the spy has been remarked at least since the (pre-Harlem) English Renaissance. "A writer-spy like Marlowe," contends John Michael Archer, knew that his work on both sides of the hyphen depended on the "necessary lie" and on "observation of men and manners [that] made their manipulation through spectacle possible" (75). But what of the figure and impact of the critic-spy or ghostreader, whose observation of authors and texts is enabled not only by decryption, identity theft, and hermeneutics of suspicion—techniques almost every literary critic shares with the intelligence agent—but by FBI manipulation?

The ingredients of the Langston Hughes file testify that more than a few Americans trusted in the better knowledge of such ghostreading, and conceived of the bureau as the final critical authority on African American modernism. Dozens of letters from the likes of Arizona State College, the Kankakee Chamber of Congress, and the Springfield, Illinois Urban League quiz Hoover about the meaning of Hughes's poems, in large part because of his public unveiling as a Hughes explicator in the widely distributed FBI pamphlet "Secularism—Breeder of Crime." A brave correspondent from the Methodist Church seeks illumination on whether the intentional fallacy applies to black Bolsheviks, noting that Hughes himself had claimed that "Goodbye, Christ" was "not an expression of his own view but . . . a poetic mechanism describ[ing] what a Communist thinks" (U.S., Hughes file, March 3, 1948). The bureau's reply failed to enlighten, but as late as 1970, then Congressman George H.W. Bush thought nothing of forwarding the FBI director a constituent's critical inquiry concerning both Hughes and the history of black theater. "I seem to remember," wrote a confused citizen from Bush's Houston district, that *A Raisin in the Sun* "was a highly controversial production . . . by a Leroi Jones and that Jones is something of a professional trouble maker and rabble rouser. If you cannot furnish information pertaining to this play and its author please advise where I might obtain such details" (U.S., Hughes file, July 6, 1970).

None of this correspondence goes to show that the FBI wisely fulfilled the office later assumed by the encyclopedia *Africana* (1999) and the *Oxford Companion to African American Literature* (1997). The bureau's readings and responses were abrupt, sometimes mistaken, and generally up to no good. It would take the emergence of the CIA and James Jesus Angleton—1941 Yale English B.A., admirer of I.A. Richards, eventual chief CIA mole-hunter—to acquaint federal surveillance with the intricacies of the intentional fallacy and other formalist doctrines of the New Criticism, drawn upon in Angleton's theory of spycraft as "the practical criticism of ambiguity" (Epstein 84). Fully formalist spy-reading, devoted to wrestling with subtle indeterminacies, might therefore be described as "CIA reading," the conquering method of the second Red Scare, when this intelligence agency exceeded the FBI in anti-Communist cachet and the New Criticism grew from Southern Agrarian dependent to national collegiate champion. "FBI reading," on the other hand, the master method unveiled during the first Red Scare of the late teens and 1920s, reflects both the bureau's place at the top of an intelligence hierarchy free from Ivy League intruders, and the theoretical grounding of the biographical-historical literary criticism of its own day. McKay's file, for one, steadily exhibits the brusque, gossip-hungry diligence of such FBI reading: the infatuation with the independent literary artifact still imagined as an exotic confessional; the always close but never "New" criticism. Plucked from dozens of available McKay poems, the sonnet "America" (1921) is found valuable enough for exacting transcription, but is stripped of most internal traction: "Although she feeds me bread of bitterness, / And sinks into my throat her tiger's tooth, / Stealing my breath of life, I will confess / I love this cultured hell that tests my youth!" (ll. 1–4). A straightforward political meaning for the poem—support for America-hating enemy aliens—is thought clear enough: the sonnet directly precedes information that McKay "appeared . . . at Ellis Island, New York, as a witness in behalf of . . . a British Communist" within months of its publication (U.S., McKay file, January 26, 1924). The affected principle of FBI interpretive theory is proclaimed earlier in the same memorandum: "McKay's views, beliefs, principles, et cetera may properly be inferred from quotations from his writings" (ibid.). Avoidance of the "biographical fallacy" thus remains in the CIA-New Critical future, and the only thing New Critically ambiguated by the bureau's approach to McKay's poem is its author's patriotism.

The sheer volume of public trust in the FBI's old-school critical authority is nonetheless instructive. An accurate impression of the bureau's comprehensive interest in African American literary intelligence escaped beyond the Beltway, as did word of Hoover's intent to outwrite black criticism in public pronouncements as well as in his agents' secret files. As I'll discuss in a moment, the lawless appetite of FBI ghostreading could create interpretive advantages, feeding paranoid insights into the transnational range of African American modernism. Authors of bureau pulp criticism would have been happy to see Hughes and company chucked into the nearest jail, but they also managed to perceive the far reaches of the Black Atlantic before their academic rivals.

Thesis Three: The FBI Helped to Frame the Twentieth-Century Black Atlantic, both Orienting and Criminalizing Its Flows

Hughes's file repeatedly quotes his claim that "Negroes are growing in global consciousness" (U.S., Hughes file, June 3, 1947). His file and others, meanwhile, confirm that the bureau concluded it should grow in the same way. Unlike Foucault's eighteenth-century prisoners, prototypical citizens of his penitentiary modern state, African American modernists were known to see widely as they were seen; FBI dossiers recognized them as subjects in communication with international movements even as they became the objects of national police information. The bureau's domestic jurisdiction was thus often exceeded in the hunt for black literary offenders. McKay's file, for instance, includes such artifacts of international surveillance as articles on the New Negro summarized from Soviet newspapers; reports on McKay's Moscow speeches by American diplomats in Riga, Latvia, then a nest of anti-Communist espionage; and clipped schedules of Europe-bound shipping traffic.

Like other narratives of black transnational voyagers, McKay's bureau dossier underscores political pilgrimage, economic immigration, and other passages typically absent from classic European travel writing. More pertinent here, however, this dossier also exposes blind spots within prevailing maps of modern black internationalism, not excluding Paul Gilroy's *The Black Atlantic: Modernity and Double Consciousness* (1993), the high sea in which so many recent accounts of Afro-modernism have found their bearings. For Gilroy, the Black Atlantic world is not simply a spawning ground of liberating transethnic exchanges among dispersed black populations; his central chronotope of the sailing ship, chosen to "rethink . . . the African disapora" via the history of the "western hemisphere," is intended to recall the racial violence of the Atlantic slave trade that built the Black Atlantic in the first brutal instance (17). Yet Gilroy joins a good deal of the work done in his wake by suggesting that the willful transatlantic roaming of black moderns handily cancels or undoes the coerced motion of the Middle Passage, its involuntary scattering of millions alchemized into free flights of reconnection. "What was initially felt to be a curse—the curse of homelessness or the curse of enforced exile," Gilroy explains, is "affirmed [and] reconstructed as the basis of a privileged standpoint from which certain useful and critical perceptions about the modern world become more likely" (111). The evidence buried within the FBI's alternative history of the Black Atlantic offers a markedly different account of the effort to transpose the negative meanings of imperative movement, documenting that *blocked* and *forced cosmopolitanisms* were common among precisely those modernist intellectuals most dedicated to the subversive promise of Black Atlantic travel.

For some of the diaspora-minded black moderns pursued by the bureau, radical internationalisms led to U.S. house arrest. The passport of founding Pan-Africanist W.E.B. Du Bois was withdrawn at the peak of the Cold War, three years after Paul Robeson's, and Hughes barely escaped the same restriction. For other of these moderns, Atlantic crossings led to American banishments: paradoxically, their rewritings and reversals of the Middle Passage brought unwilled returns. Think of the obligatory Black Atlanticism of Jamaican arrival Claude McKay, whose American de-migration parallels both Garvey's Harlem-to-Kingston extradition and C.L.R. James's deportation back to England from the ironic dock of Ellis Island. As I have detailed elsewhere, FBI vigilance ensured that McKay could not easily come home to Harlem before 1934, when New Negro elders finally intervened with contacts at the State Department (Maxwell 47–51). Wright's decampment to France was partly motivated by bureau-prying, a fate he shared with Baldwin, whose 1964 flight to Turkey to escape Hoover's watch provoked an official FBI travel warning. Baldwin's political itinerary, like McKay's before him, was rewarded with a bureau "Stop Notice" under which the INS was ordered to "immediately notify the FBI if [Baldwin] passes through the area" (qtd. in Campbell, "I Heard" 172).

No wonder that Wright considered an Atlantic cruise no place to forget the bureau's roving eye. The State Department might send Louis Armstrong, Dizzy Gillespie, and fellow jazzmen on goodwill tours of Europe, Africa, and the Middle East, convinced that international news of racial discrimination was America's Achilles heel in the global battle with Communism (Von Eschen 5). The CIA might fight what Frances Saunders terms the "cultural Cold War" by urging European roles for soprano Leontyne Price and other black opera divas, reasoning that the presence of African American artists abroad countered what one agency surrogate called "the 'suppressed race' propaganda," forestalling "all criticisms to the effect that we . . . wouldn't let our own 'out'" (qtd. in Saunders 119). The FBI, by contrast, aspired to keep African American authors running scared when not down on the farm, reflecting those interests in the federal bureaucracy pleased with the Cold War state's relative complacency toward the enforcement of racial equality and black liberty on the home front (Von Eschen 5). Study of the FBI's patrolling of the Black Atlantic reveals a dialectic of Cold War recruitment of black culture poised between Hoover's wary ghostreaders and the eager listeners of the Company and the diplomatic corps, between the strategic export of African American music and the desired containment of African American literature's free transit at home and abroad.

As Wright knew intimately, to be trailed and propelled by the FBI was not to be entirely defined by it. Bureau files capture Hoover's spy-critics acting as G-Men Dr. Bledsoes, devising secret letters and scheming to keep black modernists running in tight circles. Their efforts met with disturbing successes, but never installed an intelligence apparatus sharp enough to discover, let alone dictate, all the routes within a vast oceanic territory. In the last analysis, however, the consequences of Hoover's early exposure to cartography cannot be ignored by Black Atlantic theory. His FBI strived to outmap a whole navy of black radical voyagers, and managed to penetrate the time and space of the Black Atlantic system. The nonsynchronous present of this system, formed in the barbarous modernity of the slave trade, was punctuated by concrete echoes of a past of forced transportation courtesy of bureau deportation orders. The diasporic geography of this system was fractured internally not only by differences of class, gender, ethnicity, and so on, but also by the renationalizing atomization of bureau Stop Notices and passport seizures. In both cases, a peculiarly race-conscious national surveillance bureaucracy influenced the making of a major black transnationalism, thus arguing that the state powers most opposed to discourses of adversarial globalism may still help to inspire, direct, and translate these discourses into action.

Thesis Four: Knowledge of and Opposition to FBI Ghostreading Informs a Surprising Quantity of Afro-Modernist Writing

To an observer jaundiced by the FB eye, the contentious milieu of black Paris during Wright's final expatriate years looks like the intended result of U.S. covert operations. By the late 1950s, the *Rive Noire* of the city Brent Hayes Edwards casts as the reigning symbol of black transnational "interaction, exchange, and dialogue" (5) was rife with separation, information hoarding, and denunciation. "Everybody thought that everybody else was spying on someone or other for somebody," reported an observer of the scene at the *Café de Tournon*, once a spot where black and white expatriates tried to drink off their American racial masks, now a magnet for anxiety over American state sleuthing (qtd. in Campbell, *Exiled* 120). Spy stories ricocheted off the café's walls and settled onto everyone inside. Chester Himes wondered if William Gardner Smith received payments from the CIA, and vice versa; both charged Ollie Harrington with spying; Wright had marked doubts about the loyalties of failed author Richard Gibson, and only slightly less concern about everyone else with whom he worked, spoke, or slept (Campbell, *Exiled* 196–97). For his trouble, Wright himself was suspected of being a G-Man. "There is a story, a rumor about you that is going about," Kay Boyle warned in a letter all the way from Connecticut, "you are known to be working with the State Department, or the FBI. . . . " (qtd. in Campbell, *Exiled* 197). This tangle of mutual suspicions rose to the surface during the so-called Gibson Affair, a case of ghostwriting under Harrington's signature perhaps directed by the FBI. They exploded after Wright's sudden death in 1960, which Harrington was only the first to attribute, probably too creatively, to the bureau. At a minimum, the FBI succeeded in persuading the literary intellectuals of the *Rive Noire* that their French harbor was as navigable by U.S. intelligence as were the major crossings of the Black Atlantic.

But Hoover's bookish agents, capable of suggesting plots to the Tournon regulars, would not have the last word on overseas surveillance. The same FBI scrutiny that tested personal alliances inspired a notable family of *roman à clefs*, each running changes on the theme of U.S. state reconnaissance and black counterintelligence. Wright's unpublished final novel, *Island of Hallucinations*, ships Fishbelly, the Mississippi-bred protagonist of *The Long Dream* (1958), to the City of Light, where he uncovers intrigues among African American expatriates stoked by an American secret service. William Gardner Smith's fourth long fiction, *The Stone Face* (1963), plants a suspected G-Man among a crew of Tournon habitués whose Francophilic idyll is bruised by the Algerian revolution. Chester Himes's philosophical police procedural *A Case of Rape* (1963) enters the mix with a would-be detective character that inherits Wright's habit of tracing the criminal jeopardy of black Parisians to government conspiracies. Common to all three novels is the task of out-investigating the FBI, of solving the mysteries of the black metropolis in public case records designed to expose future bureau informers. As Himes's contribution clarifies in particular, the books pioneer a novelistic subgenre of their own, that of the counterfile, in which the tropes of the police dossier are aired and angled against their usual ghostreaders.

Minus many of the Parisian stage sets, the challenge of the counterfile is accepted in a deep pocket of real and imagined twentieth-century black literature. For nearly a decade, James Baldwin, the author of *The Evidence of Things Not Seen* (1985), threatened retaliation against the bureau in the form of a never-glimpsed exposé named *The Blood Counters.* Revenge against the national security state was taken more tangibly in the publication of Sam Greenlee's *The Spook Who Sat by the Door* (1969), Melvin Van Peebles's *A Bear for the FBI* (1968), and John A. Williams's *The Man Who Cried I Am* (1967), the great historical novel of the Tournon intrigue and a weighty brief for Wright as Hoover's cagey, document-hoarding, politically antithetical twin, thus the century's representative black intellectual. Before such texts of Black Power were even conceivable, Claude McKay had answered the bureau's manhandling of his work with spiked, cunning sonnets including "America" (1921)—as we have already seen, among the bureau's favorite McKay offerings. Here, lofty and ambivalent diction baits a known readership of intelligence agents with an aura of foreign agency, but accepts this readership's advice for avoiding the "profane, scurrilous, or abusive" anti-American language prohibited under the Sedition Act. "[A]s a rebel fronts a king in state," contends McKay's speaker, "I stand within her walls with not a shred / Of terror, malice, not a word of jeer" (ll. 8, 9–10). There are many reasons why McKay's post-Creole verse sidestepped most aspects of the formal revolution of high modernism, from his early Jamaican training in the splendor of Keats, Milton, and the Elizabethan lyricists, to his conviction that the Poundian theater of modernist rebellion was nothing but formal, mere "bourgeois attitudinizing of the social revolutionary ferment" (McKay, letter to Max Eastman, April 25, 1932). The least negotiable reason why his Standard English poems retained an uncolloquial, sometimes misty high-Romantic diction, however, was the need to elevate and obfuscate "anti-American" speech, therefore assuring that this speech would remain free. "America" and the like consciously excited bureau attention with their whispered promises of direct action, but their backward-looking anti-Imagism, their *in*direct treatment of the mutinous thing, successfully thwarted bureau-led censorship by observing the letter of sedition law. In this sense, FBI "counter-modernity," taking shape as an interdiction against profane or unreservedly critical political discourse, wound up invigorating McKay's brightly torn brand of black poetic modernism, in which expressive double agency, or speaking as a fervent rebel but without "a word of jeer," is the highest prize.

The ghostreaders partly responsible for McKay's sonnets prompt a final speculation on the readership that shaped the production of Afro-modernism. The Edgar Allan Poe critic Terence Whalen sensibly observes that "writers necessarily have some notion of audience which, above and beyond post-publication feedback, guides them in the production of texts" (10). McKay and the impressive company of black modernists shadowed by the FBI were badgered by what Whalen calls the "Capital Reader," the personification of the logic of literature as commodity who "pre-reads" any text produced for a capitalist marketplace (10). As much criticism on African American literature appreciates, McKay and his peers were also preread by a racially divided general audience that carved out distinct interpretive paths before the first page was printed. McKay was not alone among black moderns, I conclude, in supposing that the next most powerful prereader of twentieth-century black letters was the "Capitol Reader"—accent on the "o"—the school of Hoover based in Washington's most book-aware Seat of Government. In the case of McKay's work—and that of Hughes, Wright, Childress, and many of the rest, aware of the FBI's hot pursuit—the Capitol Reader provoked defining pre-revisions, not all regrettable, even when the manifest subject wandered far from the "FB Eye Blues."

WORKS CITED

"ACLU Says FBI Spying on Religious, Protest Groups." *Reuters* December 2, 2004. http://today.reuters.com/news/default.aspx accessed on December 2, 2004.

Agamben, Giorgio. *State of Exception.* 2003. Trans. Kevin Attell. Chicago: U of Chicago P, 2005.

Archer, John Michael. *Sovereignty and Intelligence: Spying and Court Culture in the English Renaissance.* Stanford: Stanford U P, 1993.

Campbell, James. *Exiled in Paris: Richard Wright, James Baldwin, Samuel Beckett, and Others on the Left Bank.* 1995. Berkeley: U of California P, 2003.

———. "I Heard it Through the Grapevine." *Granta* 73 (Spring 2001): 151–82.

Culleton, Claire A. *Joyce and the G-Men: J. Edgar Hoover's Manipulation of Modernism.* New York: Palgrave Macmillan, 2004.

Edwards, Brent Hayes. *The Practice of Diaspora: Literature, Translation, and the Rise of Black Internationalism.* Cambridge: Harvard U P, 2003.

Epstein, William H. "Counter-Intelligence: Cold-War Criticism and Eighteenth-Century Studies." *ELH* 57, 1 (Spring 1990): 63–99.

Foucault, Michel. *Discipline and Punish: The Birth of the Prison.* 1975. Trans. Alan Sheridan. New York: Vintage, 1979.

Gilroy, Paul. *The Black Atlantic: Modernity and Double Consciousness*. Cambridge: Harvard U P, 1993.

Hack, Richard. *Puppetmaster: The Secret Life of J. Edgar Hoover*. Beverly Hills: New Millennium, 2004.

Huggins, Nathan Irvin. Ed. *Voices from the Harlem Renaissance*. New York: Oxford U P, 1976.

Keen, Mike Forrest. *Stalking the Sociological Imagination: J. Edgar Hoover's FBI Surveillance of American Sociology*. Westport, CT: Greenwood, 1999.

Kornweibel, Theodore, Jr. *"Seeing Red": Federal Campaigns Against Black Militancy, 1919–1925*. Bloomington: Indiana U P, 1998.

Lewis, David Levering. Ed. *The Portable Harlem Renaissance Reader*. New York: Viking, 1994.

Maxwell, William J. "F.B. Eyes: The Bureau Reads Claude McKay," in *Left of the Color Line: Race, Radicalism, and Twentieth-Century Literature of the United States*, Bill V. Mullen and James Smethurst, eds., Chapel Hill: U of North Carolina P, 2003. pp. 39–65.

McKay, Claude. "America." 1921. *Complete Poems*. Ed. William J. Maxwell. Urbana: U of Illinois P, 2004. p. 153.

———. Letter to Max Eastman. April 25, 1932. Claude McKay Manuscripts. Lily Library, Indiana University, Bloomington.

Mitgang, Herbert. *Dangerous Dossiers: Exposing the Secret War Against America's Greatest Authors*. New York: Donald I. Fine, 1988.

Mullen, Bill V. and James Smethurst. Eds. *Left of the Color Line: Race, Radicalism, and Twentieth-Century Literature of the United States*. Chapel Hill: U of North Carolina P, 2003.

Robins, Natalie. *Alien Ink: The FBI's War on Freedom of Expression*. New York: William Morrow, 1992.

Rowley, Hazel. *Richard Wright: The Life and Times*. New York: Henry Holt, 2001.

Saunders, Frances Stonor. *The Cultural Cold War: The CIA and the World of Arts and Letters*. 1999. New York: New Press, 2000.

United States [U.S.]. Federal Bureau of Investigation. Chester Himes file obtained under provisions of the Freedom of Information Act. Assorted documents dated June 13, 1944 to November 18, 1964. File no. 105-2502.

United States [U.S.]. Federal Bureau of Investigation. Claude McKay file obtained under provisions of the Freedom of Information Act. Assorted documents dated December 16, 1921 to May 31, 1940. File no. 61-3497.

United States [U.S.]. Federal Bureau of Investigation. Langston Hughes file obtained under provisions of the Freedom of Information Act. Assorted documents dated [?] 1925 to July 17, 1970. File no. 100-15139.

United States [U.S.]. Federal Bureau of Investigation. Marcus Garvey file obtained under provisions of the Freedom of Information Act. File no. 198940.

United States [U.S.]. Federal Bureau of Investigation. Richard Wright file obtained under provisions of the Freedom of Information Act. Assorted documents dated November 2, 1942 to May 9, 1963. File no. 100-157464.

Von Eschen, Penny M. *Satchmo Blows Up the World: Jazz Ambassadors Play the Cold War*. Cambridge: Harvard U P, 2004.

Walters, Wendy W. "Policing the Borders of the Text and the Body of the Writer: Chester Himes and the FBI." Paper presented at the American Studies Association Conference, Washington, DC, November 2001.

Washington, Mary Helen. "Alice Childress, Lorraine Hansberry, and Claudia Jones: Black Women Write the Popular Front," in *Left of the Color Line*, Mullen and Smethurst, eds., pp. 183–204.

Whalen, Terence. *Edgar Allan Poe and the Masses: The Political Economy of Literature in Antebellum America*. Princeton: Princeton U P, 1999.

Wright, Richard. "The FB Eye Blues." 1949. *Richard Wright Reader*. Ed. Ellen Wright and Michel Fabre. New York: Harper & Row, 1978. pp. 249–50.

CHAPTER 2

Raising Muscovite Ducks and Government Suspicions: Henry Roth and the FBI

Steven G. Kellman

In 1921, 15-year-old Henry Roth was caught pilfering fountain pens from classmates at Stuyvesant High School in Manhattan. It was the only serious crime to which he ever confessed, though the official record of his transgressions was expunged when Roth agreed to withdraw permanently from the school. Five years later, he was working as a clerk at a Loft's candy shop in the Bronx when an agile thief made off with $10 from the cash register. The missing money was unjustly deducted from Roth's weekly salary of $16, but he made up the difference by pocketing $10 in candy sales without registering the transactions. However, when a fellow worker urged him to collude in skimming the store's profits, Roth, mindful of his disgraceful departure from Stuyvesant High School, refused.

Born in 1906 in Tysmenitz, Galicia, then part of the Austro-Hungarian Empire, Roth arrived at Ellis Island in 1907. Until his death, in Albuquerque, in 1995, he was a law-abiding citizen of the United States. Nevertheless, the Federal Bureau of Investigation (FBI) considered Roth enough of a threat to public safety to keep him under sporadic surveillance from 1946 until 1955.[1] He joined the Communist Party of the United States in 1934, shortly after completing work on his first novel, *Call It Sleep*, and he remained loyal to its shifting positions throughout and despite Stalinist repressions and aggressions.

It was only as late as 1967 that Soviet hostility to Israel finally induced him to break with the party.

For most of this 33-year period, Roth was not an eminent literary figure. A one-book author whose one book was soon out of print and out of the public mind, he gave up on the literary life in New York and went off to Maine, where he raised ducks and geese. Roth was not nearly as famous as Ernest Hemingway, Theodore Dreiser, John Steinbeck, Thomas Mann, Georgia O'Keeffe, and other leading cultural figures whom J. Edgar Hoover's bureau also monitored.[2] Like literary celebrities such as Langston Hughes and Richard Wright, Roth did show up on Hoover's Security Index, a list of those considered dangerous enough to be interned in case of war.[3] But he remained on the Index only four years, from 1951–1955. Nor did his leftist associations and activities have any demonstrable impact on the national security of the United States. However, Roth's life was profoundly affected by knowledge that he was the subject of scrutiny by federal law enforcement agents.

Roth experienced the longest writer's block of any major figure in American literature—60 years between the publication of his first novel, *Call It Sleep*, in 1934, and his second novel, *A Star Shines Over Mt. Morris Park*, in 1994. In 1964, when *Call It Sleep* was republished, rediscovered, and canonized as a masterpiece of immigrant fiction, many readers, surprised to learn that its author was still alive, were curious about his long silence. The FBI, which tracked him during the years of artistic dormancy, should not have shared that surprise. The Henry Roth of popular legend was the Rip Van Winkle of American letters, a self-taught literary prodigy who, devastated by indifference to his ambitious first book, abjured his rough magic to rusticate in Maine for 30 years. A miraculous rediscovery suddenly brought him fame, fortune, and a passion to resume writing, which he did, in a final, fierce, creative sprint. However, Roth's long life was more complex than the popular narrative of artistic renunciation, extended silence, and autumnal resurgence would admit. Anxiety over his dissident political views was a significant factor in shaping that life.

Though *Call It Sleep* sold fewer than 2,000 copies, and its publisher, Robert O. Ballou, went out of business a year and a half after its appearance, it is not true that the novel was either ignored or scorned. Its critical reception was in fact as enthusiastic as any author—especially one who had never before published a book—could hope for. Of the 14 reviews that appeared in six newspapers and eight magazines, most were highly favorable.[4] Praising the novel as "a work of superior craftsmanship, more than that a work of significance, authority and depth," Fred T. Marsh declared in the *New York Herald Tribune:* "I believe it to be the most compelling and moving, the most accurate and profound study of an American slum childhood that has yet appeared in this day when, be it said to the credit of our contemporary critics, economic color-lines are no longer drawn in our literature."[5] In *the Nation*, poet Horace Gregory hailed *Call It Sleep* as a "first novel of extraordinary character" and "an experience which few readers of contemporary fiction can afford to ignore."[6]

It might have been easy for Roth to let these rapturous reactions go to his head, but one negative review punctured his heart. An anonymous critic for the *New Masses*, a Marxist weekly, dismissed the novel as too subjective and impressionistic to be of much political use. "It is a pity that so many young writers drawn from the proletariat can make no better use of their working-class experience than as material for introspective and febrile novels," he complained, faulting the work as well for being at least two hundred pages too long and for focusing on "the sex phobia of this six year old Proust."[7]

The pan provoked a controversy within the pages of the *New Masses*, and the next three issues featured letters defending Roth's book. It also exposed a major fault line within modernist culture—do artists bear a primary responsibility to the perfection of their art or to the struggle against injustice? One respondent to the review in the *New Masses*, poet David Greenhood, applied the same Marxist principles to praise *Call It Sleep* as the anonymous reviewer had used to condemn it: "*Call It Sleep* is about the working-class bottom, written by one of its own naturals who became articulate long before he wrote the novel, and who while he wrote it was engaged, as he has never ceased to be, in the one struggle that counts."[8] Another Roth supporter, Edwin Seaver, praised the author for having created in young David Schearl a budding hero of the working class. "When we close the book," he insisted, "we honestly feel that such a childhood can mature into a revolutionary manhood."[9]

However, more sensitive to sticks than carrots, Roth got stuck on the first *New Masses* review. None of the praise heaped on his novel affected him as much as that assault on his radical credentials. "I thought I was a good Communist," he recalled. "I thought I was doing the right thing for the Party and the Revolution."[10] Roth internalized the standards of socialist realism and vowed that next time out he would write an exemplary Marxist novel. Though Michael Harrington, a prominent socialist, would later judge *Call It Sleep* "the finest proletarian novel of the Thirties,"[11] Roth continued to disparage his own literary effort as bourgeois—too fixated on the merely personal, too much invested in the version of modernism exemplified by Joyce and Proust.

Roth soon found a chance to redeem himself from reactionary aestheticism through friendship with a proud, pugnacious worker named Bill Clay. Though a hook took the place of his right hand, which was mangled in an industrial accident in Los Angeles, Clay was admired as the leading salesman for the Communist Party's *Daily Worker*, a paper that, he, because illiterate, did not read. Born in the heartland, in Cincinnati, Clay, who came of

German stock, was echt American in ways that Roth, a Jewish immigrant, could never be. Claims that he had been a middleweight boxer and even an armed robber merely enhanced the revolutionary romance of Comrade Clay, and Roth revered him as a hero of labor. Though Roth tried to teach him to read, it was Clay who served as mentor and scourge, berating him for bourgeois tendencies, tendencies that Roth believed had tainted his first novel.

Determined to create historically grounded fiction that would advance the cause of the working class, Roth began writing a new novel about a midwestern proletarian hero named Dan Loem whom he based on Bill Clay. He began the story on the mean streets of Cincinnati, with the young ruffian Loem's attempt to rob the paymaster of a slaughterhouse. Marxism has not yet redeemed him from the loutish life of a hooligan. "It seemed to me," he later told an interviewer, "that all I had to do was to explore his life's experiences and exploit the picturesque language that he used and I had a novel."[12] It was not that simple.

After completing approximately 100 pages, Roth sold his book to Scribner's, to the most celebrated book editor in the United States, Maxwell Perkins, whose stable of authors also included Erskine Caldwell, F. Scott Fitzgerald, Ernest Hemingway, Ring Lardner, Marjorie Kinnan Rawlings, and Thomas Wolfe. Perkins paid a $1,000 advance for Roth's Dan Loem novel, but Scribner's never published it, because, aside from a prologue, Roth never produced another page. Roth soon became disillusioned with Clay as a braggart and a bully, and he found himself uninspired by the formulas of socialist realism.

During the five years it took him to write *Call It Sleep*, Roth lived in the Manhattan apartment of Eda Lou Walton, a poet and a professor at New York University. His senior by 12 years, Walton served as his patron, mentor, and lover. Pygmalion to Roth's Galatea, she took an uncouth young Jewish immigrant and transformed him into a Greenwich Village intellectual. Throughout the Depression, Walton provided Roth with food, clothing, and a place to live and write. He did not have to contend with bread lines, soup kitchens, and Hoovervilles, but he did have to cope with the shame of feeling kept by an older woman. His gratitude toward his benefactor became tinged with resentment. "And I was being supported by Eda Lou, so I didn't have to mature," Roth later concluded.[13] "It was a real continuation of infancy to be supported by a woman so long."[14] Walton's vehement opposition to Roth's membership in the Communist Party helped convince him to join. But so did the sorry state of the world. During the Great Depression, joining in the call for radical solutions to the global crisis was not in itself a remarkable act. In 1935, Earl Browder, leader of the Communist Party of the United States, claimed 31,000 dues-paying members.[15] Less than 20 years after the Bolshevik Revolution, many idealistic Americans still regarded the Soviet

Union as a magnificent experiment in social and economic democracy. Jews, in particular, welcomed an end to the Tsarist régime that promulgated discriminatory restrictions and quotas and fomented pogroms. Many, including Roth, believed, naively, that its Marxist successor, many of whose leaders came from Jewish families, meant to put a stop to the virulent anti-Semitism that had for centuries blighted Eastern Europe. In the United States, where jobs were often insecure, dangerous, and underpaid and where lynching was still commonplace, the Communist Party promised an end to economic and social injustice.

Roth attended meetings of the John Reed Club, an organization dedicated to the principle that artists should side with workers in the class struggle. Named for the flamboyant American literary radical who was buried beside the Kremlin wall, the John Reed Club was founded by Joseph Freeman and Michael Gold in 1929 to advance the cause of the CPUSA among the intelligentsia. By 1934, 30 chapters had spread throughout the United States, but Roth was a member of the original one, at 430 Sixth Avenue in Greenwich Village. It was a site for poetry readings, exchange of manuscripts, and debates over the social role of literature, as well as for the sore eyes of idealists distressed by what they saw in contemporary society. Their manifesto called upon "all honest intellectuals, all honest writers and artists, to abandon decisively the treacherous illusion that art can exist for art's sake, or that the artist can remain remote from the historic conflicts in which all men must take sides."[16] Roth became convinced that he wrote his first novel under that "treacherous illusion," and he resolved to change his ways. Henceforth, he would use fiction not to make a fetish of rarefied art but to advance the interests of the working class. Enlistment in the cause might dissipate the shame that burdened Roth, as if political revolution meant personal redemption. "Here I was—warm, taken care of, well-clothed, well-fed, doing what I wanted to do—and outside all that turmoil, all that suffering," Roth recalled.[17] Using his pen to address that turmoil and that suffering might relieve him of the discomfort he felt over his unmerited fortune. As Roth later explained: "I think that one of the reasons I joined the Communist Party was to feel that I was doing something to redeem myself. . . ."[18]

Though it was enough to attract the attention of federal investigators, what Roth was doing to advance the revolution was rather meager. While trying to write his abortive Dan Loem novel of proletarian heroism, he was signing petitions and handing out leaflets. During one misadventure, in spring of 1935, Roth went to the New York wharves to try to persuade dockworkers to shift their allegiance from the accommodationist American Federation of Labor to the more radical Congress of Industrial Organizations. Urged on by the business agent of the local of the International Longshoreman's Association, a group of union thugs pounced upon him, beating him up and breaking his nose. Yet, though he burned the manuscript of his proletarian work-in-progress, Roth was not silenced politically. He publicly expressed support for Joseph Stalin's cynical ploy to eliminate rivals and consolidate personal power when, during the Moscow show trials of 1936–1938, more than a dozen leading Kremlin *nomenklatura* were arraigned on specious charges of treason. Most were convicted and executed. Roth signed onto a list of 150 American artists and intellectuals who supported the show trials. The author of the forgotten *Call It Sleep* was not the most conspicuous name on a roster that included Nelson Algren, Harold Clurman, Malcolm Cowley, John Garfield, Dashiell Hammett, Lillian Hellman, Langston Hughes, Dorothy Parker, Irwin Shaw, Raphael Soyer, and Richard Wright, but the FBI, at least, would eventually take note.

After Leon Trotsky, the principal theorist of the Bolshevik Revolution, was purged from the Soviet leadership and fled into exile in North America, philosopher John Dewey headed up an independent commission of inquiry into whether Stalin had committed an injustice against his chief rival as Lenin's heir. An "Open Letter to American Liberals" condemned the Dewey Commission in print. Its signators, according to Earl Browder, comprised "the most distinguished list of names ever gathered on a single document in America in support of the Soviet Union."[19] Henry Roth was one of the least prominent of those 88 names, which included Theodore Dreiser, Lillian Hellman, Granville Hicks, Ring Lardner, Jr., Dorothy Parker, and Nathanael West. In a short essay of his own, "Where My Sympathy Lies," published in the *New Masses* on March 2, 1937, Roth reaffirmed his confidence in the guilt of the Moscow show trials defendants, his commitment to the struggle for human liberation from exploitation, and his conviction that "the Trotskyite mentality" was an obstacle to that liberation.[20] "Whoever hungers for justice," he wrote, "must ally himself, if only in sympathy, with all those forces that struggle to liberate humanity from slavery and want." In 1937, Roth identified those forces with Stalin. By supporting the purge of Trotsky, né Lev Davidovich Bronstein, he, like many other American Stalinists, was also repudiating his own Jewishness.

"I once saw Israel Amter plain," wrote Allen Ginsberg in his 1956 poem "America." "Everybody must have been a spy." Few of the literary leftists of the 1930s and 1940s were spies, but many would have endorsed Ginsberg's suggestion—echoing Robert Browning's awestruck question: "Ah, did you once see Shelley plain?"—that a glimpse of Amter, a legendary leader of the American left who died in 1954, was like the sighting of a saint. Roth signed a nominating petition to put Amter on the ballot as a Communist in the race for governor of New York State in 1942. The following year he signed a nominating petition for Carl Brodsky, a Communist candidate for city council of New York City, and served on the defense committee for Morris Schappes, a Communist who was dismissed from his position in the English department at City College and sentenced to prison for 18–24 months. While most American Jews were not Communists, many American Communists were Jews; according to one estimate, "close to 50 percent of the aggregate of those who appeared regularly in Party-affiliated publications and joined Party-led organizations such as the John Reed Clubs and League of American Writers" were Jewish,[21] just a shave and a haircut removed from Orthodox piety. The Party, with its prophetic rhetoric and its organizational discipline, provided them with a secular substitute for religious life. In part to camouflage the Ashkenazic coloration of the Communist Party of the United States of America, it even provided them with new names that sounded more indigenous. The *nom de guerre* assigned to Roth was "Berry." For Roth, a self-proclaimed atheist who nevertheless remained nostalgic over his immigrant childhood in what he always called the "Jewish mini-state" of the Lower East Side, joining the Communist Party was like belonging to a shul. Berry/Roth accepted its dogmas longer than most others, but eventually, like heretics Louis Fischer, André Gide, Arthur Koestler, Ignazio Silone, Stephen Spender, and Richard Wright, who in 1950 published a collective recantation titled *The God That Failed*, he, too, would recognize that he had been worshipping false idols of a fickle tribe. Disillusioned with the Party, Berry would finally sour, but it took more than 30 years since the time that he joined.

However, Roth became disillusioned with New York literary culture much earlier. After attending adult industrial education classes offered free at a vocational high school in New York, he became proficient in precision grinding of tools, gauges, and dies. During most of World War II, Roth held skilled jobs at a series of machine shops in the New York area. His occupation also spared him the call to arms, since as a precision metal grinder he was assigned the Selective Service classification of 3A: Deferred for essential work. Late in the war, Roth was eager to leave New York, to get "as far away from the geographic epicenter of my neurotic frustration as I could."[22] He thought about seeking work in the thriving aviation industry that had grown up in southern California. But in May 1945, he took a job in Providence, Rhode Island, at a firm called the Federal Products Company. A month later, he was working as a tool maker for the Keystone Manufacturing Company in Boston and moving with his wife, Muriel Parker, whom he married in 1939, and their two young sons into a squalid tenement in Cambridge.

At work, Roth was active in local 246 of the CIO-affiliated United Electrical, Radio, and Machine Workers of America, serving as finance chairman of its strike committee. He also edited the union newsletter, *UE Projector*, and on February 28, 1946 ran an article that excoriated Keystone for its treatment of an employee who had just returned from military service and found his wages reduced and his seniority ignored. In a meeting that took place on April 11, management dismissed the charges as inaccurate and malicious, but Roth responded with a temper tantrum that puzzled and embarrassed the other union representatives. On May 17, 1946, Roth attended a class in union leadership at the Samuel Adams School for Social Studies, which was cited by the attorney general as a Communist organization. He became president of the Industrial 1-A (Metal) Branch of the Communist Party of the United States for District 1, Boston.

By July 2, 1946, when the FBI, through its Boston office, filed its first report on Roth, the Soviet Union, an erstwhile ally in the crusade against fascism, was now an adversary, and suspicion was cast on its American sympathizers. While he was being ignored entirely by biographical dictionaries and encyclopedias, Henry Roth became a subject of interest to federal agents investigating Communist subversives. Though it emphasizes his union activities and Communist associations, the biographical synopsis composed for the FBI report is similar in format to the Roth entry that would appear in *Who's Who in America*, eventually, in 1966.

Roth is described by an informant, who, though his name is blacked out, was apparently a fellow employee, as "quiet, a good worker," but the informant also recounts the episode in which Roth challenged management over its treatment of a returning veteran and calls his attitude "arrogant and hostile." However, Roth himself was evidently cooperative enough to furnish an FBI investigator with information about his immigration, education, and employment. Additional field reports from St. Louis (where Roth's father, Herman, was naturalized), dated August 2, 1946, and, from New York, dated March 15, 1947, supplement the initial file. The information from all sources led the FBI Boston office to conclude, in a memo sent to Director J. Edgar Hoover on April 22, 1947, that: "The Bureau does not feel that the subject's activities are such that the preparation of a Security Index card is justified."

Roth might have felt relieved, but he of course never saw that memo. Instead, the fact that the FBI had come around interrogating him and others about him troubled Roth. Amid a climate of political repression, he wondered whether it might be prudent to be less visible. In addition, he was concerned about the stutter that his older son, Jeremy, had developed. Doctors attributed the problem to the pressures of urban life, and, though he should have read enough of Marx to make him wary of "the idiocy of rural life," Roth entertained romantic fantasies of abandoning the city and living off the land. He purchased 110 acres in Montville, Maine (about midway between towns named Liberty and Freedom), quit his job at the Keystone Manufacturing Company, and, on Labor Day, 1946, moved into a tumbledown house that lacked central heating, indoor plumbing, and electricity. Late one afternoon that October, Roth, anxious to obliterate any documents that might prove incriminating, completed his personal purge. With his two young sons as witnesses, he went behind the house and set fire to his manuscripts.

Rural Maine had no more call for a precision tool grinder than it did for an autobiographical novelist, and Roth attempted to support his family through odd jobs including cutting wood, gathering blueberries, picking apples, gathering maple syrup, fighting forest fires, and tutoring Latin and math. He would be best known during the years in Maine for raising ducks and geese. From 1949 to 1953, while holding a job as an attendant at Augusta State Hospital (when his own mental state often made him feel indistinguishable from the inmates), Roth tried to organize his fellow workers and to pressure management to improve wages and working conditions. Word of his activities reached the governor of Maine, Frederic G. Payne, who directed state police to investigate. He also alerted the FBI, which reopened its files on Henry Roth. On February 8, 1951, during a meeting with an FBI agent named Thornton, Payne reported that Roth "WAS A QUOTE RABBLE ROUSER UNQUOTE, WHO WAS ATTEMPTING TO ORGANIZE THE EMPLOYEES OF THE INSTITUTION FOR A PAY INCREASE."[23] Spurred by the governor, agents began again to investigate the one-time novelist.

In 1948, Roth was briefly encouraged by the prospects of a job teaching math and science at nearby Liberty High School. The school superintendent seemed enthusiastic about hiring him, even suggesting that Roth might also coach one of the varsity teams. However, when he tried to follow up a few weeks later, the superintendent suddenly turned cold, denying that there was an opening at the school and refusing to discuss the matter further. Roth was convinced that the FBI had gotten to the school administrator and had poisoned his attitude toward the outsider. He suspected that the hostility he felt from many of his neighbors was also the result of pressure from intrusive federal agents.

Even paranoids have enemies, and Roth's sense of being victimized by surreptitious government operations may have been justified. FBI files indicate that investigators, alert for any evidence of subversive activity, did interrogate Roth's neighbors and associates about him. In the process, they probably reinforced hostility that many already felt toward a stranger with unconventional customs and attitudes. The FBI documents report that some could find nothing negative to say about Roth, except that, in the words of one unnamed informant, "They are very quiet people who seem to remain to themselves and have no friends in that area."[24] However, another informant asserted that Roth "was always talking down the American way of life and favoring Communism because he felt that it was the only plan that helped the working class of people."[25] Another unidentified source told FBI agents that, during the Korean War, Roth insisted: "The Communists in North Korea were fighting for a real cause and are putting into force a worthwhile program."[26]

Nevertheless, an FBI memorandum on Roth dated October 30, 1953 states: "Recent investigation failed to reflect any subversive activity on the part of subject for the past several years."[27] Still, in the hope that he might furnish them with information about other suspects, a pair of FBI agents attempted to interview Roth himself on December 29, 1953. Thirty-five years later, Roth would tell a literary scholar that he believed part of the reason the FBI took an interest in him in Maine was that the breed of ducks he was raising was called Muscovite.[28] The two agents, whom Roth remembered for their distinctive snap-brim hats, approached him outside his house. Initially friendly toward the strangers, he became angry and defiant when they identified themselves. "If you want to know the closest thing for which I stand," he told them, "I'm a Titoist."[29] Thereafter, according to their report, "Subject stated he would answer no questions, could give the agents no help, turned and got something from his car and entered his home saying on the way in that he had nothing to say to the agents."[30]

The suspicion and hostility that Roth, an avowed leftist, a Jew, and a foreigner (a New Yorker, born in Europe), encountered in isolated, frigid Maine during the Cold War was not unique. Much more dramatic was the case of the maverick psychoanalyst Wilhelm Reich, who was ultimately, in 1957, harassed to death, in Lewisburg Federal Prison. Like Roth, Reich was a Jew born in Galicia. He was a prominent disciple of Sigmund Freud in Vienna until forced to flee Nazism in 1938. Rural, insular Rangeley, Maine, where he settled in the 1940s, was not the ideal place for a German-speaking refugee with bizarre theories about orgone energy, and wary locals became convinced that he was a spy. The FBI was active not only in investigating but also persecuting the unfortunate Reich, whose mind became unbalanced. Like Roth's, his papers were incinerated, but in contrast to Roth, who burned his own manuscripts, Reich was the victim of arson by agents of the Food and Drug Administration (FDA). Citing its mandate to protect the public health, the FDA has, on several occasions in addition to its encounter with Reich, seized and destroyed literature that promotes alternative therapies.

An FBI memo dated May 3, 1951 recommends that a Security Index card be prepared for Roth. But by May 7, 1955, a memo from the Boston office to the FBI director recommends removing him from the Security Index, stating that: ". . . there is no evidence that the Subject has been a member of a basic revolutionary organization within the last five years. The only overt act has been the contribution of an unknown sum of money in July of 1950 . . . . There is no evidence that the Subject has been a member of or performed overt acts in furtherance of a front organization of a revolutionary group within the last three years." Thus, at least according to the documents made available under the Freedom of Information Act (FOIA), ended the FBI's surveillance of Henry Roth.

Within less than a decade, with the rediscovery of *Call It Sleep* in 1964, Roth, belatedly acknowledged as a literary master, would become subject to a different kind of scrutiny. Journalists and scholars converged on Maine to try to understand a novelist they portrayed as the Rip Van Winkle of American literature. Roth himself seemed no more pleased to be the focus of their attention than he was to be under FBI surveillance. The bestselling new edition of *Call It Sleep* was blowing his cover as an unexceptional Yankee farmer. "You're undermining my position," he complained to Peter Mayer, the enterprising editor responsible for bringing the novel back out as a hugely successful Avon paperback.[31] Coverage by the local *Kennebec Journal* as well as *Life* Magazine ensured that Roth's neighbors now knew him to be a novelist, not just an immigrant Jewish Communist. In contrast to Frederick G. Payne, the governor of Maine who had targeted Roth as a suspicious subversive, a new governor, John H. Reed, paid tribute to him. On January 24, 1965, Reed saluted the achievement—or at least the sudden national fame—of a fellow Mainer by presenting Roth with a gold-bound copy of *Call It Sleep*.

For the last three decades of his long life, Roth did not entirely renounce his radical beliefs. However, he did undergo a personal and political transformation. As late as 1963, Roth wrote: "I can only say, again, that I feel that to the great boons Jews have already conferred upon humanity, Jews in America might add this last and greatest one: of orienting themselves toward ceasing to be Jews."[32] However, in June, 1967, Roth, shocked by the prospect of Israel's destruction in an imminent war, spurned the pro-Arab stance of the Soviet Union and finally rejected Communist doctrine. He embraced his Jewish identity and, though he never carried through on plans to settle in Israel, became a Zionist. He participated in the campaign to pressure the Soviet Union to allow its Jews to emigrate, and he wrote letters urging Congress to oppose selling weapons to Israel's hostile neighbors. Though he used to support Communist candidates, in 1976 Roth favored Henry "Scoop" Jackson, a conservative Democrat from Washington state, in his unsuccessful bid for the presidential nomination, primarily because Jackson sponsored a law that tied American trade concessions to Soviet policies on Jewish emigration and because he was a staunch champion of Israel.

However, in many other ways, Roth remained a contrarian. As early as March, 1965, when Lyndon Johnson's administration was still beginning its buildup of forces in Vietnam, Roth sent a letter to Maine's Senator Edmund Muskie urging an end to American military actions in southeast Asia. His opposition to the war in Vietnam, complicated by the fact that each of his sons was in uniform, Jeremy in the National Guard and Hugh in the Army Corps of Engineers, became more strident as American involvement became more massive. He contributed his name and his money to an antiwar ad designed by the literary couple Denise Levertov and Mitchell Goodman that ran in the *New York Times*, and in private, in a letter to his Italian translator, Mario Materassi, he declared his identification with the enemies of the United States. "I'm a Vietcong or a North Vietnamese," Roth wrote his Italian friend. "The bigger the toll they take of us, the better I like it."[33]

In the late 1960s, while Newark, Detroit, Watts and other urban areas exploded in racial riots, Roth took heart in the rise of black militancy. "I not only hope it becomes the great stumbling block, even a paralyzing one, of American society, but its ultimate undoing," Roth wrote Materassi, whose first wife was African American. "I don't believe the American society, taking it by and large, deserves to exist morally; and if it doesn't morally it doesn't deserve in any other way."[34] FBI agents might have found many other pungent remarks to insert in their reports if, following the fall of Senator Joseph McCarthy, the bureau had not ceased to take an interest in Henry Roth. Though he was now a prominent and influential figure, the aging novelist might now have seemed like a harmless relic of the Old Left. If the FBI kept track of Roth during the final years, no record has been made available. In his late eighties and suffering from rheumatoid arthritis so severe that creating prose became a physical not just psychological torture, Roth managed to produce 5,000 manuscript pages that were clearly autobiographical and acutely embarrassing. Relishing the self-laceration, he was compensating for the pages he had burned many years before. It was Roth not the G-Men who had the last word.

NOTES

1. Most of the information about Roth's leftist associations and activities and his surveillance by the FBI was obtained under the Freedom of Information Act (FOIA) from the Boston office of the FBI. For a detailed discussion of FBI interest in Roth within the context of his life, see: Steven G. Kellman, *Redemption: The Life of Henry Roth* (New York: Norton, 2005).
2. Herbert Mitgang's *Dangerous Dossiers: Exposing the Secret War against America's Greatest Authors* (New York: Dutton, 1988) discusses the cases of these and others but does not mention Henry Roth.
3. Natalie Robins, *Alien Ink: The FBI's War on Freedom of Expression* (New York: William Morrow, 1992), p. 79.
4. Julie Eastlack Hopson, *The Literary Reputations of Henry Roth*. Unpublished M.A. thesis, Harvard University, June 1990, p. 4.
5. Fred T. Marsh, "A Great Novel about Manhattan Boyhood," *New York Herald Tribune Books*, February 17, 1935, p. 6.
6. Horace Gregory, "East Side World," *The Nation*, 140 (February 27, 1935): 255.
7. "Brief Review," *The New Masses*, 14 (February 12, 1935): 27.
8. David Greenhood, "Another View of *Call It Sleep*," *The New Masses*, 14 (February 19, 1935): 21.

9. Edwin Seaver, "Caesar or Nothing," *The New Masses*, 14 (March 5, 1935): 20.
10. *Call It Sleep*, a film directed by Peter Lataster and Petra Lataster-Czisch, 1996.
11. Michael Harrington, "Afterword," in Michael Gold, *Jews without Money* (New York: Avon, 1965), p. 233.
12. 1977 interview with John S. Friedman, reprinted in: Henry Roth, *Shifting Landscape: A Composite, 1925–1987*. Ed. Mario Materassi (Philadelphia: The Jewish Publication Society, 1987), p. 23.
13. Bonnie Lyons, *Henry Roth: The Man and His Work* (New York: Cooper Square, 1976), p. 162.
14. Lyons, p. 176.
15. Walter B. Rideout. *The Radical Novel in the United States 1900–1954: Some Interrelations of Literature and Society* (Cambridge, MA: Harvard UP, 1956), p. 141.
16. "Draft Manifesto of John Reed Clubs," *The New Masses*, 7 (June 1932): 3–4.
17. William Freedman. "A Conversation with Henry Roth," *Literary Review* 18, 2 (Winter, 1975): 154.
18. Lyons, *Henry Roth: The Man and His Work*, p. 162.
19. Harvey Klehr, *The Heyday of American Communism: The Depression Decade* (New York: Basic Books, 1984), p. 360.
20. Roth, *Shifting Landscape*, pp. 48–50.
21. Alan Wald, "Jewish American Writers on the Left," in Michael P. Kramer and Hana Wirth-Nesher, eds., *The Cambridge Companion to Jewish American Literature* (New York: Cambridge UP, 2003), p. 171.
22. Henry Roth, "Batch Two." Unpublished manuscript. American Jewish Historical Society, p. 1487.
23. Teletype message, labeled "very urgent," from agent Thornton in Boston to Inspector A.H. Belmont in Washington, February 9, 1951, p. 1.
24. FBI report 100-17564, filed in Boston, May 3, 1951, p. 4.
25. FBI report 100-17564, filed in Boston, May 3, 1951, p. 3.
26. FBI report 100-17564, filed in Boston, May 3, 1951, p. 3.
27. Office Memorandum, from SAC, Boston (100-17564) to Director, FBI (100-345488), October 30, 1953, p. 1.
28. Interview in Albuquerque with Alan Wald on December 21, 1988, as reported by Wald to the author in a May 2, 2006 email.
29. Alan Wald email, May 2, 2006.
30. Office Memorandum on Henry Roth from SAC, Boston (100-17564) to Director, FBI (100-345488), January 4, 1954.
31. A conversation with Peter Mayer on September 21, 2001.
32. Henry Roth, "The Meaning of *Galut* in America Today," *Midstream* 9, 1 (March 1963): 33.
33. Letter from Henry Roth to Mario Materassi, July 25, 1966. Henry Roth Papers, American Jewish Historical Society.
34. Letter from Henry Roth to Mario Materassi, July 25, 1966. Henry Roth Papers, American Jewish Historical Society.

Works Cited

"Brief Review." *New Masses* 14 (February 12, 1935): 27.

Call It Sleep. Dir. Peter Lataster and Petra Lataster-Czisch, 1996.

Crossman, R.H.S., ed. *The God That Failed.* New York: Harper and Row, 1949.

"Draft Manifesto of John Reed Clubs." *New Masses* 7 (June 1932): 3–4.

Federal Bureau of Investigation, Boston office, file on Henry Roth. Released to the author under the Freedom of Information Act.

Freedman, William. "A Conversation with Henry Roth." *Literary Review* 18, 2 (Winter 1975): 149–57.

Friedman, John S. "On Being Blocked and Other Literary Matters: An Interview." *Commentary* 64 (August 1997): 28–38.

Greenhood, David. "Another View of Call It Sleep." *New Masses* 14 (February 19, 1935): 21.

Gregory, Horace. "East Side World." *The Nation* 140 (February 27, 1935): 255.

Harrington, Michael. Afterword. *Jews without Money.* In Michael Gold. New York: Avon 1965. 227–34.

Hopson, Julie Eastlack. *The Literary Reputations of Henry Roth.* Unpublished M.A. thesis, Harvard University, June 1990.

Kellman, Steven G. *Redemption: The Life of Henry Roth.* New York: Norton, 2005.

Klehr, Harvey. *The Heyday of American Communism: The Depression Decade.* New York: Basic Books, 1984.

Lyons, Bonnie. *Henry Roth: The Man and His Work.* New York: Cooper Square P, 1976.

Marsh, Fred T. "A Great Novel about Manhattan Boyhood." *New York Herald Tribune Books* (February 17, 1935): 6.

Mayer, Peter. Interview with the author. September 21, 2001.

Mitgang, Herbert. *Dangerous Dossiers: Exposing the Secret War against America's Greatest Authors.* New York: Dutton, 1988.

Rideout, Walter B. *The Radical Novel in the United States 1900–1954: Some Interrelations of Literature and Society.* Cambridge, MA: Harvard UP, 1956.

Robins, Natalie. *Alien Ink: The FBI's War on Freedom of Expression.* New York: William Morrow, 1992.

Roth, Henry. "Batch Two." Unpublished manuscript archived with the Roth papers at the American Jewish Historical Society, New York City.

———. Letter to Mario Materassi. July 25, 1966. Henry Roth Papers, American Jewish Historical Society.

———. *Shifting Landscape: A Composite, 1925–1957.* Ed. Mario Materassi. Philadelphia: The Jewish Publication Society, 1987.

Seaver, Edwin. "Caesar or Nothing." *New Masses* 14 (March 5, 1935): 20.

Wald, Alan. Email to the author. May 2, 2006.

———. "Jewish American Writers on the Left," in *The Cambridge Companion to Jewish American Literature,* Michael P. Kramer and Hana Wirth-Nesher, eds., New York: Cambridge UP, 2003. pp. 170–89.

Chapter 3

Telling Stories from Hemingway's FBI File: Conspiracy, Paranoia, and Masculinity

Debra A. Moddelmog

As he did with so many other writers, J. Edgar Hoover, the director of the Federal Bureau of Investigation from 1924–1972, authorized and contributed to a hefty confidential file on Ernest Hemingway. Made available to the public for the past two decades, this file runs 127 pages, with approximately 15 pages withheld or mostly blacked out "in the interest of national defense." The file begins October 8, 1942 and ends January 25, 1974, almost 13 years after Hemingway's death and two years after Hoover's. However, references in the file indicate that the FBI kept tabs on Hemingway as early as the 1930s, by which time he had established himself as a celebrated expatriate writer and "modern master" (Raeburn 17). In short, for 40 years, FBI agents gathered confidential reports on the activities of Hemingway.

Given Hoover's assumption that modernist writers were especially inclined to leftist radicalism and Communism, it is not surprising that he set his sights on the young Hemingway. After all, his early fiction portrayed the brutalities of war, blaming inept politicians and military leaders for the loss of millions of lives in World War I, and it unapologetically explored sexual relations outside of marriage. Such topics would surely have concerned the ultra patriotic and conservative Hoover. References in Hemingway's file reveal that during the 1930s, the FBI paid particular attention not only to his Loyalist support during the Spanish Civil War but also to "his pronouncements on avoiding the next war and his indictment of the government in *New Masses* for the death of [hundreds of] veterans in the 1935 Matecumbe hurricane" (Reynolds, *The Final Years* 379n.64), which indicate that the FBI was particularly interested in charting his political allegiances.

But while reports in the file suggest that the FBI was struggling to learn, as they tried to do with so many other modernist authors, whether Hemingway was a Communist or a Communist sympathizer, they are finally inconclusive on this subject. Hoover himself eventually dismissed the charge. In the margins of a report dated January 6, 1964, he wrote, "Knowing Hemingway as I did I doubt he had any communist leanings. He was a rough, tough guy and always for the underdog" (Hemingway's FBI file, Paperless Archives).[1] This notation has led Natalie Robins to propose that "for all the years Hoover spent tracking Hemingway, he did it not because of any Communist connections, but because Hemingway had been critical of the FBI" (213).

As I will detail shortly, Hemingway's critical attitude toward the FBI does seem to have played a part in Hoover's interest in his whereabouts and activities. It has also been the source of speculation by some contemporary writers who have interpreted this interest as a vendetta for something Hemingway said or did while he was working in the service of the U.S. government in Cuba in 1942–1943. For these writers, the FBI file on Hemingway provides indisputable evidence for reinvigorating his popular persona as a culture hero. This need to pour new life into Hemingway's heroic image seems, in part, to be a response to the demythologizing that has taken place since his death as biographers and critics have circulated information about the complexity of his behavior and desires: his occasional cruelty, his bouts of vulgarity and boorishness but also his sexual and gender deviations from the norm of heteromasculinity.[2] This revisionist Hemingway—supported by posthumous publications such as *The Garden of Eden*, *Islands in the Stream*, *True at First Light*, and most recently, *Under Kilimanjaro*—has entered the public sphere to some degree, causing unease among those who want to view him as an uncomplicated model of heterosexual manhood.

But a related argument I will make is that if we are to understand Hoover's interest in Hemingway, we must recognize it as a personal interest that went beyond his desire to discover political allegiances and consider, instead, both men's response to the model of masculinity that was prominent in their day. While each man positioned himself similarly within this model and Hemingway sometimes produced male heroes or portraits of himself that promoted the model, he also wrote against it. His literary resistance to the heteromasculine model emerged especially in the works he was composing in the 1940s and 1950s when Hoover's FBI and Senator Joseph McCarthy were publicly and oppressively enforcing it. By ignoring the evidence of these works and of Hemingway's life that reveal his own deviations from the heteromasculine norm, contemporary male writers who have written about Hemingway and the FBI miss what might have been Hemingway's most courageous act of defiance against the conservative environment promoted by Hoover's FBI and McCarthyism.

HEMINGWAY: HOOVER'S PUBLIC LITERARY ENEMY #1?[3]

As the FBI file discloses, Hemingway and Hoover developed an antipathy for each other (Hemingway's antipathy extended to the whole of the FBI) during 1942–1943 when Hemingway was running a counterintelligence organization in Cuba and searching for German U-boats off the Cuban coast. Although his operations originally had the approval of the U.S. government, Hoover and Raymond Leddy, the FBI agent sent to report on Hemingway's clandestine activities and findings, quickly soured on him and urged that his services be discontinued. Leddy seems to have been especially irritated that Hemingway introduced him at a Jai Lai match as a member of the American Gestapo, a description that Hemingway later, probably disingenuously, shrugged off as a jest. Nonetheless, Leddy continued to gather reports that Hemingway and his assistant Gustavo Durán had "personal hostility to the FBI on an idealogical [*sic*] basis, especially Hemingway, as he considers the FBI anti-Liberal, pro-Fascist and dangerous as developing into an American Gestapo" (Hemingway's FBI file, stamped July 17, 1961). Hoover, too, recognized early that "Hemingway has no particular love of the FBI" and insisted that Hemingway is the last man to be used in any [counterspying] capacity. "His judgment is not of the best, and if his sobriety is the same as it was some years ago, that is certainly questionable" (Hemingway's FBI file, December 19,1942).

A few critics contend that Hoover was jealous of Hemingway's intelligence operation. Herbert Mitgang states, "Hoover considered him a rival, not a patriot trying to help his country at war in a self-assigned dangerous role" (62). If this is so, it provides an example of the absurdity of Hoover's paranoia since Hemingway's makeshift unit of bartenders, waiters, priests, pelota players, former bullfighters, exiled counts and dukes, several Loyalists and Francistas, and "wharf rats" (Spruille Braden qtd. in Reynolds, *The Final Years* 60) was in no way comparable to the federal bureaucracy of investigation that Hoover directed. Although Hoover was, at this time, attempting to consolidate the power of the FBI in relationship to other "competing" military and naval intelligences agencies such as the Army's MID and the Navy's ONI (see Theoharis and Cox 178–92), Hemingway's "Crook Factory" was clearly not on the same playing field as these others.

More obviously, Hoover was anxious about Hemingway's power as a public celebrity and famous writer who was unafraid to speak his mind. As early as December 19, 1942, Hoover cautioned his agents not to interfere with Hemingway's relationship with the U.S. Ambassador to Cuba; for given Hemingway's negative view of the FBI, Hemingway would "no doubt embark on a campaign of vilification" (Hemingway's FBI file). A couple of memos (August 21, 1943 and October 14, 1943) convey Hoover's concern over reports that Hemingway might write a book about his intelligence activities in Cuba. This apprehension seems to have been provoked by the possibility that a writer of Hemingway's stature could tarnish the reputation of the FBI by portraying its agents as "the dull, heavy-footed, unimaginative professional policeman type" (memo to Hoover from Leddy, Hemingway's FBI file, August 13, 1943). For someone as obsessed with the public image of the FBI as Hoover was, the possibility that a famous writer might depict the agency in a negative light had to be disconcerting.[4]

That Hoover continued to dislike and distrust Hemingway is suggested by the presence of a derogatory newspaper article, "He Never Was a Hemingway Fan," placed in Hemingway's file around the time of his suicide. Written by Westbrook Pegler, a right-wing columnist who supported McCarthyism and one of Hoover's favorite journalists, this article attacks both Hemingway's writing and his character. Pegler describes Hemingway's style as unintelligible and affected, and claims that Hemingway was "the creature of a claque of sycophants, most of them book reviewers." He insists that Hemingway's "obsession with pugilism as a personal activity was juvenile and brutal," concluding, "this man was a personal, physical bully and his adventures in and around battle, though exciting and dangerous, were only the routine experiences of thousands of other men and kids all around him" (Hemingway's FBI file, stamped July 17, 1961). By adding to Hemingway's confidential file an article that hacked away at his reputation as both an avant-garde modernist author and a courageous man, Hoover reveals that his interest in Hemingway was as much personal as it was political. Hemingway was barely in the grave when this clipping was placed in the file, a kind of posthumous thumbing of the nose at the famous writer.

Hoover's suspicion that Hemingway, not only the most famous modernist writer of his time but arguably the most well-known American writer of any era, might portray the FBI negatively and his personal aversion to the author help to explain why the FBI continued to track Hemingway up to the time of his suicide in 1961. However, as I mentioned previously, some contemporary authors and Hemingway fans have imagined a more elaborate backstory and ascribed more sinister motives to the FBI's surveillance of Hemingway. As with other authors the FBI investigated, this surveillance was kept secret both during Hemingway's life and for some time after. Hemingway frequently insisted that the FBI was tailing him, an assertion that his wife and friends attributed to paranoia and to mental problems that surfaced as he aged. When the FBI file on Hemingway was finally released, it confirmed Hemingway's suspicions, even if he might have been wrong at times that there were agents spying on him from the bathroom or a nearby table at a restaurant (Reynolds, *The Final Years* 351, 358). Thus, to some of his fans and scholars, the existence of the FBI file has been taken as evidence that Hemingway was not paranoid after all or, if he was, that his case proves that "even paranoids have real enemies" (Meyers, 543).

Indeed, one of the most intriguing memos in the file indicates that the FBI was involved in some way with the Mayo Clinic in Rochester, Minnesota, where Hemingway was secretly brought in January 1961. Suffering from a number of ailments and too confused to fill out the forms, Hemingway was checked in by his doctor-friend from Idaho, George Saviers, who used his own name to expedite the process (Reynolds, *The Final Years* 349). Hemingway then began to worry that the FBI would become suspicious because he had registered under an assumed name. While his wife, Mary, assumed this was another manifestation of his paranoia, an FBI memo dated January 13, 1961, reveals that someone from the clinic had, in fact, asked permission from the FBI to tell Hemingway that they were *not* concerned that he had registered under another name, permission they subsequently granted. Behind this mini-theatre of the absurd ("pay no attention to that FBI agent behind the curtain!") lies a connection that some have seen as sinister. Clearly, this memo reveals not only that the FBI knew where Hemingway was, despite attempts to keep his hospitalization a secret, but also that they had an association with the clinic. That Hemingway's psychiatrist, Dr. Howard Rome, delivered a sequence of debilitating electro-shock treatments to the writer in January and April of 1961, has sparked a number of speculations about the FBI's involvement in Hemingway's death, including the possibility that they were responsible for it.

Finding the "truth" about the FBI's role in Hemingway's death seems impossible to ascertain. The secrecy with which the FBI conducts its activities, the death of so many actors (Hoover, Leddy, Hemingway, Rome) who might have provided missing information, the cover-up or destruction of "sensitive" information in the files, the passage of time—all of these variables make it difficult to tell the truth, or what might pass for truth in our postmodern age, about the FBI's involvement in the end of Hemingway's life. In any case, it is not my mission here. What I am interested in, instead, is the public desire to imagine *the* truth, even to pronounce it, as captured in a series of narratives and novels published by armchair internet detectives as well as by professional writers. The effort to revitalize the heroic Hemingway is connected to a need to reconcile the man who embodied courage, including the courage to speak his mind, with the man who committed suicide and to rescue one of the most famous representatives of macho masculinity from evidence that he had queer desires or a less-than-admirable personality. Significantly, in these efforts to recuperate Hemingway, the FBI plays the role of both the catalyst for his restored heroism and the villain who caused his intolerable suicide. Not surprisingly, the form these stories take are investigative report, *noir* detective story, and spy thriller, all genres associated with heroic men of action.

INTERNET INVESTIGATORS, PRIVATE EYES, AND 007

The most radical claim about Hemingway and the FBI can be found in pseudo-investigative reports posted on the Internet. From the perspective of these cyber private eyes, the FBI caused Hemingway's mental decline, his suicide, or both. In this scenario, the FBI cleverly got rid of Hemingway by driving him to suicide or, in more extreme formulations, by murdering him, making the murder look like a suicide. For example, in "Ernest Hemingway: Life Is Courage," the anonymous author asks, "Can anybody reasonably justify the claim that Ernest Hemingway committed suicide?" and answers, "We should think not." Listing some of Hemingway's acts of courage that contradict the notion that he might have committed suicide, the author declares that the FBI tracked Hemingway to the Mayo clinic and convinced Hemingway's psychiatrist to give him a series of "electro shocks to the brain." "Clearly," the writer concludes, "it is futile to argue that J. Edgar Hoover was not directly responsible for the brain damage that shock therapy produced." For this armchair sleuth, the FBI surveillance and persecution of Hemingway is another example of how "repressive societies never fail to destroy penetrating thinkers." As the title of the essay reveals, the author resurrects Hemingway's heroic status by insisting that his outspokenness and his liberal ideas were so threatening to a conservative establishment that it had to kill him. Hemingway, the writer claims, "possessed the perception, the passion and the ability to shred deceit, to expose the barren truth, and to cause those who did not share his extraordinary gifts, to challenge his very sanity" ("Ernest Hemingway: Life Is Courage").

This posting was clearly influenced by "investigator" Mat Wilson's research on Hoover's dealings with public figures such as Hemingway, Marilyn Monroe, and John F. Kennedy. In "Dirty Politics: Hoover, Blackmail, Hemingway and Murder," Wilson states, "the claim that Hemingway committed suicide is patently absurd" (8), and he maintains that "Hemingway was essentially murdered through shock therapy" ordered by Hoover (7). Part of Wilson's evidence is the argument that Hemingway "was obsessed by the incredible passion to live—he even gave up drinking for it,"[5] and "repeatedly equated the act of committing suicide with cowardice" (7). As with the anonymous writer of "Ernest Hemingway: Life Is Courage," Wilson resists the possibility that a man with Hemingway's reputation should have taken his own life, since he believes suicide is a coward's act. Instead, Hemingway was the victim of an insidious plot by the FBI, first, to make him seem delusional by keeping their surveillance a secret; and, second, by authorizing the electro-shock treatments that destroyed his capacity to think and write, in effect "murdering" him. In Wilson's hands, Hemingway deserves to be called a hero because he saw the truth about the FBI while others were ignorant of their repressive tactics; and because his death was a murder, not a suicide.

The intentions of investigators such as Wilson are not hard to identify. Playing fast and loose with the "facts," their reports are full of inaccuracies and of theories passing for truth. The leaps of logic they take are masked by rhetoric that dares the reader to presume otherwise: "Can anybody *reasonably* justify the claim that Hemingway committed suicide?" "*Clearly*, it is futile to argue that J. Edgar Hoover was not directly responsible for the brain damage that shock therapy produced" ("Ernest Hemingway: Life Is Courage"; my emphasis). "Hemingway, who was *invariably always* followed by Hoover's FBI, has been posthumously vindicated" (Wilson 5; my emphasis). "It [Dr. Rome's confidentiality about Hemingway] all sounds very ethical, but under the circumstances, an orchestrated cover up is the *only* rational explanation which accounts for the extreme secrecy" (Wilson 6; my emphasis). In our post-McCarthy, post-Watergate climate of suspicion about the U.S. government, suspicion that has been heightened by disclosures about the tactics of Hoover's FBI, these conclusions sound convincing. But regardless of the degree of truth behind these reports, my point is that half a decade after Hemingway's death, some are reading Hemingway's FBI file as evidence that he should be reclaimed as a cultural icon of masculinity.

The intentions of two novelists, Leonardo Padura Fuentes and Dan Simmons, who have written about Hemingway's association with the FBI are less obvious because their knowledge of both Hemingway's life and the FBI files is more extensive, because they are more skillful writers, and because beatification does not seem to be their first motive. However, the effects of their novels are similar to that of the investigative reports of the Internet sleuths. Indeed, although Padura and Simmons both state that they are writing fiction—the former, a detective story; the latter, a spy thriller—they deliberately blur the line between fiction and nonfiction. As a result, their novels take the form of postmodern biographies in which Hemingway emerges as humanized but still the ultimate hero.

Adiós Hemingway (2005) centers on Inspector Mario Conde, who has appeared in other detective novels by Leonardo Padura Fuentes, one of Cuba's most famous contemporary writers. In his "Author's Note," Padura relates that his Brazilian publisher convinced him to contribute to their "Literature or Death" series in which each story revolves around a real author. Padura chose to write about Hemingway, with whom he has had a "fierce love-hate relationship" for years (viii) and brought Conde, his detective-writer, back into service.

Just as Padura revives Conde in order to contribute to his publisher's series, so Conde is persuaded to come out of retirement by the discovery of skeletal remains on Hemingway's Cuban estate, the Finca Vigía. Although the body has been decomposing under an old boxing ring for 40 years and Hemingway has been dead for almost as long, Conde figures out that the man who was killed was an FBI agent, John Kirk. Through a series of interviews with men who were employed by Hemingway and through forensic study of the body, Conde speculates that Hemingway and Kirk struggled, whereupon two of Hemingway's employees shot Kirk who was about to kill Hemingway. Hemingway subsequently engaged in the cover-up, helping to bury the body and relocate one of the killers to Mexico.

Having developed understanding of, even compassion for, the writer he once emulated and later hated, Conde decides that the full truth cannot be ascertained and that publicizing his findings would ruin Hemingway's reputation. So the case is closed without any publicity or repercussions. One of his drinking buddies, Skinny Carlos, says, "That's the best thing about this story. [. . .] It's as if nothing had ever happened. There was no dead man, no killer, nothing. I like that . . . ." Conde responds that something did happen: "Hemingway doesn't seem the same to me now . . . somehow" (220). He now sees Hemingway as he was—complicated—not as the myth he helped to create, just as Hemingway finally saw himself at the end of his life: "He was seeing himself [in a photo contained in a Hemingway biography that Conde has read], without an audience, without any disguises, without any lights. He was seeing a man overcome by life. A month later he shot himself. [. . .] he was free of the character he'd invented for himself. That's the real Hemingway" (217; my ellipses).

The resolution of *Adiós Hemingway* is thus psychological, as Conde comes to terms with his love-hate relationship with the writer he originally "worshipped" (80) but later could not stand once he learned the truth about his brutish treatment of animals and people. At one point, he tells Inspector Manolo Palacios, "But the fact is I don't know him. What's more, I don't think anyone knows him. Let me find out who he was: that's what I want to do" (80). Crucial to this biographical investigation is the question of whether Hemingway was actually courageous or simply a poser (77, 96, 119), a question that arises partly because Hemingway never killed anyone. Although he still has not killed anyone by the end of the novel, Conde suggests that Hemingway *was* courageous—he stood up to the FBI agent and protected his friends—even as he was also a "bastard."

This final assessment of Hemingway is bolstered by the narrative structure of the story in which Conde's present-day investigation is juxtaposed with scenes from Hemingway's perspective in 1958. This allows Padura to introduce the FBI file, as well as information from Hemingway biographies, as part of Conde's evidence but also to incorporate this biographical information into his characterization of Hemingway. Conde tells Manolo, "Look, what I can't get my head around is what the hell that FBI agent was doing in the house. Keeping him under surveillance is one thing, attacking him is quite another . . . And Hemingway was no jerk whom they could pressurise just like that" (213). Manolo responds, "I'd love to see the fifteen missing pages from the FBI file ['on grounds of national security' 114]. [. . .] I don't know why, but I think that the key to everything that happened that night lies there" (214).

But if Manolo and Conde cannot know what is missing from the FBI file, we are privy to part of it, at least as imagined by Padura. In the sections narrated from Hemingway's point of view, we learn that John Kirk was spying on Hemingway, one of many agents assigned to the task over the years. "You know Hoover doesn't like you, don't you?" Kirk asks Hemingway (205). Kirk's cover was blown when he left his badge at Hemingway's house. When he returned to retrieve it, Hemingway refused to give it to him until Kirk told him what was in his FBI file. This led to the fight between the two men that, in turn, led to Kirk's murder and, Conde believes, to Hemingway's death: "There are secrets that can kill . . . And that one [what happened on October 2, 1958] killed at least two men: the agent and Hemingway" (214). In Conde's formulation, the FBI tailed Hemingway even more relentlessly after their agent went missing, and the inability of others to believe him when he said the FBI "was after him" resulted in a medical misdiagnosis that ended Hemingway's life: "The doctors believed that this was a figment of his imagination, a kind of persecution mania. And in order to cure him they gave him twenty-five electroshocks. [. . .] They gave him a living death" because he could no longer write. In short, they "castrated" him in the head, and that is why he shot himself (190–91).

The postmodern joke, conveyed through the words of Skinny Carlos quoted above, is that there was no John Kirk, no killer, "nothing," since Padura has made up this part of the story. However, by reminding the reader that the FBI file has been redacted, a redaction that is interpreted as having sinister implications; by attributing the FBI's surveillance of Hemingway to the events of October 2, 1958, two days before he stopped work on

The Garden of Eden and left Cuba for Idaho; by linking that surveillance to Hemingway's demise; and by presenting part of the story from Hemingway's perspective "as if it really happened that way," Padura creates a tale where the line between fiction and fact blurs impossibly. If John Kirk did not exist and the events of October 2, 1958, did not happen as laid out here, surely, his story suggests, *something* must have happened to cause the FBI to pursue Hemingway. This novel, he writes, "is just a novel and many of the events narrated in it, even when they have been drawn from the most ascertainable reality and the strictest chronology, are filtered through fiction and mingled with it to the extent that, at the present moment, I'm incapable of telling where one ends and the other begins" (viii–ix). While Padura's Hemingway is more complicated, more self aware, and definitely more gross than the Hemingway memorialized by Internet sleuths, he still emerges as heroic in this postmodern blend of fact and fiction. As with the Hemingway constructed by Internet detectives, Padura's Hemingway is heroic in the way he resists a corrupt, insidious, and invidious government police force.

Dan Simmons's *The Crook Factory* (1999) resembles *Adiós Hemingway* in its extensive use of Hemingway's FBI file and the biographies written about him, and in its conscious merging of fiction and fact. Simmons's protagonist, Special FBI Agent Joe Lucas, is, like Conde, on a mission to discover the "real" Hemingway. A masterful killer for the Special Intelligence Service, a counterintelligence division of the FBI created during World War II, Lucas is sent personally by Hoover to spy on Hemingway as he starts up his Cuban espionage operation, the Crook Factory, in 1942. Ostensibly serving as Hemingway's "liaison" with the U.S. Embassy in Cuba, Lucas is actually on a mission, as Hoover describes it, to "Get close to Hemingway [. . . .] Report to me on who the man is. *What* he is. Use your skills to ferret out the truth about this phony. I want to know what makes him tick and what he really wants" (44). Like Padura, Simmons has read the biographies on Hemingway, including recent ones that paint a complex picture of his personality, his sexuality, and his masculinity. However, he does not reference these biographies directly, and the sexual and gender complications are breezily mentioned, then dismissed. Instead, Simmons is most intrigued by Hemingway's personality and how to reconcile stories about his vulgarity and cruelty with the heroic myth. Lucas immediately sizes up Hemingway as a man "who probably could be simultaneously the most interesting person you'd ever meet and a tiresome son of a bitch" (73). The novel bears this out, but in the end, Hemingway's "interesting" side clearly dominates.

In this complex tale of espionage, Simmons imagines Hemingway's Crook Factory, his submarine patrol, and Hemingway himself as central to the events of World War II. In contrast to the view of some of his acquaintances that Hemingway's intelligence activities in Cuba were "a lark, a way to get rationed gasoline" for his boat (Reynolds, *The Final Years* 78), Simmons constructs a narrative in which the Crook Factory and sub patrols are not only legitimized, they are at the crux of the FBI's attempt to pass on secrets about Britain's war time plans to the SD (part of Heinrich Himmler's Reich Nazi internal security agency) in exchange for information about the Abwehr (the German Military Intelligence and an enemy of the SD).

In Simmons's story, Hemingway's motley crew of agents is very effective at the business of intelligence gathering. The crew of Hemingway's fishing boat, which is outfitted to search for and possibly attack German U-boats, not only spots two subs (123–24, 530–33), but Lucas is also able to intercept and decode radio reports indicating German crews will land on Long Island. Their report of the planned insertion of German spies onto U.S. soil is apparently ignored by the FBI, the Navy, and the U.S. Embassy at Cuba (286), but newspaper accounts later confirm their intelligence (242–43). In addition, Lucas decides that the Crook Factory is working "astonishingly well" as it begins to uncover the corruption of the Cuban National Police, including proof that the head of the police is taking payments from both the Nazis and the FBI (258–59).

The most important discoveries and adventures involve Hemingway and Lucas, who frequently separate themselves from the others in order to pursue threatening plots they are uncovering on their own. Together, they witness the deaths of two Nazis killed by snipers; these men have papers revealing German plans for disembarking agents onto the coast of Maine (417). Lucas and Hemingway also decode German radio messages indicating the Germans have broken the British Royal Navy's code and thus have access to their battle plans (452–53, 458). Their collaboration culminates in a confrontation with two German operatives, one who is killed by Lucas and one who is killed by Hemingway, but not before both Lucas and Hemingway are seriously injured themselves. While recovering at the Finca Vigía, they are visited by Wallace Beta Phillips and Ian Fleming. Phillips was once employed by the Office of Naval Intelligence and now works for the Coordinator of Intelligence, a unit that eventually became the CIA. Fleming was an agent for the British Foreign Intelligence and would later become the inventor of the fictional Agent 007, James Bond. Phillips and Fleming clear up the remaining mysteries, revealing that Hoover used the Crook Factory as a front for the flow of intelligence between the Germans and the FBI. He also planned for Hemingway and Lucas to be the fall guys in case the intelligence transfer was discovered. All of this is top secret, with neither Lucas nor Hemingway telling anyone about their escapades and discoveries.

Until now. The story is narrated in retrospect by Lucas, who states at the beginning of the novel that he vowed on the day of Hemingway's suicide, July 2, 1961, which was coincidentally Lucas's forty-ninth birthday, to do two things before he died: first, find and "liberate" the FBI files on Hemingway and, second, write this story (9). It took him more than a decade to do the former and more than three decades to complete the latter. Near the end of the novel, we learn that Lucas is now almost 86 years old and dying. His last act, but one, is to write the story we are reading. In effect, then, his story is a vindication of Hemingway from allegations of paranoia and from the assumption that his suicide was a coward's act. Charged by Hoover to find out who Hemingway really is, Lucas's story reveals that far from being a phony, he was a real hero. Before they head out on their missions, Hemingway admits to Lucas that he has never killed a man, but by the end of the novel not only has he killed a man in hand-to-hand combat, he has killed "the single most able intelligence agent in the entire German war effort" (517) who was also the man who probably killed John Dillinger, Baby Face Nelson, and other criminals (518). In the process, he saved Lucas's life. Indeed, at one point, it seems that Hemingway himself is dead; the Nazi agent has taken off the back of his head with a gaff, knocking him unconscious. However, Hemingway staggers from the pool of his own blood in order to engage the agent in a tenacious battle. "You're one tough son of a bitch," the German says. "That blow would have killed most men" (500). The fight ends when Hemingway is able to pull the man's finger on the trigger so that the Nazi shoots himself in the head (503–04).

Because he killed the agent who was transferring secrets between Hoover and Himmler and because he knows about Hoover's role in handing over British secrets to the Nazis,[6] Hemingway becomes a target of relentless FBI surveillance. Besides the Nazis and a corrupt lieutenant in the Cuban police force, the villain in the story is Hoover, who does terrible things out of fear of losing power. Lucas emphasizes that Hoover would not try to kill Hemingway. He prefers to destroy people through "leaks, innuendo, blackmail, and the IRS" (335). Ian Fleming agrees: "Rather more his style to haul you up in front of a Senate committee investigating Communist infiltration and discredit you or send you to jail." When Hemingway responds that there's no such thing as a "witch-hunt committee like that," Fleming assures him, "There shall be, dear chap. There shall be" (519), thus predicting Hoover's role in Joseph McCarthy's "Un-American" investigations that ruined the lives of so many people.

If Hoover is the ultimate villain of this story, Hemingway is clearly the ultimate hero. This dynamic is underscored when Lucas transfers his allegiance from the former to the latter; and begins to think of Hemingway as a father, as the "Papa" that others call him (504, 534). As an insider, Lucas *knows* that the FBI followed Hemingway, bugging his phone and his house, and preparing a tax case against him in collusion with the IRS (6–7). They even discussed "the advisability of Hemingway's electroshock treatment even before the writer or his wife was presented with the option" (8). Given what he knows about Hemingway's secret history with the FBI, Lucas determines that his suicide was not the desperate act of a sick man but a "message": "a last, violent move to declare stalemate to a decades-old game rather than suffer checkmate at the hands of a patient but relentless enemy" (11). In an act that confirms his view that Hemingway's suicide was courageous and binds him permanently to the writer who served as his surrogate father, Lucas commits suicide in Ketchum, Idaho, a short distance from Hemingway's grave (557–58).

If this neat ending seems melodramatic, we are brought back to reality by Simmons's "Author's Note" at the end of the novel. Here he informs us that "The incredible story of Ernest Hemingway's Cuban spy-catching, submarine-chasing, World War II adventures . . . is—I think—all the more incredible for being 95 percent true" (559). He then lists parts of the story that are true, including the fact that the FBI kept a file on Hemingway and did follow him as the writer claimed. But Simmons does not identify the parts that are *not* true. As with *Adiós Hemingway*, the reader is left with the impossible task of sorting fiction from history, imagination from biography. We are also left with the impression that Hemingway, while far from perfect, was a hero, the man's man that he has so often been advertised as. It is no accident that Ian Fleming shows up in the novel. Although he did serve in the British Intelligence Service during World War II, he is also an index to the kind of heroism that Simmons suggests Hemingway achieves. If Simmons's Hemingway (who identifies as Agent 08) is not nearly so suave, effective, or destructive as Fleming's 007, he nonetheless manages to defeat both Nazi spies and the FBI. The story resembles a James Bond novel, but in the end, it's also a postmodern biography of Hemingway. And in that regard, who is to say which five percent is fiction?

PARANOIDS, SISSIES, AND HEROES: HOOVER, HEMINGWAY, AND MASCULINITY

Just because paranoids have real enemies does not mean they cannot also be paranoid. What is illuminating about the stories explored in the previous section is that they deny or downplay the possibility that Hemingway might have been responsible for his own suicide or they turn that suicide into a courageous act of revenge. They also avoid evidence that illness might simply have struck him, as it does so many of us, in old age. His heavy drinking, his many accidents (including two plane crashes in 1954 that gave him his fifth concussion; paralyzed his sphincter muscle; cracked two spine discs; ruptured his liver, kidney, and spleen; and dislocated his right arm; Meyers, *Hemingway* 575); his declining health; the depression that apparently ran in his family (his father, brother, one sister and possibly two, and granddaughter all committed suicide)—none of these is finally advanced as the cause of Hemingway's death. That role is given to the FBI. By ignoring or deemphasizing these other factors and by imagining a conspiracy in which the FBI sought Hemingway's end, he is restored as a hero for his time and for ours.

In saying this, I do not mean to dismiss the role that Hoover and the FBI might have had in Hemingway's life and death, or in the harrowing experiences of many individuals who were investigated by the organization. Athan Theoharis and John Stuart Cox claim, "Hoover had more to do with undermining American constitutional guarantees than any political leader before or since" (17). Moreover, it was not the case that Hoover demanded antiradical investigations only to confirm or deny Communist associations: "Convinced that the nation confronted an unprecedented peril, the Director, whenever assured that the FBI's activities could not become publicly known, discreetly used such information to purge, or try to purge, supposed radicals of every stripe from positions of power" (Theoharis and Cox 8). Undoubtedly, Hoover's obsessions were fueled by paranoia; and while I agree with biographers who argue that his psyche was complex, I do not think I am stretching to suggest that some of Hoover's problems, like Hemingway's, were the result of overcompensation in an attempt to achieve an idealized form of masculinity.

The son of a forceful mother, with whom Hoover lived until her death, and an ineffectual father, Hoover developed an "overriding preference for male companionship" (Theoharis and Cox 39). The homosocial world of the FBI was a perfect place to live out this preference. He enjoyed a 45-year relationship with Clyde Tolson, assistant FBI director, who is now buried next to him. Neither man married, nor did they seem to have romantic relationships with women. If their relationship was not sexual, it certainly encouraged those suspicions. One FBI agent reportedly said of Hoover, "If he isn't queer, then he's weird" (qtd. in Theoharis and Cox 108). Determined to expose homosexuals as "traitors," Hoover was sensitive to rumors about his own sexuality, and vigorously pursued those who suggested he was a pervert (Theoharis and Cox 108, 208–12). Curt Gentry notes that a 1938 *Collier's* article that hinted at Hoover's homosexuality, referring to his fastidious dress and "mincing step," caused Hoover to remedy that impression, including planting an article in *Liberty* magazine, which stated that his "compact body, with the shoulders of a light heavyweight boxer, carries no ounce of extra weight—just 170 pounds of live, virile masculinity" (159). Hoover's tough bulldog persona seems to have been, at least in part, overcompensation for his sense that his masculinity was inadequate, his sexuality, queer.

Some of this story sounds remarkably similar to that of Ernest Hemingway, and the similarity suggests that part of Hoover's problem with Hemingway was that he identified so strongly with the author that he had to disavow the identification by questioning Hemingway's potency as both a man and a writer. Born four years after Hoover, Hemingway, too, was the son of a domineering mother and a weak father. His mother even dressed him and his older sister as "twins" for several years when Hemingway was a young child, which meant that he sometimes looked like a girl and wore girl's clothes. Later in life, he felt most at home in the homosocial world of bullfighters, soldiers, fishermen, hunters, and drinking companions—although, unlike Hoover, he had several heterosexual relationships, including four marriages. He was also sensitive to suggestions that he might be effeminate or homosexual, an association often made of male artists and intellectuals of the late nineteenth and early twentieth century.[7] Such sensitivity motivated his hypermasculine persona, especially in the 1930s, at the same time that Hoover was building the legend of his own bulldog toughness.

Michael Kimmel argues that masculinity in America underwent a major crisis in the 1930s, during the Depression, when many men had a hard time finding steady work and were forced to spend more time in the domestic sphere than they had previously. To compensate for this loss of achievement in the public sphere, American masculinity was "reconceived as the exterior manifestation of a certain inner sense of oneself. Masculinity could be observed in specific traits and attitudes, specific behaviors and perspectives." Men who were able to express their manhood in this manner were perceived as "real men"; those who could not were in danger of becoming homosexual. "A key psychological question for the 1930s," Kimmel concludes, "was whether homosexuality could be 'cured' by a healthy dose of manhood" (206). Hoover's and Hemingway's personal anxieties about their masculinity thus played out within a national model that provided specific behavioral parameters for proving they were true men. Still, their very public performances of virility and bravado seem overdone even in a time when overdoing was the order of the day. While Hoover was planting articles in popular magazines that promoted his toughness, Hemingway was developing a hair-trigger sensitivity to attacks on his virility that became more common after the publication of *Death in the Afternoon* (1932). One of the most famous exchanges took place between Hemingway and Max Eastman, who, in a review of *Death*, accused him of "wearing false hair on the chest" in both art and life, which Hemingway refuted in a letter to the *New Republic* by implying that his sex life was quite satisfactory. This quarrel culminated four years later in a celebrated brawl between Hemingway and Eastman in Max Perkins's office (Raeburn 60–61).

It would seem, then, that Hemingway was doubly dangerous to Hoover, arguably more dangerous than any other modernist writer, not because he had Communist ties, which even Hoover finally recognized he did not, but because he had been able to attain a fame in which his literary reputation and his reputation as a man's man were inextricably bound. Unlike other modernist writers, Hemingway became a public personality whose face and words were known around the world. His words were read by millions, and millions admired him and his writing. If he criticized the FBI, it was on a different order from that of any other writer; and if the FBI tailed him, they had to be especially careful since the world was watching his every move and might be outraged to learn the FBI was, too. Moreover, Hemingway proved that the respected male artist need not be a cultured effete, but could be even more masculine than most men. In some ways, Hoover's own stylized masculinity looked an awful lot like the heroic model Hemingway had created for himself and other men in such works as *Death in the Afternoon* (1932) and *Green Hills of Africa* (1935). It seems understandable, even inevitable, that Hoover and Hemingway, both overly sensitive and anxious about their masculinity, would develop an antipathy toward each other.

But, as I mentioned above, recent scholarship has constructed a more complicated picture of Hemingway, drawing upon biographical evidence that was previously suppressed or dismissed and upon his writings, especially those that were unpublished in his time. In these more complex portraits, Hemingway's heterosexuality and masculinity intermingle with other proclivities such as fetishism, homosexuality, masochism, cross-racial desire, and cross-gendered play. Significantly, this more complex portrait of Hemingway's masculinity and sexuality is alluded to by some of the writers examined in this essay, most particularly Padura and Simmons. But as much as these authors rely upon biographies that portray Hemingway's flaws as well as his strengths, they refute evidence suggesting he deviated from masculine or heterosexual norms. Indeed, if we need more proof that Hoover is the enemy and Hemingway the hero of *The Crook Factory*, Joe Lucas informs us that Hoover was a "mama's boy," and although "an undercurrent of Presbyterian Sunday school correctness would have made [a secret homosexual] life all but unthinkable for him" (47), he was still "a mean fat boy dressed in nice clothes—a vindictive sissy who had cultivated the speech and mannerism of a tough guy" (73). Hemingway, on the other hand, really is a tough guy, which he proves by killing a Nazi spy and by fighting Lucas *mano a mano* after Lucas calls him a *maricón* [homosexual] for performing a "fake" suicide (343). In addition, while he might engage in disgusting "locker room" talk about women, Hemingway "seemed truly interested" in what women had to say and was at his best around intelligent women (214–15).

Perhaps the most interesting recovery of Hemingway as a "manly man, tough and virile" (Raeburn 39) comes in Padura's *Adiós Hemingway*. His Hemingway works on *The Garden of Eden*—the unfinished novel depicting a ménage-a-trois, lesbianism, sodomy, and gender-switching in bed—but he is also determinedly heterosexual, as is represented most memorably by his possession of Ava Gardner's black lace knickers. At one point, Conde has a "wet dream" in which he imagines himself as Hemingway making love to Gardner in his pool at the Finca Vigía (109–12). Not only does this dream confirm the heterosexuality of Conde, who is single and close friends with a homosexual man (Manolo), but it also figures Hemingway as the lover of a beautiful and willing female movie star.

With his suicide explained as FBI bullying or retaliation, Hemingway, the courageous man of action and the skillful lover of women, is back, and he is more pumped up than ever. As has been the case before, Hemingway's celebrity is located not in his literary contributions—which depict men with vulnerabilities (Raeburn 202–03), even with "deviant" sexual desires—but in the cultural myth of his macho heroism. A major irony in these contemporary efforts to rescue Hemingway from the cowardice of suicide and to present him as one of the few people who "understood the serious threat that Hoover's FBI posed" ("Ernest Hemingway: Life is Courage") is that they reinstate an image of Hemingway that he was actively writing against in his later years and thus miss what might be interpreted as a truly courageous act of resistance against the repressive society that Hoover's FBI promoted and enforced. As I have explored elsewhere (*Reading Desire* 85–88), Hemingway worked, intermittently, on *The Garden of Eden* from 1946–1958, a time during which the U.S. government deemed homosexuality an invisible menace (Cong. Rec. 96.4, March 29–April 24, 1950), and Senator Joseph McCarthy made it his special mission, assisted by the FBI, to ruin the lives of known or suspected "sexual deviants." In this intimidating environment, Hemingway created a male protagonist, David Bourne, who played the "girl" to his wife's "boy" in bed, who enjoyed sodomy, and who was struggling to come to terms with "abnormal" desires. David, a writer, is particularly concerned with how his private life might affect the reputable public self he has created through his fiction. Through this portrayal, Hemingway reveals his recognition that creating a character like David might damage the public persona that he had helped to create and that had the power "to impress, to make money, and to inspire imitation" (*Reading Desire* 86). That Hemingway never published—or, for that matter, finished—*The Garden of Eden* is a testament to the power of the homophobia that was the legislated order of his day and part of his own psyche. That he attempted to write this novel at all suggests he understood that one way to fight repressive societies and their psychic effects is by imagining an alternative.[8]

Joe Moran states in *Star Authors* that literary celebrities such as Hemingway "are complex cultural signifiers who are repositories for all kinds of meanings, the most significant of which is perhaps the nostalgia for some kind of transcendent, anti-economic, creative element in a secular, debased, commercialized culture" (9). Certainly, this nostalgia is present in the works

I have discussed here, which represent Hemingway as the creative individual fighting to express himself in the face of conservative elements that threaten his very existence. However, the nostalgia expressed in these narratives is also for a form of virile masculinity that confronts, and sometimes defeats, evil in the world, be it the evil of Nazi terrorism or of a repressive government that monitors every aspect of its citizens' lives. And *this* time, these writers suggest, the myth of Hemingway that has been such a lasting sign of this nostalgia is not a myth; it is the *real* Hemingway.

NOTES

1. Because it is easily accessible, I typically cite Hemingway's file provided on the FBI Web site; however, in this case, I have had to cite the paperless archives CD, which provides access to a memo that seems to be redacted from the FBI Web file. In 1991, Curt Gentry stated, "Since the 1950s the FBI has assigned a permanent staff to the National Archives, to determine what FBI and Justice Department records will be retained, made public, withheld from examination, or destroyed" (390). This clandestine oversight makes it difficult to state authoritatively what is "in" the Hemingway file much less whether the file is "complete."
2. See Kenneth Lynn, *Hemingway* (New York: Simon and Schuster, 1987); J. Gerald Kennedy, *Imagining Paris: Exile, Writing, and American Identity* (New Haven: Yale UP, 1993); Nancy R. Comley and Robert Scholes, *Hemingway's Genders: Rereading the Hemingway Text* (New Haven: Yale UP, 1994); Rose Marie Burwell, *Hemingway: The Postwar Years and the Posthumous Novels* (Cambridge: Cambridge UP, 1996); Carl Eby, *Hemingway's Fetishism: Psychoanalysis and the Mirror of Manhood* (Albany: State U of New York P, 1999); Debra A. Moddelmog, *Reading Desire: In Pursuit of Ernest Hemingway* (Ithaca: Cornell UP, 1999); Michael Reynolds, *Hemingway: The Final Years* (New York: Norton, 1999); and Richard Fantina, *Ernest Hemingway: Machismo and Masochism* (New York: Palgrave Macmillan, 2005); among others.
3. The phrase "public literary enemy #1" comes from Mat Wilson's essay.
4. Jeffrey Meyers points out that Hemingway mentioned the FBI in several books: "In *To Have and Have Not* [1944], he wrote that 'Edgar Hoover exaggerates the publicity' he received for capturing famous gangsters in the thirties. And in *Islands in the Stream* [published posthumously in 1970], the grubby old salt calls the Agents 'draft-dodgers' and satirizes the obtrusive, ineffectual, 'inescapable FBI men, pleasant and all trying to look so average, clean-cut-young-American that they stood out as clearly as though they had worn a bureau shoulder patch on their white linen or seersucker suits'" (381).
5. This is misleading, to say the least, since Hemingway might have stopped drinking periodically at his doctor's insistence, but he never "gave it up" for good. The year before he died, Hemingway's intake of alcohol had "risen dramatically from the prescribed two glasses with supper. [The Hemingways'] January to June [1960] liquor bill from Licores Manzarbeitia in Havana was $1550.49 for eighteen bottles of liquor and fifty-five cases of wine during a period with almost no Finca visitors" (Reynolds, *The Final Years* 343).

6. Lucas does not suggest that Hoover, a supreme patriot, was sabotaging U.S. war efforts; only that he was divulging British secrets in order to acquire more important secrets from the Nazis for helping the U.S. war efforts.
7. For example, in 1926, Zelda Fitzgerald reportedly said of Hemingway that no one could be that masculine (Reynolds, *Hemingway: The American Homecoming* 46); and in her review of *Men Without Women* in 1927, Virginia Woolf called him too "self-consciously virile" (qtd. in Raeburn 34).
8. As Rose Marie Burwell notes, during the 1940s and 1950s, Hemingway worked on three other books (besides *The Garden of Eden*) that were unfinished at the time of his death: *A Moveable Feast* (1964), *Islands in the Stream* (1970), and *True at First Light* (1999). In the latter two works in particular, he also portrayed men and women with sexual proclivities considered deviant in his time, including miscegenation and polygamy. Several of these works ask why different cultures have different norms. As Patrick Hemingway, editor of *True at First Light*, puts it, "Hemingway is at pains to point out, in this story the space and time aspect of ethical behavior in different cultures" (315). Burwell notes that Hemingway was certain that he would be unable to publish these works (except perhaps for *A Moveable Feast*) while he was alive. In the summer of 1956, he wrote to Robert Morgan Brown, "I don't think it [*True at First Light*] would ever be acceptable at Fordham and I think maybe it would be better to wait until I'm dead to publish it. But it is an awfully good story and I was born to write stories not to please the authorities" (qtd. in Burwell 188n.5).

WORKS CITED

Anonymous. "Ernest Hemingway: Life is Courage." http://justice4jfk.users3.50megs.com/dick.htm accessed July 30, 2004.

Burwell, Rose Marie. *The Postwar Years and the Posthumous Novels*. New York: Cambridge UP, 1996.

Ernest Hemingway FBI file. http://foia.fbi.gov/foiaindex/ernesthemingway.htm accessed on July 17, 2005.

Ernest Hemingway FBI file. CD-ROM. File number 64-23312.

Gentry, Curt. *J. Edgar Hoover: The Man and His Secrets*. New York: Norton, 1991.

Hemingway, Patrick. "Cast of Characters." *True at First Light*. By Ernest Hemingway. New York: Scribner, 1999. pp. 313–16.

Kimmel, Michael. *Manhood in America: A Cultural History*. New York: Free P, 1996.

Meyers, Jeffrey. *Hemingway: A Biography*. New York: Perennial, 1985.

Mitgang, Herbert. *Dangerous Dossiers: Exposing the Secret War Against America's Greatest Authors*. New York: Donald I. Fine, 1988.

Moddelmog, Debra A. *Reading Desire: In Pursuit of Ernest Hemingway*. Ithaca: Cornell U P, 1999.

Moran, Joe. *Star Authors: Literary Celebrity in America*. London: Pluto P, 2000.

Padura Fuentes, Leonardo. *Adiós Hemingway*. Trans. John King. Edinburgh: Canongate, 2005.

Raeburn, John. *Fame Became of Him: Hemingway as Public Writer.* Bloomington: Indiana U P, 1984.

Reynolds, Michael. *Hemingway: The American Homecoming.* Oxford: Blackwell, 1992.

———. *Hemingway: The Final Years.* New York: Norton, 1999.

Robins, Natalie. *Alien Ink: The FBI's War on Freedom of Expression.* New York: William Morrow, 1992.

Simmons, Dan. *The Crook Factory: A Novel of Suspense.* 1999. New York: Harpertorch, 2000.

Theoharis, Athan G., and John Stuart Cox. *The Boss: J. Edgar Hoover and the Great American Inquisition.* Philadelphia: Temple U P, 1988.

Wilson, Mat. "Dirty Politics—Hoover, Blackmail, Hemingway and Murder." http://dirtypolitics.50megs.com/hoover.htm accessed on July 11, 2005.

CHAPTER 4

Most Wanted: Claude McKay and the "Black Specter" of African American Poetry in the 1920s

Josh Gosciak

Specters are curious phantoms that tell a lot about society. They are composed of our deepest fears, and have been known to quell popular revolt and civic distrust, if conjured wisely and judiciously. In the past, Elizabethans invoked them in morality plays as a cautious reminder to obey and submit. Specters soon took on regal personas, discoursed in monosyllabic ways, and soon reflected the modern predilection for full-bodied desire: They became ghostlike with complicated pedigrees and acted with a sense of entitlement, seeking balance and justice rather than retribution. (The Ancients, of course, were more inclined to dispense with balance altogether and made their specters visceral and elemental. But that is a bit too crude for our more diversity-driven era.) Though still sinister, the newer ones, in the twentieth century, tended toward the exotic, fed on what the Jamaican poet Claude McKay called "color lines and race differences."[1]

Sightings especially arose after World War I as conscripts from India, Africa, and the Caribbean—former colonials and peasants who had learned the ways of modern warfare—began to descend en masse upon Paris,

London, and New York to ply their newfound trades. Many became busboys, sidewaiters, pantrymen, and cabaret dancers. All of course were down on their luck and unaware of their potential. While most sought jobs and opportunity, others, disappointed, cried for retribution and back pay. McKay brilliantly captured this Great Migration, of vanished borders and vanquished peoples, in the poem "Outcast."[2]

> I would go back to darkness and to peace,
> But the great Western world holds me in fee,
> And I may never hope for full release
> While to its alien gods I bend my knee.
> Something in me is lost, forever lost,
> Some vital thing has gone out of my heart,
> And I must walk the way of life a ghost
> Among the sons a thing apart.[3]

Like that grinning Cheshire Cat in Lewis Carroll's *Alice's Adventures in Wonderland*, these newer specters seemed to vanish at whim, then reappear spookily, at once ubiquitous yet undefined. Almost anyone, it seemed, might easily crossover to become a feared bogeyman—busboys, nannies, janitors, even poets like McKay—in this jumble of shifting terrain and homelands.

Such a crossover and detour became embarrassingly apparent to the author at the debut on Broadway in the spring of 1922. McKay attended the opening of Russian playwright Leonid Andreyev's *He, the One Who Gets Slapped*, at the invitation of the Theater Guild. He was listed as the theater critic for the *Liberator*, a monthly New York progressive magazine, edited by Max Eastman and his sister Crystal, the well-known suffragist. Possibly the Guild anticipated good reviews from the *Liberator*, since the play takes swipes at the Western pecking order through clownish slapstick, and so did not check on McKay or his credentials. Apparently the Guild did not think it was necessary, given that theater critics were high brow and civilized. For McKay, the production and setting seemed an unlikely place for what he described later as a "brooding darkly, madly, burnt, seared and pierced" specter—except, perhaps, on stage.[4] But there they were, a gyre of fears and terror that swirled about the poet creating panic among the ushers. The befuddled poet was quickly engaged and silently escorted from the orchestra seat and up into the balcony and out of sight. (A hard and fast rule for these modern specters, which we too, of late, have learned, is to be felt but not seen, which really has little to do with how one's politics sit.) So quick was the reflex on the part of the ushers, so precise and orchestrated the actions, that the poet hardly had time to react. (He later wrote about this faux pas on the part of the Guild in a review titled "He Who Gets Slapped," which appeared in the May 1922

Liberator.) One moment he was a respected drama critic, the next an untidy nuisance. Only at the conclusion of the play did it all come jarringly together:

> Andreyev's masterpiece, they call it. A masterpiece? A cleverly melodramatic stringing together of buffoonery, serious-comic philosophy, sensational love-hungriness and baby-doll impossibilism, staged to tickle the mawkish emotions of the bourgeois mob! So I thought. I sat there apart, alone, black and shrouded in blackness, quivering in every fiber, my heart denying itself and hiding from every gesture of human kindness, hard in its belief that kindliness iks to be found in no nation or race. I sat there inwardly groaning through what seemed a childish caricature of tragedy. Ah! If the accident of birth had made Andreyev a Negro, if he had been slapped, kicked, buffetted, pounded, niggered, ridiculed, sneered at, exquisitely tortured, near-lynched and trampled underfoot by the merry white horde, and if he still preserved through the terrible agony a sound body and mind sensitive and sharp to perceive the qualities of life, he might have written a real play about Being Slapped.[5]

Indeed, with dramatic irony and unwilling audience participation, it dawned on the poet that *he* was the one slapped: A wraith in black face that had intruded upon one of "the holy places of the whites." And like the clown in the Andreyev piece who was the butt of comic relief, McKay extended the conceit: He, a presence tugging at society's sleeve, "always darkly peering through the window, giving them no rest, no peace." McKay sheepishly looked inward and had found denouement! He marveled at this remarkable change where previously he was commonplace and invisible. Why, he chuckled, "How they burn up their energies trying to keep you out."[6] As he pondered the irony of this mis-en-scène from the heights of his newly realized "Nigger Heaven," such insights into the underpinnings of New York high society would become routine in just a few months as forces greater than those of Broadway or Tinseltown worked at transforming a sentimental familiar bogeyman (McKay) into a potent international threat—a specter, if you will.[7] He'd become the clown in a dead-serious obsession, brought about by an alarmingly paranoid State Department and Bureau of Investigation concerned with shifting alliances and borders, whose whereabouts provided a potent soliloquy of "no rest, no peace."[8]

Such behavior, particularly when the obsession is upon one individual—and a poet no less—might be viewed with a bit of cynicism. But it is interesting how those bizarre, irrational actions soon become the norm. Such was the case then—and it is true even more so today. Lately, we have seen a whole new set of specters mutate and multiply, burning up energy, setting our course and national policy, influencing agencies, creating new ones, such as Homeland Security, and generally dictating the tenor of our lives. We call these rifts and shifts in the fabric of society paradigms, and what is interesting is that the generation born into one paradigm does not know what the quality of life was like in the other. We accept the delays, searches, break downs as givens. Back then, in the 1920s, specters were more likely to be blacks than Arabs, though, and what made them such a potent threat were the riots that had taken place in East St. Louis, Illinois, Tulsa, Oklahoma, and elsewhere. But the era also had an anomaly: An extremely secretive and ambitious agent, J. Edgar Hoover, and his mentor, Attorney General A. Mitchell Palmer, who set the bar by which agents would infiltrate and track, detain, deport, and harass undesirables. Of course, though complexions and demographics have changed, we still possess undesirable elements and our governments are no less officious in burning up a great deal of energy, time, and money in keeping under wraps any slippage, permeability, and articulation. In our media-driven world, to invoke specters is to work at crowd control, create markets, channel revenue, suppressing dissent—or the truth. In the early twentieth century, when there was much promise for racial and social harmony, to blur lines and barriers, government policy seemed singularly fueled by World War I and the great Migration on one side, and J. Edgar Hoover on the other and his obsession with blacks. Truth was less important than policy, and a higher good was conveniently invoked for crusade or war. Naturally, as we have discovered since 9/11, such climatic changes demand—more and more, it seems—personal sacrifices, and we soon become the thing we feared, and are terrorist hardened, flint-nosed, and less concerned with reality than with imagined specters. In such a world, truth easily travels from lie to innuendo, and is the cog of a secure democracy.[9]

As one poet and editor familiar with the cultural terrain of the early century noted: The nineteenth-century world of innocence, honesty and truthfulness had come to an end, and in its place was a terrifying one "preempted by propagandists who insist that the artist bear only one kind of fruit."[10] Even race leader W.E.B. Du Bois suggested, with some bravado, that our modern twentieth century needed a good dose of propaganda to correct its injustices—and this "ever must be, despite the wailing of the purists." But when truth is compromised and propaganda becomes our social remedy, we actually begin to erode diversity of expression and meaning, to "unbend the wild curve" of humanity, as the Russian Yevgeny Zamyatin had written in his futuristic novel *We*, "to straighten it tangentially, asymptotically." We become, Zamyatin reckoned, "OneState"—in mind and body—and a sublime efficiency kicks in and moves us toward a "great, divine, precise, wise straight line—the wisest of all lines."[11] McKay surmised the allure of this line, especially the racial one designed to keep blacks in line (Du Bois' "Criteria of Negro Art," Alain Locke's "Enter the New Negro," among others), and marveled at the energy devoted to "the nature of the propaganda that is conducted among them." Will they become mere pawns of the bourgeois elite, or truly class conscious? he asked. The problem went beyond a mere change in demarcation, and would require, he concluded, a more "emancipated Negro intelligentsia of the future"—at least beyond the current mindset of race leaders and intellectuals.[12]

ON THE LAM

Government interest in McKay began as "If We Must Die" circulated in 1919, a signature year for radical upheavals, and marked his own slippage from that precise, straight line into an asymptotic morass. The poem debuted in a June *Liberator* under "Songs and Sonnets," during an equally uneasy Red Summer, when violence erupted from June to September in Washington, D.C., Chicago, Charleston, Knoxville, Omaha, and elsewhere. The year 1919 was a key moment in international affairs—for feminism as well as racial conscious-raising. The slow, brutal winnowing away of promises in the aftermath of World War I was not limited to women, but the lost political ground was felt by African Americans as well. The first of many Pan-African conferences occurred in 1919, and were reported on by W.E.B. DuBois in *The Crisis*; the Red Scare and the Palmer raids were at their height; the United States had gone to war first with Mexico, and then Haiti; and there was unrest in England and Europe. In Germany, Rosa Luxemburg would be jailed and mysteriously murdered along with her companion. The summer of 1919 has been an indelible mark for scholars of the Harlem Renaissance as returning World War I veterans and unemployment, mixed with racism, ignited riots throughout the country.[13] The poem stubbornly resurfaced in the Riot Issue of the *Messenger* a few months later, a sort of summary of events over the summer, and used as the frontispiece for a guest editorial demanding a "New Negro."[14] (We should distinguish this earlier anomaly from the more streamlined Harlem Renaissance version that was fashioned through the tireless efforts of philosopher Alain Locke six years later.) Unlike Locke's later manifesto, the *Messenger's* New Negro tugged deceptively at America's provincially white picket fence, whose foundation was low wages, poor working conditions, and institutional discrimination (things Locke's New Negro never broached out of good taste—or fear). With an inclination toward union organizing that reflected the Wobbly approach (One Big Union, for instance, with lateral as well as horizontal organization), the *Messenger* connected the sentiments in "If We Must Die" to a more globally positioned Negro: one who possessed "stiffened back bone, dauntless manhood, defiant eye, steady hand and a will of iron."[15]

> If we must die—let it not be like hogs
> Hunted and penned in an inglorious spot,

While round us bark the mad and hungry dogs,
Making their mock at our accursed lot.
If we must die—oh, let us nobly die,
So that our precious blood may not be shed
In vain; then even the monsters we defy
Shall be constrained to honor us though dead!

Oh, Kinsmen! We must meet the common foe;
Though far outnumbered, let us still be brave,
And for their thousand blows deal one death-blow!
What though before us lies the open grave?
Like men we'll face the murderous, cowardly pack,
Pressed to the wall, dying, but—fighting back!

Used this way, the poem became a clarion. This was no soulful croon sentimentalizing the black condition. Whether read as poetry or propaganda, its message was unmistakably sharp and clear and need not pass the censors for evaluation in the anti-Bolshevik furor of 1919, a frenzy that resulted a few years earlier from the successful overthrow of the czar by Russian peasants.[16] Much like his later experience at the theater, McKay's poem was revelatory and touched a nerve, becoming a bellwether for black angst. Thus it was reported to have been read into the *Congressional Record* as an example of this New Negro's potential: a militantly suicidal and international renegade who seemed determined to "face the murderous, cowardly pack" against any odds.[17] The *Messenger* echoed such sentiments: "If death is to be their portion, New Negroes are determined to make their dying a costly investment for all concerned."[18] The warning in McKay's verse, further corroborated by the *Messenger's* no-nonsense approach, reflected a continuation of a strategy conceived by Frederick Douglass and Ida B. Wells in the latter part of the nineteenth century when Jim Crow, segregation, and lynchings first became institutionalized. It is a sentiment driven by hopelessness and humiliation, of failed leadership and spotty policy. And it continues today, though those driven up against the wall are jihadist of various persuasions, radicals and poets, women and children. (Then and now we continue to misread those early warning signs of discontent, or we deny our part in nurturing that dissatisfaction.)[19]

What began as an instructive literary encounter on Broadway, embellished with allusions to a specter haunting Western civilization, moved quickly from fantasy to reality as government agents acknowledged the threat this verse—and poet—now posed.[20] McKay hardly fit the profile of a demonic specter, though, and was more the soft-spoken lyricist, mentored in obscure Victorian romances and Elizabethan conceits. What was to be done with this image? A black poet who preferred Shakespeare, and who actually copied the bard's sonnet style into much of his work, even the notorious "If We Must Die"? To add to the problem, he was a bit of a hedonist and admired the decadents—those late-nineteenth-century English poets who wrote not of revolutionary zeal but debauched exuberance—which was unheard of among the sophisticated Black Belt. (McKay, on the other hand, arrived in the United States in 1912 from rural Jamaica to study agriculture at Tuskegee Institute.) The Irish rebel Oscar Wilde was in his circle of admirers, and he read Algernon Charles Swinburne, William Ernest Henley, Ernest Dowson, and other formal English writers. His friends included lesbians and suffragists, stuffy Fabians, philosophers such as John Dewey, linguists C.K. Ogden and I.A. Richards, as well as a mix of homosexuals and street hustlers. Yet one bureau agent, in his report to the director in Washington, D.C., characterized McKay as "a typical black American Negro" of the mulatto variety, which would have amused McKay since he considered himself very black—and proud of that fact.[21] The poet's attitude on life and politics derived from an old rhyme he learned as a child in Jamaica: "Keep in the middle of the road / Though the road be deep and wide / There's a ditch on either side."[22] Indeed, far from the racial call to arms that excited the *Messenger*, "If We Must Die" had a deliberate middle-of-the-road message, one that appealed to "black or brown yellow or white, Catholics, Protestants or pagans, fighting against the Terror."[23] This ubiquitous "Terror," alluded to by the poet, was part of a sinister propagandistic line taking shape in the early twentieth century, where ideologues of the right and left, black and white, dug their pens in for the long haul. It was a characteristic of this author, as an enfant terrible of Harlem, to keep those emerging borderlines, in his poetics as well as politics, as Zamyatin suggested, wild and asymptotic.[24]

That might be due also to McKay's creative inclination. He viewed himself first and foremost as a poetic rebel, though later wrote three novels and worked as an editor for the *Liberator*, a radical New York magazine, and the *Dreadnought*, published by Sylvia Pankhurst, in London. Still, by 1922, he was hardly a literary name, though fast becoming a black American militant—to his chagrin. (Before coming to the United States, he had published two volumes of verse, *Songs of Jamaica* and *Constab Ballads*.) His militant rhetoric, however, paled in comparison to such well-known figures as Eugene V. Debs, Emma Goldman, even Big Bill Haywood. He explained at one gathering how awkward he felt behind the podium: "my public speaking is so bad," he admitted, "that I have been told by my own people that I should never try to make speeches, but stick to writing, and laughing."[25] He was a pacifist, another oddity, and a committed one, on good terms with the antiwar agitator Crystal Eastman, founder of the Women's Peace Party in New York City. Although as a struggling poet he might have appreciated the government's interest in his work, he was completely unaware of the frenzy he had created after he dropped from the radar and vanished in the fall of 1922 as a stoker aboard a freighter en route to Liverpool. He had just finished up with his first book of American verse, *Harlem Shadows*, which was put together with the help of *Liberator* editor in chief Max Eastman, brother to Crystal. The two then made plans to meet up at Fourth Congress of the Third International in Moscow. The Congress, the fourth in a series that highlighted issues of concern to socialists around the globe, particularly interested McKay because the Negro Question would be put on the party agenda. This delighted the poet, who was curious as to how the international community would address regional problems of racism.[26] Remarkably, though unaffiliated with the Communist Party or the official Comintern, the organizing arm of the international Communist Party, McKay was nevertheless invited to speak on the question, and so impressed Lenin and Trotsky that he was asked to write on the problem at length. (He had a more radical notion of farming than what he learned of agriculture at Tuskegee Institute and later Kansas State College, which was more in line with Henry George's land reform schemes of "liberating millions of city folk to go back to the land."[27])

From Liverpool, he traveled to London and visited with old acquaintances: Cambridge intellectuals he had met while working on the *Dreadnought* in 1920: C.K. Ogden, James Wood, I.A. Richards. He dropped in to the highbrow 1917, a London literary salon that was home to radicals and Bloomsbury intellectuals, such as Virginia and Leonard Woolf, to drum up financial support for his trip to Moscow, but with little success. He worked his way to the Baltic Sea where he boarded an "old potato boat" for Petrograd. To his surprise he found himself in the company of the English CP delegation. Among them were those who had given him the shoulder in London. They were all—officially and unofficially—on their way to the Fourth Congress of the Third International.[28]

Much of this resistance was due to McKay's brand of politics, which was a curious amalgam for a black poet, and especially for someone mistaken as an American Negro associated with the Harlem Renaissance. He was an internationalist, part of a movement that grew out of opposition to World War I. Unique among radical groups, it was inspired by women associated with the international suffrage movement of the late nineteenth century. Internationalist's fierce opposition to the war made it a flash point of concern for governments around the world. (Interpol, at this time, was just falling in place, and passports were becoming de rigueur as an identity card.) Viewed by trade unionists, traditional socialists, and labor organizers as feminine, porous, and undefined, internationalism was ideally suited for specter sightings and scapegoating. But it was, nevertheless, an exciting time for these footloose radicals as national boundaries became less meaningful and their cause quickened. Important publications such as *Women's Dreadnought* in

England and *The Liberator* in America, broadened their perspectives. (The *Dreadnought* became the *Workers' Dreadnought* and shifted its focused to colonial issues, while the *Liberator* rekindled the radical tradition of Frederick Douglass.) Everywhere was the image of the new: the New Woman, the New Century, the New Negro, and the New Worker. For American blacks it was an exciting—albeit cautious—beginning to a new century. As its chief black proponent, McKay warranted extra scrutiny from U.S. authorities unfamiliar with the ways of black folk, particularly internationally minded ones.

As early as July 21, 1922, William J. Burns, director of the Justice Department, had become curious about this McKay character and his nomadic inclinations, and he pressed W. L. Hurley of the State Department, who had earned his stripes keeping track of Germans and other suspicious-looking immigrants during World War I, for more information. According to Burns' sources McKay, referred to as "the well known radical of New York City," was due to embark for Europe in August. More information was needed since McKay was considered (reported another memo) to be a highly placed representative for the black cause and dangerous. He was also of some literary merit, another agent reported, though how to describe those merits of a black 32-year-old author was beyond him. (Two books, *Songs of Jamaica* and *Constab Ballads*, written in dialect and published in Jamaica; another, *Spring in New Hampshire*, off an obscure press in London.) He had just published *Harlem Shadows* in New York, but the merit of that work still needed to be assessed. (Yet his biographer, Wayne F. Cooper, believed that McKay was robust and in his prime, creatively and intellectually, when the bureau's interest in him was perked.) There were delays in leaving (probably due to finding a vessel that would take him since he did not have an American passport), but he finally steamed out of New York harbor on September 20, 1922. It was a journey that was part publicity tour for his new book, part curiosity, and would take him into political exile for 20 years.[29]

The Third International convened on November 5. It was a month-long meeting that brought together radicals from around the world, those who were committed such as Rose Pastor Stokes as well as the curiosity-seekers like McKay. (This, in many ways, was a very glamorous event, and attracted many for whom this would be a exotic vacation.) But among the hardcore there was a lot of business at hand: whether to affiliate with traditional political parties and labor unions, and how best to engage colonials, blacks and the dispossessed, in the factories and on the field. Thus, there was a fresh dynamic at this particular meeting. U.S. officials, of course, were concerned with the intentions of the American delegates once the congress concluded in December. What message would they be bringing home to the awaiting masses? Immediately after, Burns wrote Hurley (on December 22), with more reliable information, this time from the American minister in Riga, detailing the routes these delegates would take home. McKay, he noted, was believed to be in the company of three other "Negro delegates": Saycsh, Claude McKay, a communist by the name of Johnson, and a J. Billings.[30] "I would greatly appreciate being informed by your office," Burns politely inquired, "as to the definite route which these individuals will use if they return to this country, in order that they may be given appropriate attention upon their entry. It is further suggested that you endeavor to find out whether or not passports have been issued to these subjects, and if so, I would appreciate photostat copies." After these black delegates pressed the Negro Question, U.S. officials were now concerned that these representatives would not continue to disseminate bad press abroad, as they zigzagged around the Continent as footloose "sailors"—an euphemism the State Department used for rogue militants. (Unaffiliation seemed to worry U.S. officials more than affiliation. Interestingly, a central debate at the Fourth Congress was whether the Communist Party should move above ground, affiliate with more tradition labor groups, and work more as a political party on progressive issues.) As field agents moved out into the international arena (a trend necessitated by World War I), the semantics of the *Messenger's* warning that "the international method of dealing with problems is the method of the future" became a matter of urgency.[31]

Suddenly McKay, along with three other vagabonds, reappeared on the government radar, transformed from a humble poet to a seething specter, and the mad scramble began. Between January and March of 1923, the Justice Department, with the assistance of the State Department and Customs, put out an all-ports bulletin. Officials at all possible access points (at this period in time mostly seaports) were telegrammed—the West Coast (Seattle, San Francisco, Los Angeles), the Midwest (Chicago, Milwaukee, and the Canadian border towns), the Southeast (Delaware, South Carolina), the Northeast (Boston, New York, Baltimore), and the Gulf coast (Texas, Louisiana)—asking that McKay be intercepted, detained, and interrogated. This became a demand after rumor worked into an officious report that the poet had personal and coded directives to organize "the black race in America" in overthrowing the U.S. government.[32] The FBI pulled out all stops, and recruited more black agents to infiltrate domestic organizations such as the NAACP and the African Blood Brotherhood, a primarily Caribbean political organization that also published the *Crusader*. The most infamous agent with the bureau was James E. Amos, the first official black G-Man to cut his teeth infiltrating the Marcus Garvey organization, and whose information was used against the black leader in his subsequent mail fraud trial.[33] Caucasian agents assigned to the case included Edward J. Brennan, Harold Nathan, a New York special agent who along with Brennan were later accused of counterespionage, and special agents A.C. Sullivan, who traveled to Copenhagen in an attempt to snare the poet, and of course Hoover, a mason and negrophobe, who headed the newly formed General Intelligence Division and acted as a go-between William J. Burns of the Justice Department and Secretary of State W.L. Hurley.[34] There were others, who reported on and relayed information from "the field"—moles, informants, loyal Americans concerned about the race problem. Brennan may have perked Hoover's interests in pursuing the Negro poet by alluding to McKay's sexual inclinations, which was not an unusual characterization for blacks, in a biographical sketch on December 13, 1922. Like many of the writers of the Harlem Renaissance—Langston Hughes, Countee Cullen, Harold Jackman, even Alain Locke—there was much gossip as to who was doing what with whom. Harlem Renaissance and the gay cabaret scene were considered by many, from senators to agents, to be decadent and criminal—a place where lines of race and sexuality were disgustingly blurred. And for that senator from Missouri or Illinois, it was a place to be outlawed and monitored. Of course, McKay was a central figure in that gossip, and it did not take much effort to exaggerate some of those claims, especially from those envious of his talents.

It was soon circulated among all the bureaus that the group of rogue delegates might return via Chita or Shanghai, so customs officials in San Francisco and Seattle were particularly put on alert, and reminded by the Justice Department to give them "a very thorough examination" upon entry.[35] "They no doubt went out and will return as sailors," Burns advised, of the most convenient method of travel among radicals and vagabonds.[36] In Los Angeles, field agents were asked to lean heavily on informants who might have contacts within "the Communist Party of America." In addition, "confidential informants on Negro Activities" were marshaled up to see if there were any racially coded signs or sightings. Other bureaus as well were asked "to watch out for subjects," and the postal service was enjoined to reroute McKay's letters to friends in New York City to the Justice Department for ciphering. Even at the *Crisis* and *Liberator* there were moles who dutifully passed along gossip and news pertaining to McKay's whereabouts when pressed by agents (and one wonders what types of tactics or intrigue were used to gain this information so readily). An "Agent Titus" (Earl B., possibly an alias for Amos, who went under several pseudonyms) relayed information, supposedly from Grace Campbell, a Harlem socialist whom McKay admired and trusted, insisting that McKay never intended to return to the United States. (Pseudonyms for black agents were very important and kept them alive, since they were viewed as betraying the race.) Despite these assurances, the bureau continued its search for the elusive poet. Agent Titus was engaged again to go undercover, this time traveling to

Chicago where he filed a report on January 18, 1924, after a meeting of the African Blood Brotherhood, which was called to discuss strategies in working with Communists and, curiously, a February "Sanhedrin" conference. The meeting included Edward L. Doty and 13 other unidentified Blood Brotherhood members.[37]

But McKay did not enter the United States, and instead, at the invitation of Lenin and Trotsky, was asked to remain in Russia and expand on the Negro Question for the next congress. In fact, while in Moscow, he was treated like a celebrity, much like Doty described, and corroborated in reports from Max Eastman, who had shared the spotlight with the Jamaican while in Moscow. There are scenes of him being hoisted in the air by jubilant throngs of well wishers, and adopted "as a kind of mascot" by the Red Army and Navy. Eastman wrote, with a bit of envy, that the Jamaican was "entertained everywhere at the state's expense, given a Grand Duke's bedroom and study to live and work in, [and] exhibited on tribunes with the great leaders and orators of the revolution." The ivy-league-educated radical marveled at how this humble peasant was able to have "the time of his life."[38]

Yet McKay was very serious about the Negro Question and his attempt to call radicals, particularly in the States, on the carpet. "The situation in America is terrible and fraught with grave dangers. It is much uglier and more terrible than was the condition of the peasants and Jews of Russia under the Tzar."[39] McKay informed Eastman that he planned to condemn American radicals in a postscript to *Negroes in America*, which he began while in Moscow.[40] This was the ultimate betrayal, and Eastman went into frenzy. "I think it would be a great mistake," he warned in a terse letter on April 12, 1923, to even consider pressing radicals on the race question. The issue needed more time and judicious care. "The proletarian revolution has occurred," Eastman announced, "or is occurring here. The persecution of Jews has ceased. The two most powerful men in the government at this moment are Jews. The race problem in its basic outlines has disappeared. For you, the leading revolutionary figure in the Negro world, to come out at this moment with a statement that it is 'indulging in the chimerical fancies of a child' to imagine that the race problem will be solved by the proletarian revolution (the triumph of labor) is really a tragedy."[41] McKay had received that line so often from party regulars that he was shocked and saddened to hear it from his dear friend and editor:

> Do you think I was playing when twice in 1921 you saw colored men and women at the *Liberator* office discussing politics and race problems with me—and you did not like it from fear of the Justice Department? You have been entirely deceived by me, Max. I suppose it is due to this everlastingly infectious smile of mine.[42]

There were simply too many lynchings, and for the movement to win the hearts of Negroes, McKay believed, it was necessary for the Communist Party, particularly in the South, to make a powerful showing above ground.[43]

With Trotsky's help, McKay suggested ways that Negroes might be comfortably included in a revolutionary movement, but he shied away from heavy-handed attempts at converting party regulars to his way of thinking. They possessed, he concluded, a peculiarly narrow way of interpreting the struggle, regrettably much like his friend Eastman, and "bore themselves as if they were holy messengers of Jesus, Prince of Heaven, instead of working class representatives."[44] Indeed, McKay knew how to have a good time, and sought out, instead, nonpartisans and other anti-Bolsheviks, those who were less dogmatic such as the poet Vladimir Mayakovsky and the futurist writer Yevgeny Zamyatin, a pariah among Communists after his warning of slippage toward totalitarian regimes of the right *and* left in *We*. The countryside and peasantry enthrall him, and he began to see the revolution in terms of poetics rather than polemics. In Russia, he explained, was where "all the races of Europe and of Asia" met and mixed, which made for a new aesthetics and sensibility. He was especially fond of the Domino Café, a shabby Moscow watering hole popular among "young anarchists and menshevists." As was his hedonist inclination, he admitted to enjoying the city's "second-rate cabaret" atmosphere to the official goings-on.[45] He even had time to take trips to the countryside, and he found the newness and mix of places like Petrograd especially exciting, with red flags everywhere and streamers that magically fluttered against the stark whiteness of the snow. For him, it was a lyrical moment: "Railroad trains, street cars, factories, stores, hotels, schools—all wore decorations," he blushed, and the people, well, they were "beautifully naïve"—in that warm peasant sort of way that reminded him of Jamaica.[46] He stayed on in the city until May 1923 and wrote a poem about May Day in Petrograd, which only caused further speculation among federal agents as to his intentions: was he carrying bombs and special instructions for the Negroes of the world, or a cache of new incendiary poems? And where would this wraith set landfall? Indeed, such indecision on the poet's part set off reams of official conjecture, with close readings of his verse for secret messages. (One lengthy memorandum dated January 26, 1924, for instance, quoted numerous poems.) Amid this whirl of intrigue, McKay was far less the subversive than impish literatus. But the State Department's propaganda mill of misinformation continued on without pause, and seemed to diverge more and more from the reality of McKay's threadbare literary existence. An April 13 letter to Burns, for instance, describes McKay as nearly brainwashed after completing his studies at, of all places, "the Bolshevik propaganda academy in Moscow," where he mentored in the best ways of "rousing the negroes against the white races, whether these are American, British, or French."[47] In actuality, though, he was less inclined to lecture—or to be lectured to—and spent much of his extended visit devoted to solitary writing. He produced a book-length critical study on *Negroes in America*, as well as numerous articles. He also wrote a grouping of poems that included "Moscow," "Russian Cathedral," and a parting tribute to his beloved city titled "Petrograd: May Day 1923."[48] Near the end of his stay, he contemplated a move to Berlin and a visit to its notorious cabarets, and later when he did, was where he apparently contracted venereal disease. Understandably oblique about his plans, he wrote Eastman, "You may not be able to see me for some time. Uncertain as to time myself. But you can address me to Amer Express—Berlin."[49] It was a clip and ominous note, easily misunderstood. Was the specter about to be unleashed? The State Department in a mad scramble contacted the Danish Legation in hopes of dislodging this ticking time bomb of race-hating propaganda. But no Negroes were sighted by Danish police—anywhere in Denmark! It was a nice, clean, racially ventilated state. Furthermore, it was reported, "during the past year no Danish authority, authorized to grant visas, has permitted any negro to enter Denmark under any visa." In fact, it was reported, with some reluctance, "Six months ago, two negroes, coming from Coblenz, calling themselves musicians by profession, requested visas of the Danish Legation at The Hague, which were refused them."[50] So much, it seemed, of the possibility of specters infiltrating Denmark.

There were sightings of McKay in Germany, briefly gulping the prefascist atmosphere with trepidation, and by June a description of him was broadcast as "the well known negro agitator." All this was done with little exhortation or effort on the part of the poet, and it seemed his due, having graduated summa cum laude from "the Propaganda and Agitation School in Moscow."[51] But writing—and making a living as a writer—were what preoccupied his thoughts. On July 8, 1923, he wrote Walter White, the influential NAACP organizer, about approaching Du Bois at the *Crisis* to see if he would be interested in a two-part feature on Russia. It would be an objective, nonpartisan cultural expose from a black Jamaican viewpoint. This was hardly the incendiary prose anticipated by Hoover and field agents, and the bureau seemed uniformly disappointed. They were not deterred though in their mission to block the author's entry into America, should be decide to return. For McKay's part, he simply wanted to begin the process of broadcasting his analysis of white international communism, and to engage radicals on the Negro Question, since most mainstream publications, including radical ones like the *Liberator*, newly edited by Mike Gold, seemed far from receptive.[52] And from a colonial vantage, in this post–World War I gyre of politics, his comments would be very instructive and prophetic. But he burnt too many bridges it seemed, among black and white progressives, and was fortunate enough to have White intercede for him in placing his request before Du Bois without much hand-wrenching or mudslinging.[53] Finances and making ends meet as a writer were on his mind again when he wrote Arthur Schomburg later in September: "I can't go home to America now, for I haven't the money. Besides I don't want to—I want to stay abroad and write some things. But I am quite broke—want to go to Italy where it is warm and cannot. Frightfully cold here."[54] Finally, in December 1923 and January 1924, his two pieces on Russia appeared in the *Crisis.* Immediately, the FBI intensified its surveillance, moving Amos back into the field. Might this be the long-awaited coded message for black readers of the *Crisis*? Amos dogged Mrs. Cyril Briggs and others, beginning in January 1924.[55] (Her husband, Cyril Briggs, an acquaintance of McKay's, had organized the African Blood Brotherhood, which had the not-so-revolutionary intention of total integration as its aim.[56]) Amos and another agent, Earl Titus (or his pseudonym), had the inside scoop on the goings-on between McKay and Grace Campbell, White, and others, through casual interviews. From Cyril Briggs, who Titus befriended, he learned that McKay was in Germany "and was to stay there until something happened." Titus also befriended W.A. Domingo, a fellow Jamaican and friend of McKay's and one of the editors, along with Briggs, of the *Crusader*. He was able to tag along with the group to Briggs' home at 213 West 135 Street, in Harlem. Titus made a mental note of his conversation with Briggs and Domingo, who talked about his trip to Philadelphia with Otto Huiswood, where they spoke at several churches. Wasn't Huiswood with McKay in Russia? Titus felt like he had hit pay dirt. Titus also asked Domingo his opinion of Garvey, another fellow Jamaican who had been the focus of recent bureau surveillance, but in jail at the moment. Domingo mentioned that the NAACP was "a good organization and getting good results, but Garvey has the ability of organizing."[57] Valuable information, and reason to keep a sharp eye on developments in Garvey's Universal Negro Improvement Association, should it become a mass movement.

Whether it was McKay's good luck or naiveté, such scrutiny eluded him. And by staying put in Europe, he avoided the harassment, arrest, and deportation that Garvey experienced at the hands of Amos, Hoover, and company. Europe also offered up the opportunity to expand on his poetic sensibility, something he was not allowed to do while in America. And in places like Petrograd, with its blundering naiveté and bold banners, in contrast to Harlem, he had discovered his own "gateway to the strange."[58]

SIGHTINGS AND MISINFORMATION

The key to the effectiveness of specters, though, is the way they anonymously emanate signals deep inside caves or impenetrable fortresses, with demonic gargoyles and sentries on guard. Here they can work under disguise, while maintaining a powerful field and presence. Thus, it was better that McKay remain in Russia to build up his imaginary arsenal, since it would only add to the suspense and intrigue should anything real occur. As late as October 1923, the U.S. government persisted in placing McKay in Russia awaiting plans for the overthrow of the West by a black vanguard. Yet by his own reckoning, the poet was in Hamburg having "the bummiest holiday in my life," down on his luck with the grippe and no money. "My life here is very unsatisfactory for a propagandist," he complained to Campbell. The great propagandist, who personally trained with Trotsky and Lenin, had been reduced to "cadging a meal off people who are not at all sympathetic to my social ideas."[59] But the plan worked, and the government's misinformation on McKay began eventually to filter back into the right hands. It was used by white leftists and Harlem Renaissance writers who had little regard for McKay to begin with, and used such information to jockey their own careers to stardom and fame.

Eric Walrond, a fellow West Indian and one in Locke's stable of young protégés, and William Stanley Braithwaite, don of Negro criticism, who weighed in with an appraisal of "If We Must Die," when it first appeared, accused him of losing sight of his artistic integrity. Now those reports of McKay at the Moscow Academy of Propaganda seemed only to fan the flames. He had become a poet enmeshed in a "dilemma," Braithwaite observed, one who was "caught between the currents of the poetry of protest and the poetry of expression," who had become sadly a "violent and strident propagandist, using his poetic gifts to clothe arrogant and defiant thoughts." What had happened to the "pure lyric dreamer" who contemplated "life and nature with a wistful sympathetic passion?" Braithwaite wondered. Why, he "hovers for a moment, pardonably perhaps, over the race problem." In such poems as "If We Must Die," his allegiance should be to poetry, not race or racial injustice, and to that "it must soar." McKay seemed not to be holding his own very well in the States.[60] Walrond, on the other hand, found McKay too bitterly un-American (strange to hear from a fellow British colonial), and floated the rumor that the poet was an agent, in the employ of the Soviets—which immediately unnerved McKay.[61] "A lie," McKay countered later. "I had to peddle autographed copies of poems, bum my friends and work as a fireman from N.Y. to Liverpool to get to Russia. And although the Bolsheviks tried to make me represent the Negro race, I let them know that I was a free spirit, a poet although politically my sympathies were communist."[62] The left, interestingly, seemed a tad too quick in chastising McKay for behaving as a decadent.[63]

But the poet seemed less and less concerned with his racial image in America and focused, instead, upon the sinister shifts in political winds that were faintly forecasting an even mightier foe to American democracy, the rise of Naziism throughout Europe. (Too bad, agents from the United States were not as concerned with this new form of propaganda.) He wrote Schomburg of the abuses by "the German Right against their moderate and radical opponents." Berlin had become the epicenter for "the resentful spirit of all Germany," and began to resemble, he noted sadly, "a brutal might," where critics, such as Luxemburg, are simply kidnapped and executed by thugs in the government's employ. From his vantage, McKay saw little difference with what was taking place in the American South where lynching was a commonplace occurrence and held as social events in which entire families—fathers, mothers, sons, and daughters—participated. Usually this involved a grisly burning as well, as in the 1919 lynching of William Brown in Douglas County, Nebraska, which may have spurred McKay to write these lines. In all, some 4,000 Negroes were lynched, from 1883 to the late 1960s.

> His spirit in smoke ascended to high heaven.
> His father, by the cruelest way of pain,
> Had bidden him to his bosom once again;
> The awful sin remained still unforgiven.
> All night a bright and solitary star
> (Perchance the one that ever guided him,
> Yet gave him up at last to Fate's wild whim)
> Hung pitifully o'er the swinging char.
> Day dawned, and soon the mixed crowds came to view
> The ghastly body swaying in the sun:
> The women thronged to look, but never a one
> Showed sorrow in her eyes of steely blue;
> And little lads, lynchers that were to be,
> Danced round the dreadful thing in fiendish glee.
>
> "The Lynching," *Cambridge Magazine*
> 10 (Summer 1920): 56.

Curious to understand this frenzy, here in the very center of Ayran nationhood, he characterized it as a "futuristic forest" where "Wandervogel everywhere like a plague of flies" hovered; a modern day Frankenstein, "in which the dynamo / Of Europe throbbed with sinister intent."[64] From here, emanated segregation, race laws, apartheid, discrimination, the true heart of darkness. But McKay needed urgent medical care, and so moved on to Paris, where he was treated for his illness. Forced to work while not fully recovered, the poet contracted influenza, the result of modeling nude in damp, drafty studios for a few bucks. (The well-known militant seemed to have attracted a following and his body was in demand. Neither his poetry nor his views on the Negro Question generated much interest.)[65] "But to the astonishment of the doctors I recovered within a month," he wrote in a letter to an acquaintance named Charlie, which had been intercepted and filed away by the FBI. The letter was hardly the promised instructions to the black masses, but described McKay's situation in Europe. "My ankle was swollen and I was limping in my left foot, but I pulled through o.k. and now am quite safe and sound," he explained.[66] Yet as news of his ill health reached colleagues and friends in Harlem, the FBI blundered along, reporting on not one but multiple sightings of the phantom, in Russia and Copenhagen. He was even believed to have made furtive appearances in Milwaukee, San Francisco, and New York. He seemed to be, conveniently, every place but where he actually should have been: in a dingy Parisian hospital charity ward where he took up pen to write tortured lyrics reminiscent of the hospital poems of the late Victorian William Ernest Henley. He also became severely depressed (possibly a result of a syphilitic attack), and began developing a paralysis in the left side of his face (a condition due to hypertension, which would affect him later and ultimately cause his death): "my face gradually became puffed up like an enormous chocolate soufflé."[67] He admitted to Locke later: "The treatment in Paris worked like magic; the doctors said the disease was only incipient and in six weeks my flesh was sound again. I am strong and look healthier than ever, but I must take treatment at intervals for about a year or two for the germs in my blood."[68] McKay, however, was never really the same.[69]

The deterioration of his physical condition, so sudden and unexpected, mimicked the cultural stagnation that rolled and undulated against a rising chorus of attacks by T.S. Eliot and other modernists on vernacular and mongrelized art and that preceded the rise of European fascism and the outbreak of World War II.[70] It was as if his body was an artist's palette, where hues and colors mixed in a brilliant array. McKay, too, in his own work began to interrogate this stagnation, titling one collection of verse "Miasma." These poems are highly impressionistic, and marked a turning point for the author. In such pieces as "The Desolate City" (which appeared later in a Caribbean issue of *Opportunity* in 1926 as "Desolate"), the poet's muscles and bones play out the fantasies of the exile's homeland, and become the girders of a dreamscape that has been "Glutted with baffled hopes."

> Strange agonies make quiet lodgment there:
> Its sewers, bursting, ooze up from below
> And spread their loathsome substance through its lanes,
> Flooding all areas with their evil flow
> And blocking all the motions of its veins:
> Its life is sealed to love or hope or pity,
> My spirit is a pestilential city.[71]

Understandably, given his physical condition, the poem is about blocked motions, sealed lives, quiet lodgments. (As a result we surmise the entrapment, the net of government control, the web of suspicion that was swirling around the poet.) The poem also works at a composite of traditions—the Victorian and Romantic—and evokes Lord Byron's *Childe Harold* whose persona, likewise, wore "the shattered links of the world's broken chains."[72] This desolate city is a forlorn place where even nature is unwelcome. "Clean waters beat against its high-walled shore," the poet tells us, "but cannot enter." High above the poem's walls, an empty tower and broken minaret loom ominously. (One wonders what that minaret might mean for McKay, and us today. Possibly it hangs above the desolate city in places like Berlin and Paris, much like that rough beast in Yeats' "The Second Coming"?) Exhausted by the intrigue and tiring of being up against the wall, McKay longed for a quietude beyond a "superficially racist context" to a source of inspiration through which all experiences would be uniquely his own.[73] The FBI would have none of that, and continued to anticipate a world revolution incited by a lone black poet, who wrote in stark detail of his own ill health and depression. Were those, in fact, agents mused, another coded message to the masses? Only the author knew the true intention of those slippery metaphors that lurked, like specter bubbles, between the lines of such verse as "The Desolate City."

Back in the United States, the FBI continued to secure its borders in anticipation of those powerful metaphors breaking through, and the landscape slowly began to resemble a hopeless desolation of blocked motions and sealed lives. (The rise of McCarthyism, blacklists, loyalty oaths, exemplary executions.) Much of the obsessions with this phantom, however, continued to emanate from Hoover's office and his desire to control through fear and intimidation; to, at the very least, anchor this specter to a place or historical marker. One possible entry, the FBI surmised, might be along old slave routes, from the Caribbean to the southern United States, which conjured images of past insurrections and revolt. F.L. Park, in Charlotte, North Carolina, titled his note to Hoover simply "Radical" (June 15, 1923). McKay was believed to be en route to the Southern port city via the West Indies, and Park "called on" the inspector of customs, C.O. Brown, to notify the Justice Department should "CLAUDE MACKEY, negro radical" [*sic*] disembark. (There is some irony here in this particular alert for a fugitive "negro" [*sic*] from the West Indies at this southern port city, which had been a popular routes for slaves during the antebellum era.) In fact, customs officials in major cities along the entire southern coast were asked to report any suspicious "disembarkation." (Earlier, on April 11, customs officials in Wilmington, Delaware, had been given the same instructions.) Postmaster George H. Bunker, a colonel in the American Legion post in Wilmington, warned of an imminent entry from "the West Indies." The poet, he instructed, should be given the "appropriate attention." Soon after, with Bunker reporting no sign of McKay, the Wilmington office concluded its investigation. But sightings of the poet also cropped up in Cleveland. (Apparently he had eluded the government's dragnet and was believed to have mysteriously entered the country "over a month ago.") In Galveston, Texas, another crucial entry point, the Washington bureau "took up the phone with all Federal officers" and asked that descriptions of McKay be distributed among all government agencies. But neither Texas City nor Galveston was a desirable destination for the fugitive Negro delegate.[74] Another sighting was at the Rand School and Worker's Party headquarters in New York City, a more obvious place one would expect radicals such as McKay to be. Yet when Frank X. O'Donnell, Special Agent in Charge (SAC) in New York, questioned Huiswood, the Dutch Guianan who returned from Moscow via Curacao, he was told that McKay returned with him on March 3. Whether that was true or not, the poet's "present whereabouts," O'Donnell concluded, were at the moment "unknown."[75]

Thus, for nearly two years this stubbornly unmanageable specter, which had been brought to life unintentionally in 1922, traveled openly from Paris to Nice, then Marseilles, where one novel, *Home to Harlem*, was written and on to Africa and Tangiers, where he finished another, *Banjo*, and began work on a third, *Banana Bottom*. Yet in addition to the FBI, State and Justice Departments, other agencies became involved in efforts to cordon off this demon. Immigration, Customs, Public Health officials, as well as sheriff's and police departments, in Galveston, Texas, New Orleans, Louisiana, and at the Canadian border town of Sault Ste. Marie, Michigan, were requested "to keep a sharp lookout" should the "Radical Negro Representative" suddenly appear. A photograph, not nearly as embellished as those used in the Ten Most Wanted, was circulated among immigration officials along the Canadian border. With nary a "Negro Delegate" in hand, it seemed that the Justice Department was ready to admit defeat at the hands of the notorious author of "If We Must Die." (Unlike today, governments were more diplomatic about violating another country's integrity. The United States was not yet a super power, and it needed to be more discreet in how it bargained. Thus it was very difficult to apprehend a fugitive and declared internationalist in the 1920s who was beyond one's jurisdiction.)

On January 26, 1924, just as Hoover was promoted to the FBI's new director, a memorandum on McKay was circulated among agents, some 18 pages in length. It dated from 1919, and was a summary of McKay's career and articles, particularly those published in Moscow during the Fourth Congress. The memorandum excerpted his poetry as well, sometimes quoting entire works, and included a transcription of the original questions put to McKay by Leon Trotsky. This report also contained a photo of McKay taken with Sen Kataytama, a Japanese radical, Big Bill Haywood of the IWW, and Rose Pastor Stokes. In February another lengthy report was produced, this one a summary of McKay's life based almost exclusively on a *Boston Herald* article. Agent Titus was again brought back on the case for one final go-through, and reminded Brennan and other higher ups that it was "quite apparent that McKay is not in the United States."[76] Soon after, the government shifted gears and looked more closely at Harlem and Locke's more nascent and pristine New Negro, who would debut a year later.[77] Prohibition and bootlegging, cabaret and illicit sex, would take center stage.

FAR FROM SCRUTINY

But the journey and intrigue did not end here, either in Paris or Harlem, for the well-know agitator. In the summer of 1926, McKay traveled southward on his poetic journey in an attempt to heal himself. He set landfall in Marseilles, and turned to fiction instead of the Negro Question, realizing this was not of interest to white folks. He expanded a short story into a full-length novel, *Home to Harlem*, a tribute to that community's "deep-moving African rhythm" that "still remains one of the most pleasurable sensations in my blood"—but condemned nevertheless by critics such as Du Bois for pandering to prurient tastes.[78] In Marseilles, he met sailors from Morocco and North Africa who invited him to visit, and in 1928 made the amazingly short journey by sea across the strait of Gibraltar. Immediately he found respite from the political surveillance and cultural stagnation that had engulfed him, and his health improved in the dry heat of the climate.

> The Berber youngsters pitch their little tents,
> And skip gazelle-like for the approving throng
> Of nomads purchasing the city's joys—
> African drum beat, oriental song,
> Salome-sensual dance of jeweled boys,
> Amidst the ruins of austere monuments.[79]

Finally he was able to settle down, quite content never to return to Western culture. He scrapped together what meager royalties from *Home to Harlem* as down payment on a dilapidated farmhouse on the outskirts of Tangiers. It was strange yet oh-so-familiar, and he wrote Eastman back in New York: "There are many things in the life of the natives, their customs and superstitions, reminiscent of Jamaica."[80] (Like his time in Petrograd, McKay was able to connect to a larger sensibility.) He also returned to one of his delights, cottage gardening, a pastime he had not enjoyed since his youthful days in the hillside of Jamaica. He began to embrace aspects of Islam, and paid tribute in a poem to Xauen, a small village that lies in a remote gorge in the Rif Mountains, considered by Moroccans a holy Mecca. This "lovely fountain" of inspiration seemed to cleanse him of all the "bitter memories" of Europe and America.

Oh, lovely fountain bubbling in my breast,
And cleansing all the bitter memories,
Of pilgriming over the gutters of life:
Flow tenderly along the avenue
Of my bruised body, heavy upon my knees,
And wash the incisions where the sharp-edged knife
Of circumstance has penetrated through:
Bathe me always as when I was your guest.

Oh, lovely fountain flowing like the dawn,
That comes like spiders weaving silver charm
Upon the heavy dews of Afric's night,
Perspiring for the happy days so warm
And amorous from the pressure of the light,
Playing upon the gem the Moors call Xauen.[81]

Nearby was the Suani, a tidal river that seemed "always calm and excellent for bathing when the sea is often rough because of the strait and Levant winds." No longer a swimmer because of his health, he was nevertheless "very fond of floating in deep water at high tide," especially when "the sea drives up the river." On a hilltop above his house was a village of about 500 people "and a few friends always came down from these and over from town to visit me."[82] In the Moroccan hillside, McKay finally found balance, where "lyric and amatory poetry" were so much a part of everyday life that even the most "illiterate Moor" enjoyed it. "Certainly it was the Arabian poet," McKay wrote to his agent back in New York, "who, upon the Arab conquest of Spain, introduced lyric feeling into the rude and barbaric accents of the Europeans." McKay quickly involved himself in this local folklore "like a *loco*," visiting Arabian cafes nightly in search of native music and poetry, much as he had done in Petrograd, Moscow, New York, and Paris. Here, though, instead of nomenclatures that delineated race or one's politics, he became known universally as "Claudio," an exile finally gone native. This is how the Americans Charles Henri Ford and Paul Bowles found him: "plump and jolly, with a red fez on his head." He had been living this way for some time, it seemed, "exactly like a Moroccan."[83]

Postscript to a Poet "Gone Native"

For reasons best left to future scholars to ponder, the poet *did* eventually return to the United States, and a specter—brief and faint, though hardly a threat now—shadowed him. In May of 1940, as the poet applied for

American citizenship, a dusty dossier was uncovered, jammed in the back of a file cabinet that was purchased at auction from the Post Office Building in Baltimore. (One wonders how misplaced that file really was or what the intentions had been of this citizen in bringing this lost property to light.) Harold Nathan, who was agent on the case in 1922, was contacted in Washington, and he personally notified the chief, who was now, of course, Hoover. McKay's name rang a bell and the director quickly wrote back, praising the loyalty of this citizen for providing such important material. He asked that the papers be handed over to E.A. Soucy, SAC in Baltimore, who was dispatched posthaste. Having been anonymous since his turn southward in France, McKay was now back under the government's glass. But times and intentions had changed and black specters were no longer the threat they had been back in the 1920s. The material too was old and consisted of memoranda and reports, long forgotten, by former director W.J. Burns and Secretary of State Hurley, then special agent Nathan, and C.D. McKean, dated March 12 and 26, 1923. Little came of the newly surfaced material except to have it reclassified and kept out of public view, for good measure, Hoover believed, for his own as well as others' reputations. And anyway, sightings of the famous Negro, spectral or otherwise, hardly raised eyebrows anymore. There were other, bigger fish to fry, and specters to unleash, in the post–World War II anti-Communist era ahead.[84]

Notes

1. McKay, "He Who Gets Slapped," *Liberator* (May 1922): 24–25; rept. *The Passion of Claude McKay: Selected Poetry and Prose, 1912–1948*, ed. Wayne F. Cooper (New York: Schocken Books, 1973), p. 71.
2. Although primarily known as a phenomenon that took place in the United States, there were numerous migrations from the rural areas to large metropolitans. Not only New York, which became home to thousands of southern blacks as well as immigrants from the Caribbean, but London and Paris as well. By the 1920s, there were some 40,000 African West Indians who settled in Harlem. And by 1930, they made up 25 percent of the nation's largest black community. The "Great Migration" from the American South, as well, increased dramatically in the years between about 1910 and the early 1920s. Between 300,000 and 1,000,000 African Americans moved north during this period, largely a result of the need for replacement labor during World War I. In all, six million southern blacks made the move to the north during this period.
3. "Outcast" appeared in *Harlem Shadows* (1922), and is reprinted in *Complete Poems of Claude McKay* (Urbana: U of Illinois P, 2004).
4. McKay acquired the front-row press tickets as drama critic for the *Liberator*. His companion, William Gropper, an artist on staff with the magazine, accompanied him. The play was later made into a Hollywood film by Metro-Goldwyn Pictures (MGM) in 1924.

5. *The Passion of Claude McKay*, ed. Cooper, p. 70
6. Ibid., pp. 71–72.
7. Made famous by Carl Van Vechten's 1926 novel about Harlem titled *Nigger Heaven*.
8. Ibid., pp. 71–72. All letters and memos are from the FBI files from 1922 to 1924, and reopened in 1940 at the request of J. Edgar Hoover, upon McKay's application for U.S. citizenship. Freedom of Information Act No. 400,109/ 190-HQ-1137090.
9. McKay, "The Racial Question: The Racial Issue in the United States," *International Press Correspondence* 2 (November 1922): 817.
10. Genevieve Taggard edited and wrote an introduction to *May Days: An Anthology of Verse from Masses-Liberator* (Boni & Liveright, 1925), which included works by McKay as well as Jean Toomer, e.e. cummings, Louis Ginsberg, Maxwell Bodenheim, Louis Untermeyer, Amy Lowell, Edna St. Vincent Millay, Carl Sandburg, Louise Bogan, Mike Gold, Rose Pastor Stokes, and Edmund Wilson. "*The Masses* seems to have vanished from the gaze of the literary historian," she noted, "underground it went, to cut channels in the bed rock" (5). Her comments on propaganda appear on page 14 of her introduction.
11. The race leader W.E.B. Du Bois was convinced of the efficacy of propaganda, to be used against "a dusty desert of dollars and smartness." In *Souls of Black Folk* (1903), he wrote: "all in all, we black men seem the sole oasis of simple faith and reverence" (11–12). He became convinced, as did Locke and others, that integration could only be achieved through the manipulation of artistic expression. His comments on propaganda appeared in "Criteria of Negro Art," published in 1926, a year after the New Negroes' debut in Harlem. Yevgeny Zamyatin, *We* (New York: Penguin, 1993), p. 4.
12. McKay to James Weldon Johnson, April 30, 1928. James Weldon Johnson Collection, Beinecke Rare Book and Manuscript Library, Yale University.
13. Racial unrest began as early as 1918 in St. Louis.
14. The *Messenger*, edited by Owen Chandler and Phillip Randolph, began in 1917 as a union newspaper *Hotel Messenger* for black employees of Headwaiters and Sidewaiters Society of Greater New York. When the two editors published an expose on union corruption, they were immediately fired. They began their own journal, *Messenger*, soon after, in August 1917. "Our aim is to appeal to reason, to lift our pens above the cringing demagogy of the times, and above the cheap peanut politics of the old reactionary Negro leaders," commented a November 1917 editorial. In 1918, during the war, the two were charged by Palmer with breaking the Espionage Act. Recalled Randolph: "The judge was astonished when he saw us and read what we had written in the *Messenger*. Chandler and I were twenty-nine at the time, but we looked much younger. The judge said, why, we were nothing but boys. He couldn't believe we were old enough, or, being black, smart enough, to write that red-hot stuff in the *Messenger*." "Spartacus Educational," http://www.spartacus.schoolnet.co.uk/USACmessenger.htm
15. The editorial was initialed "W.A.D," *Messenger*, September 1919, p. 4.

16. Attorney General A. Mitchell Palmer created an "antiradicalism unit" run by J. Edgar Hoover, who personally escorted Emma Gold and Alexander Berkman off American shores that year. Some 6,000 people were arrested during the height of the frenzy, in January 1920, which was aimed mainly at immigrants who did not have citizenship. Agents, acting under Hoover's direction, searched homes without warrants, refusing access to legal counsel to those suspected of terrorist activity, and most were held without specific charges. The Palmer raids were used mainly as an excuse to deported illegal aliens.
17. The primary source for much of the poem's notoriety is found in Lee Jenkins' "If We Must Die: Winston Churchill and Claude McKay," *Notes and Queries* (September 2003), pp. 333–37. At the time of the race riots in 1919, Jenkins reports that Henry Cabot Lodge supposedly called the poem a "piece of demagogic heresy that demanded investigation" (334–35). Jenkins could not find the source of Cabot's remarks, however. Also anecdotal may be McKay's own remarks that a soldier on the Russian front had carried the poem into battle.
18. *Messenger*, September 1919, p. 4.
19. Among Arabs, the term has little meaning, and is used mainly by the West to define a porous armed resistance. The modern notion of mujahedeen came about, ironically, during the Russian invasive of Afghanistan, when the U.S. government under Ronald Reagan financed the Islamic opposition, who were referred to as freedom fighters. "Ronald Reagan Presidential Library," http://www.reagan.utexas.edu/archives/speeches/1982/31082c.htm accessed on July 14, 2006.
20. William J. Maxwell argues that, indeed, McKay warranted such fear. "The paperwork surrounding this suspicion," he explains, "argues that the bureau was not simply hallucinating; McKay may have been recruited as an underground operative." In any case, Maxwell notes, "he certainly enjoyed writing as one." "F.B. Eyes: The Bureau Reads Claude McKay," in *Left of the Color Line: Race, Radicalism and Twentieth-Century Literature of the United States* (Chapel Hill: U of North Carolina P, 2003), p. 41.
21. More likely he was mistaken for another Negro. Hurley to Burns, March 21, 1923.
22. McKay, "Right Turn to Catholicism," p. 25. The Schomburg Center for Research in Black Culture, New York Public Library. This was one of the many rhymes McKay devised and sang as a child.
23. McKay, "If We Must Die," in Bontemps, ed., *Anthology of Negro Poets* [recording]. Ed Arna Bomtemps. New York: Folkways, 1954. "If We Must Die" was viewed by McKay as complementary verse, coupling "Black Fiend" with "White Fiend," or "If We Must Die" with "Pariahs." This was a literary style that originated in the Victorian era called the talking or double poem, which was "founded on debate and contest." Isobel Armstrong, *Victorian Poetry—Poetry, Poetics, and Politics* (London: Routledge, 1993), p. 13. But more to the point: "From purely racial motives," he explained to his London editor C.K. Ogden, "I shouldn't like to publish the two you have chosen without the others. You would understand why if you had lived in America and tasted the

poison of hatred." American "coloured opinion" won't relish it, he said. "Pariahs," on the other hand, had "the note of despair" that was offset by "If We Must Die."

24. In Petrograd, McKay was asked to read his poems at literary events, attended by Zamyatin and others. "There was no communist spirit in evidence at these intelligentsia gatherings," McKay noted. "Frankly, there was an undercurrent of hostility to the bolsheviks." ("Soviet Russia and the Negro," *Crisis* 27:3 [January 1924]: 116.)
25. Cooper, *Passion*, p. 91.
26. In 1920, he published a chapbook in England entitled *Spring in New Hampshire*, and reprinted almost all of those poems in *Harlem Shadows*.
27. McKay, "How Black Sees Green and Red," *Liberator* (June 1921): 20–21; rept. *The Passion of Claude McKay*, p. 61.
28. Wayne F. Cooper, *Claude McKay, Rebel Sojourner in the Harlem Renaissance* (Baton Rouge: Louisiana UP, 1987).
29. Ibid., p. 171.
30. Escla to Burns, January 29, 1923. There may have been only three delegates: Frank Billings was the pseudonym used by Otto Huiswoud, and Saysch may be a variation on McKay's own nickname, Sasha, which he used while in Russia, though this was never confirmed or questioned by the agents. Manning Johnson, possibly the mysterious third rail within the Negro delegation to the Third International in 1922, later renounced communism and worked for the FBI. His book *Color, Communism, and Common Sense* traces his journey from a Communist to a Negro in the John Birch Society. He testified in 1953 before the House un-American Activities Committee that the Communist Party recruited radicals to enter the Catholic priesthood, where there was intense Communist activity. Interestingly, McKay was associated with Dorothy Day, founder of the Catholic Worker Movement, and became a Roman Catholic in the 1940s, long before Johnson's accusations came to light.
31. "Editorials: Internationalism," *Messenger*, August 1919, p. 6. "The ignorant leaders of the country might take a tip from De Valera in the presentation of their problems. Carry the Negro problem out of the United States, at the same time that you present it in the United States. The mere fact that the country does not want the Negro problem carried to Europe is strong evidence that it ought to be carried there" (6).
32. March 2, 1923, memo from the American Legation at Riga, Latvia. So incredible was this statement, that Burns asked for a copy of the original piece by Trotsky, published in *Izvestia* 34 (February 15), in which he answers questions "propounded by the American negro Communist," to have it translated accurately. (Hurley to Burns, undated, Dispatch No. 476; Burns to Hurley). The translation, by F.W.B. Coleman, asks that Negro agitators, such as McKay, return to the United States to engage in, what Trotsky calls a "deadly struggle" against race prejudice. Later versions of Trotsky's comments have McKay carrying large sums of money with instructions to "organize a colored Soviet" (qtd. in Report by A.C. Sullivan, April 1, 1923).

33. Garvey was found guilty and served five years in prison. Amos was hired at $6 a day, and served from 1921 to 1953. He was given the diplomatic task of befriending and recruiting help in keeping track of black specters. His experience for the job, interestingly, was his 12 years as a personal bodyguard for President Teddy Roosevelt, and an understanding of the Masonic tradition in America. Amos's reminisces can be found in *Theodore Roosevelt: Hero to His Valet* (New York: John Day, 1927). Both Roosevelt and Hoover were Masons, and Amos made the transition to the Justice Department with little difficulty, by replying on that bond of secrecy. He was sworn in on August 24, 1921. Amos's biographical information appears on the FBI's website (fbi.gov) as promotion and outreach for black recruits.
34. Attorney General A. Mitchell Palmer was Hoover's role model and mentor.
35. Burns to regional bureaus, January 19, 1923. Chita, at the eastern-most tip of Russia, was a center for worker unrest in the early years of the twentieth century and a likely springboard, officials believed, for McKay's entry into the United States. During the Cold War era, Chita was off-limits to foreigners because of its proximity to the Chinese border and its military industry.
36. Burns to Roy A. Darling, Seattle, Washington, February 2, 1923. In *The Black Atlantic: Modernity and Double Consciousness* (Harvard UP, 1993), Paul Gilroy missed the significance of McKay's passing as a sailor. Although the image of the sailor connoted a libertine lifestyle—homosocial if not openly sexual—Gilroy seems ignorant of its political meaning. McKay's identification with this maritime class was also a protest against the implementation of passport system. Many radicals, particularly those of color, simply refused to submit to this fairly recent surveillance system, which they felt was enacted to control their movements. Internationalists flaunted their global citizenship, and challenged all borders that confined them.
37. January 18, 1924 report by Earl B. Titus, "African Blood Brotherhood: Radical Negro Activities."
38. Max Eastman, *Selected Poems of Claude McKay* (New York: Bookman, 1953), pp. 111–12.
39. McKay, "Report on the Negro Question," *International Press Correspondence*, 3 (January 1923): 16–17.
40. *The Negroes in America* was translated into Russian. An English edition appeared in 1979, published by Lennikat Press.
41. Eastman to McKay, April 12, 1923, *Passion of Claude McKay*, pp. 88–89.
42. McKay to Eastman, May 18, 1923, ibid., p. 89.
43. One of the issues around the Negro Question for McKay was whether the activities of the party should be covert or above ground. In the South, covert activity played into the hands of racists. McKay felt that a united front of white radicals in support of black issues would be much more effective than subversive cloak and dagger activities. Interestingly, this had been the tactic suggested by Douglass in dealing with the abolitionists in the mid-1800s, demanding that they form political parties and lobbying groups.
44. McKay, "Soviet Russia and the Negro," *Crisis* 27 (January 1924): 115.

45. Ibid., pp. 115–116.
46. Ibid.
47. Hurley to Burns, April 13, 1923. Interestingly, as a representative from the State Department, Hurley mistakenly confuses race with nationality, while placing "negro" in some *other* category.
48. "Russian Cathedral" was later published in *Survey Graphic* on March 1, 1925, and retitled "St. Isaac's Church, Petrograd" in *The Selected Poems of Claude McKay*, published in 1953.
49. McKay to Eastman, Petrograd, May 1923. In *The Passion of Claude McKay*, p. 90; also cited in *Claude McKay: Rebel Sojourner in the Harlem Renaissance*, p. 193.
50. Prince to Hurley, April 25, 1923.
51. Hurley to Burns, June 1, 1923.
52. Much of McKay's criticism of the left comes from his encounter with Gold in 1922 before his departure for Russia. Gold was known for his novel *Jews without Money*, a depiction of New York's ethnic working class. He also had become a fanatical communist, and the two argued heatedly over the role of the Negro in the party. It spilled into the pages of the *Liberator*, and there was bickering over how much space should be devoted to Negro issues. Eastman stepped in and suggested a quota system, based on the percentage of blacks in the United States. Such a comment enraged McKay and he resigned as executive coeditor. The magazine became an organ of the Worker's Party and in 1924 was renamed the *Communist Monthly*, owned by the American Communist Party.
53. Cooper, *Rebel Sojourner*, pp. 195, 196. McKay and Du Bois had a rocky relationship throughout the 1920s, and ended after Du Bois' bitterly negative review of *Home to Harlem* in 1928.
54. McKay to Schomburg, September 25, 1923. Schomburg Center for Research in Black Culture; qtd. in Wayne Cooper, *Rebel Sojourner*, p. 198.
55. Gathering information on Garvey, Amos interviewed Walter White as well, assistant secretary of the NAACP and close friend of McKay's, on October 22, 1922. White told Amos that Garvey "has and is doing more to hurt the Negro than anyone has ever done"; also if Garvey doesn't go to jail it will be "the worst calamity" for the Negroes. Amos probably also pressed White on McKay's whereabouts. ("Report by Special Agent James E. Amos," New York, NY, October 19, 1922); "Marcus Garvey," http://www.marcusgarvey.com/wmview.php?ArtID=424&term=Walter%20white accessed on June 14, 2006.
56. Cooper, *Rebel Sojourner*, p. 106.
57. Report by Earl E. Titus, November 16, 1923.
58. Quoted from "Petrograd: May Day, 1923." May Day in Petrograd, for McKay, was a celebration of "The pagan day, the holy day for all!" In "New Poems," Beinecke Rare Book and Manuscript Library, Yale University.
59. Cooper, *Rebel Sojourner*, p. 210.
60. William Stanley Braithwaite, "The Negro in American Literature," *The New Negro, An Interpretation* (New York: Boni, 1925), p. 40.

61. Waldron, born in Georgetown, British Guiana in 1898, moved to the United States in 1918, at the age of 20. His one collection, *Tropic Death*, was published in 1926 and he died in London in 1966.
62. McKay wrote Cunard on September 18, 1932. Nancy Cunard Collection. Harry Ransom Humanities Research Center, The University of Texas at Austin. Cunard, a poet, also edited *The Negro Anthology* (1934). She was born in 1896, the only child of Sir Bache Cunard. She later became a communist and campaigned to free the Scottsboro Boys in the 1930s. Her involvement with McKay dates to the mid-1920s when she requested material from him for her anthology. She died in 1965.
63. This was another rumor circulated by lefts and New Negro intellectuals to discredit McKay.
64. McKay, "Berlin," in "New Poems." James Weldon Johnson Collection, Beinecke Rare Book and Manuscript Library, Yale University. Ten years after McKay wrote this poem, Alice Hamilton chronicled the rise of Nazism in "The Sound and the Fury in Germany" for the *Survey Graphic* (November 1933): "matters were moving with lightning speed, so that people dreaded to open their morning papers lest they find some new devastating governmental decree," the author noted. "There was much that was still only foreshadowed, there was hope that the whole program might not be put through . . . . The working-class quarters of Berlin in April were waiting, breathless, silent, to hear what their fate was to be."
65. An exotic, he was in demand at bohemian high modern art studios, such as Nina Hammets's famous salon and André Lhote's art school.
66. McKay to "Charlie," February 29, 1924.
67. McKay, *A Long Way from Home* (1937), p. 231.
68. McKay to Locke, May 1, 1924. Alain Locke Papers, Moorland-Spingarn Research Center, Howard University Library; qtd. in Cooper, *A Rebel Sojourner*, p. 200.
69. In November 1932, McKay suffered another breakdown, and traveled to a sanatorium in Berlin. He had been working on *Banjo* at the time, moved to Morocco and was getting the manuscript ready for Rieder, the French publisher, when he got the attacks. McKay thought it was a return of syphilis, but realized it was a real breakdown. Sometime before, his apartment had been ransacked, and his "carte d'identite" taken. McKay admitted to Nancy Cunard that he found it "hard to do any thinking because of the continuous noises in my head." McKay to Cunard, November 28, 1932. Harry Ransom Humanities Research Center.
70. Under the banner of New Humanism and through such journals as *Blast*, these reactionary modernists disparaged the popular culture while positioning themselves as authorities on art and literature. In "A Preface to Modern Literature," which appeared in a November 23, 1923 issue of *Vanity Fair*, T.S. Eliot explained: "I am not inclined to attach to our contemporaries in America as much value as they attribute to themselves. Their work is interesting—one can see why to people in America, it has supreme importance—but it is interesting as a *symptom*," which Eliot viewed as a general breakdown of culture. (*Vanity Fair* 21 [November 1923]: 44.)

71. In McKay's 1953 *Selected*, the word "city" in the second line was added; "spirit" appears in the unpublished "New Poems" as well as in *Caroling the Dusk*, Cullen's 1927 anthology. Eastman agreed that "The Desolate City" was McKay's finest work.
72. McKay, *A Long Way from Home*.
73. Barbara Christian, 15.
74. Report by A.C. Sullivan, April 1, 1923.
75. Memo dated March 19, 1923. The Rand School of Social Science in New York, according to a March 1918 notice in *The Crisis*, was a center for progressive politics, teaching "History, Economics, and Socialism in modernwise. It is unhampered by no traditions, but is radical in its honest search for truth. Above all it extends 'a genuine welcome to colored men and women.'" (*The Crisis*, 15, 5: 218.) Later in the 1920s, the Rand School was suspected of links to international radicalism.
76. Report by James Amos, January 31, 1924.
77. Hoover became acting director of the FBI on May 2, 1924.
78. McKay, "Significant Books Reviewed by Their Authors," *McClure's* (June 1928), p. 81.
79. McKay, "Marrakesh," in "New Poems." James Weldon Johnson Collection, Beinecke Rare Book and Manuscript Library, Yale University.
80. Cooper, *Rebel Sojourner*, p. 271.
81. McKay, "Xauen," in "New Poems." James Weldon Johnson Collection, Beinecke Rare Book and Manuscript Library.
82. McKay to Cunard, April 31, 1932. Harry Ransom.
83. Bowles, *Without Stopping* (Ecco, 1972), p. 148.
84. In 1940, McKay also began assembling his complete poems, a task he never succeeded in accomplishing. A truncated version appeared in 1953, titled the *Selected Poems of Claude McKay*, edited by Max Eastman. McKay's complete poems as well as other verse were never published. After long, painstaking work, William J. Maxwell reassembled the *Complete Poems of Claude McKay*, published in 2004.

WORKS CITED

Armstrong, Isobel. *Victorian Poetry—Poetry, Poetics, and Politics*. London: Routledge, 1993.

Bontemps, Arna. Ed. *Anthology of Negro Poets*. New York: Folkways, 1954.

Bowles, Paul. *Without Stopping; An Autobiography*. New York: Ecco, 1972.

Braithwaite, William Stanley. "Some Contemporary Poetry of the Negro Race." *Crisis* 7, 6 (April 1919): 275.

———. "The Negro in American Literature." *The New Negro, an Interpretation* New York: Boni, 1925.

Christian, Barbara. "Spirit Bloom in Harlem. The Search for a Black Aesthetic during the Harlem Renaissance: The Poetry of Claude McKay, Countee Cullen, and Jean Toomer." Ph.D. dissertation., Columbia U. Arthur Schomburg Collection, Schomburg Center for Research in Black Culture, New York Public Library.

Cooper, Wayne F. *Claude McKay: Rebel Sojourner in the Harlem Renaissance*. Baton Rouge: Louisiana U P, 1987

———. Ed. *The Passion of Claude McKay: Selected Poetry and Prose, 1912–1948* New York: Schocken Books, 1973.

Du Bois, W.E.B. *The Correspondence of W.E.B. DuBois: Selections 1934–1944*. Ed. Herbert Aptheker. Amherst, MA: U of Massachusetts P, 1973–1978.

Gilroy, Paul. *The Black Atlantic: Modernity and Double Consciousness*. Cambridge, MA: Harvard U P, 1993.

———. *The New Negro, an Interpretation*.

Maxwell, William J. Ed. *Complete Poems of Claude McKay*. Urbana: U of Illinois P, 2004

———. "F.B. Eyes: The Bureau Reads Claude McKay," in *Left of the Color Line: Race, Radicalism, and Twentieth-Century Literature of the United States*. Bill V. Mullen and James Smethurst, eds., Chapel Hill: U of North Carolina P, 2003. pp. 39–65.

McKay, Claude. *A Long Way from Home*. New York: Lee Furman, 1937; Harcourt Brace, 1970.

———. "Collected Poems of Claude McKay." James Weldon Johnson Collection, Beinecke Library.

———. Federal Bureau of Investigation, Freedom of Information Act Files 400,109, 190-HQ-1137090 pertaining to Claude McKay. U.S. Department of Justice, Washington D.C.

———. Letters. Nancy Cunard Collection. Harry Ransom Humanities Research Center, University of Texas at Austin.

———. "New Poems." James Weldon Johnson Collection, Beinecke Library

———. Papers. James Weldon Johnson Collection, Beinecke Rare Book and Manuscript Library, Yale University.

———. "Right Turn to Catholicism." Arthur Schomburg Collection, Schomburg Center for Research in Black Culture, New York Public Library.

———. *Spring in New Hampshire*. London: Grant Richards, 1920.

———. *The Negroes in America*. Port Washington, NY: Lennikat, 1979.

———. *The Passion of Claude McKay: Selected Prose and Poetry, 1912–1948*. Wayne F. Cooper, ed. New York: Schocken Books, 1973.

———. "The Racial Question: The Racial Issue in the United States." *International Press Correspondence* 2 (November 1922): 817.

Taggard, Genevieve. Ed. *May Days: An Anthology of Verse from Masses-Liberator*. New York: Bovi: 1925.

CHAPTER 5

MADNESS, PARANOIA, AND EZRA POUND'S FBI FILE

KAREN LEICK

> Either there is and was a plot to ruin all goyim, all nations of Europe, or some people are stark raving crazy. (Ezra Pound, in a broadcast over Rome Radio)

ALTHOUGH MANY OF US ARE STARTLED TO LEARN THAT THE FBI MAINTAINED files on writers including E.B. White and Robert Frost, it comes as no surprise that the FBI collected 1,512 pages on Ezra Pound.[1] His large file includes correspondence between Hoover and his agents regarding Pound, transcripts of some of his pro-Mussolini broadcasts over Rome Radio, the entire text of his *Jefferson and/or Mussolini* (1935), clippings of newspaper articles about Pound and his arrest for treason in 1943, and dozens of interviews with people: some knew Pound well, some had encountered him on few occasions, and some had never met him at all. The FBI was most interested to see if any of these individuals would be able to identify Pound's voice in recordings of his radio broadcasts for his trial.

The Department of Justice was concerned that Pound could not be convicted of treason because of the way it is defined by the U.S. Constitution:

> Treason against the United States, shall consist only in levying War against them, or in adhering to their enemies, giving them Aid and Comfort. No Person shall be convicted of Treason unless on the Testimony of two Witnesses to the same overt Act, or on Confession in open Court. (U.S. Constitution, Art. 3, Sec. 3)

The government was pressed to find two individuals who could testify that they had witnessed "the same overt Act." Usually there was only one Italian working at the radio station in Rome when Pound spoke, and none of the radio technicians spoke English. Five Italian witnesses were flown over to the United States to testify, and the government sought American witnesses who would, after listening to records that had been made of the broadcasts, state under oath that the voice they had heard was definitely Pound's.[2]

Evaluating the information given to the FBI by interviewees is a challenge for any scholar. The interviews recorded in Pound's FBI file are censored, with the names of the interviewees blacked out, along with their addresses and much information that might be used to identify them. George Antheil is the only subject who was interviewed about Pound whose name was not censored. The identities of some of the blacked out names, however, can still be deduced from certain details divulged in the interviews, such as William Carlos Williams, James Laughlin, Richard Aldington, e. e. cummings, Kay Boyle, and Theodore Spencer.[3] But the credibility of all witness testimony is suspect for a variety of reasons: some of Pound's friends, such as Williams, minimized his sins, while others, such as cummings, emphasized his errors, possibly to create distance between his views and their own. Interviewees rightly feared that they could easily be targets of FBI investigations themselves, and their responses reflect this concern. Many of those interviewed had only met Pound once or twice in Italy or in the United States when he visited in 1939; their comments are frequently based on rumor or speculation. And, the timing of an interview may have affected it. Those interrogated before Pound's well-publicized indictment for treason on July 26, 1943, may not have understood what was at stake, while those who were interviewed by the FBI after this date would have been well aware that their responses might provide information for the upcoming trial. In addition, many FBI agents conducting the interviews did not know the details of Pound's case themselves. Kay Boyle reports that when an FBI agent appeared at her door asking questions about Pound on February, 20, 1943,

> The agent stayed about an hour. Well, at the end of the hour he said to me, "By the way, um, who *is* Ezra Pound?" I said, "You don't know who he is?" "No," he said. "I have no idea." I said, "Well, he's a poet and he's a great admirer of Mussolini and Hitler, and he's broadcasting for the Axis."[4]

Although the FBI interviewed a wide range of persons over the course of several years and the purpose of each interview was to find out the interviewee's relationship to Pound and his or her ability to recognize his voice, there is a striking observation that recurs, regardless of the timing of the interview, or whether the person being interviewed identified him or herself as a friend or enemy of Pound. The FBI did not know that a plea of insanity would be used by Pound's attorney, Julien Cornell, but they might have guessed that this would be an effective defense since so many of those interviewed told the FBI that they believed Pound was mentally unstable.

> [Blacked out] advised that, in his opinion, DR. POUND had gone completely insane as far as any sense of reason and judgment was concerned.[5] (February 25–March 15, 1943; March 17, 1943)
>
> [Blacked out] still considers himself a close friend of POUND's and is sorry for POUND, believing that POUND has turned traitor to the United States because of a mental condition.[6] (December 28, 1942–February 9, 1943; February 14,1943)
>
> [Blacked out] states that his attempts at conversation with Pound were successful in producing only 4 topics of conversation on the part of Pound, namely, that Martin Van Buren was the greatest president the United States ever had, that John Adams was one of the greatest men that ever lived, a strong tirade against the Jews, an equally strong tirade against international bankers . . . [Blacked out] stated that despite Dr. Pound's ability as a literary figure, he believes the man is mentally unbalanced . . .[7] (March 1943; March 6, 1943)
>
> [Blacked out] stated that he has never met Dr. Ezra Pound but has heard that POUND is mentally unbalanced. He also suggested that [Blacked out] might be able to furnish further information relative to POUND.
>
> [Blacked out] was in Italy until April 1, 1941, recalled meeting Dr. EZRA POUND in Italy on one or two occasions between February 12, 1941 and April 1, 1941. [Blacked out] believes that Pound is a "crack-pot" and recalled that Pound told him that he was really fighting for America inasmuch as he was favoring the Fascist cause, which is the only reasonable form of government. Pound also told [Blacked out] that the Jews were trying to get the United States into the war. (December 1942; January 1, 1943)
>
> [Blacked out] stated that he knew Pound since 1935. . . . [Blacked out] described Pound as a "madman" and stated that he is very antagonistic toward the British because of the alleged British treatment of the Fascist government . . . (December 1942 or January 1943; January 13, 1943)
>
> It was [Blacked out]'s opinion that Pound is a "crack-pot" and turned against the United States because he believed the Americans never appreciated his genius. (December 28, 1942–February 9, 1943; February 16, 1943)
>
> Originally [Blacked out] was very fond of Pound, but stated when he last saw Pound the latter was definitely fanatical. (February 9–March 29, 1943; April 8, 1943)

> [Blacked out] had met POUND in Rome on one or two occasions in 1935 or 1936. It is [Blacked out]'s opinion that POUND is completely "crazy." He was already, at the time she saw him, a rabid Fascist. (December 28, 1942–February 9, 1943; February 16, 1943)

> [Blacked out] considered Pound somewhat mentally unbalanced and said that Pound rambled incoherently at times . . . (February 15–March 12, 1943; March 14, 1943)

> Like many other people interviewed, [Blacked out] claims that she considered Pound "a bit insane." (July 26, 1945; August 9, 1945)

> On one occassion she heard her husband make a remark that DR. POUND was a "crack pot." (September 4,1944; September 7, 1944)

> [Blacked out] stated that he would be willing to testify against Ezra Pound, although he stated that he, as well as any acquaintance of Pound, should they be called, probably all would state that they believed he had become mentally unbalanced. (April 1943; April 27, 1943)

Critics have always greatly resisted the suggestion that Pound was unbalanced or fanatical. Those who admire Pound's work may feel that the quality or significance of his writing is diminished if a consensus is reached among scholars that Pound was mentally unstable. As Louis Sass points out in *Madness and Modernism*:

> [some believe] that whereas the artist chooses, controls, and uses certain states or forms of consciousness, the madman simply suffers them. This latter idea is one that has been with us since ancient times, and, with little doubt, it remains the most widely held assumption about the difference between insanity and "true" creativity.[8]

In 1946, the editors of the *Nation* expressed a slightly different reason for their discomfort with the charge that Pound was insane: "It seems to us an unwarranted slur on the poet to maintain that he is less responsible for his actions than other men—and we can't help begrudging to various and sundry philistines the satisfaction of having one of the most famous of modern poets declared insane."[9] The *Nation* was aware that some Americans had always felt alienated by modernist poetry and found the idea that Pound was mad to be evidence that modern poetry was unintelligible for a reason: modernist writers, they were amused to report, were crazy. This theme was repeated by many editors and columnists during the controversy that erupted when Pound received the Bollingen Award for poetry in 1949. An editorial in the Richmond *Times Dispatch* on February 24, 1949, explained that: "Entirely apart from art and treason, we are afraid the award has confirmed what a good many plain, God-fearing, hard-working, salt o' the earth Americans have suspected—that poets are nuts, and especially modern ones."[10] Likewise, an editorial in the Philadelphia *Inquirer Public Ledge* observed: "The [Bollingen] award says, in effect, we must understand a mind like Pound's if we're going to cope with modern poetry. That makes it easy for most of us to reach a decision to get along without such specialized literary fare."[11] A letter to the editors of the *Washington Post* predicted the consequences of giving the award to a possibly insane traitor: "The 'prize poet' is either a man suspected of treason, or one who is of unsound mind! The public's reaction to this dilemma cannot help but be a further estrangement between modern poets and a potentially attentive reading audience."[12]

Like Pound's loyal admirers, most serious enemies of Pound have never believed his insanity plea. The idea that there was a "conspiracy" among the doctors at St. Elizabeths to find Pound mentally unfit for trial only in order to save him from possible execution has been suggested by numerous critics, including E. Fuller Torrey, Kay Boyle, Robert Casillo, and others.[13] Alfred Kazin argued in 1986, "Whether or not he always knew what he was saying—clearly impossible in such a lifetime's flood of words—Pound was dishonest, and so were his defenders, when he finally claimed insanity as a reason for his actions. He got away with it."[14] This mistaken interpretation of events is shared by many detractors, although Pound's actions during World War II were never judged; instead, he was found unfit to stand trial. That is, his present mental condition was the only concern of the doctors (Winifred Overholser, Marion King, Joseph Gilbert, and Wendell Muncie) who reported on Pound's condition at the trial. Pound's treatment at the Disciplinary Training Centre (DTC) north of Pisa, where he had been locked in a small open cage, exposed to rainstorms and hot sun, and blinded by floodlights around the clock from May 24 to June 15, 1945 (when he began to exhibit signs of a mental breakdown), was seen as one likely cause of Pound's unstable mental condition in the fall of 1945; his wartime behavior was irrelevant. But the consensus reached by these doctors was never believed by much of the public. Like Kazin, Kay Boyle also thought that the insanity plea was a deliberate manipulation:

> [T]he whole business of being in the hospital was a trick. He either pretended to be insane or got people to tell people he was. If it was pacifism, that would have been something else, but it wasn't that. He was telling the American troops to desert. He wanted American troops to lose the war.[15]

My reading of the FBI interviews is quite different; many people were spontaneously telling officials that Pound was unbalanced without being coerced either by Pound or FBI agents, who clearly were not interested in encouraging this line of defense for the poet. Boyle's belief that Pound encouraged American troops to desert during World War II in his radio broadcasts is also not accurate, although many Americans at the time who had not heard or read transcripts of the broadcasts also believed this to be true; instead, Pound was considered treasonous for giving "comfort to the enemy" because he frequently complimented Mussolini, harshly criticized Roosevelt, and suggested that Churchill and Roosevelt were pressured by a network of Jewish international bankers and munitions dealers to bring about World War II.

During the years that numerous citizens were telling the FBI that Pound was insane, many of his friends and acquaintances also discussed this possibility among themselves. Hemingway wrote to Archibald MacLeish in 1943: "He is obviously crazy. I think you might prove he was crazy as far back as the latter [*sic*] Cantos. He deserves punishment and disgrace but what he really deserves most is ridicule. He should not be hanged and he should not be made a martyr of." Hemingway also wrote to Allen Tate that Pound "ought to go to the loony bin." MacLeish wrote to Hemingway: "it is pretty clear that poor old Ezra is quite, quite balmy."[16] And, as early as 1934, Joyce suggested that Pound had lost his mind after he had a disturbing dinner with Hemingway and Pound in Paris; Hemingway reported in a letter: "Joyce . . . asked me to come around when Pound was present because he was afraid he might do something mad."[17] E. Fuller Torrey dismisses the significance of all of these comments, claiming that Hemingway was exaggerating Pound's mental instability in a deliberate attempt to orchestrate an effective insanity plea for him, and that these comments as well as all of the references to Pound's insanity in his FBI file evince this effort. But Torrey is forced to quote certain comments in the file out of context, such as the individual who said that "he as well as any acquaintances of Pound's, should they be called to testify, probably would all state that they believed he has become mentally unbalanced." Torrey fails to mention that this person explicitly said that he would be willing to testify *against* Pound.[18] Humphrey Carpenter speculates that because Hemingway's report of the meeting with Joyce "was written after Hemingway had seen a transcript of one of Ezra's wartime broadcasts, when the question of his sanity had begun to be raised. . . . Hemingway's recollections were probably influenced by this."[19] That Pound's friends wondered about his stability in private might counter claims that the insanity defense was without substance and simply invented by a clever attorney, but critics have not regarded this discourse as significant. According to Carpenter, MacLeish's or Hemingway's comments in their correspondence should not be taken seriously because "there was a considerable difference between calling him 'cracked' in private letters and publicly claiming, as a legal defense, that he was clinically insane."[20]

William M. Chace contends that "no one had thought him seriously ill in a clinical sense, although Hemingway was fond of offering the opinion, that of an amateur in such matters, that Pound was 'wacky' or 'balmy' or 'goofy.'"[21] To prove that Pound was not really unbalanced, Chace uses as evidence the letter that Julien Cornell, Pound's attorney, wrote to Dorothy Pound before the trial that stated that Pound's "mental aberrations" were "not anything new or unusual, but are chronic and would pass entirely unnoticed by one like yourself who has lived close to him for a number of years." Cornell concluded the letter: "I am sorry that you may have been startled and alarmed by reports of your husband's condition and I hope that you can understand that he may appear to a stranger in quite a different way from the way in which he appears to you."[22] Chace does not mention that important closing, although it clearly indicates that Cornell was giving Dorothy a rosy assessment of Pound's condition to mollify her fears.

Many other anecdotes suggest that those who met Pound did not find his behavior normal. For example, in1941 in Italy, Luigi Villari of the Institute of Overseas Cultural Relations tried to warn Radio Rome about the advisability of letting Pound broadcast: "There is no doubt in my mind that Ezra Pound is insane! He is a pleasant enough madman and he is certainly a friend of Italy, but in the course of two interviews I recently had with him, I heard criticism, circumspection, accusations, etc. that have rather alarmed me."[23] Pound's eagerness to share his paranoid conspiracy theories with politicians and other influential figures only served to alienate him from the few individuals whom he managed to see. He specifically traveled to the United States in 1939 to convince officials in Washington that the United States should stay out of the war and managed to arrange a meeting with William Borah, Republican senator from Idaho; Charles E. Corker, Borah's office clerk, reports that after the senator spent about 20 minutes with Pound he made two memorable remarks: "Do you know how that poet makes a living?" and "I think he's crazy."[24] And it was not just Pound's warped political perspective that caused concern among those who encountered him. Romano Bilenchi recalls that during the war Pound told him that "the only thing that might cause us to lose the war in the long run is the scarcity of butter. But I've found the answer: sow peanuts in the Alps . . . One of these days after I've talked it over with Pea at Viareggio, I'll go to Rome to explain the problem to Mussolini." Pound did discuss this plan with Pea, who concluded: "The fellow is crazy, crazy, completely crazy."[25]

These reports and many others suggest that Pound's eccentric ideas in the late 1930s and early 1940s alarmed many of his friends and acquaintances. Pound's singular obsession with select political topics of conversation, his maniacal attempts to convince others of an international Jewish conspiracy, and his confidence in his own wisdom with regard to the tragic events unfolding in Europe all fostered speculation about his mental stability. Once Pound was incarcerated at St. Elizabeths in December 1945, visitors had concerns as well. James Laughlin was disturbed that Pound told him that he had not realized he was being arrested for treason and had thought that the government, recognizing his expertise on Eastern philosophy, was planning to send him to Tokyo as a political ambassador of some kind. Laughlin also was troubled by Pound's insistence that another patient taste his food to be sure that it was not poisoned by "Berny Baruch [and] the Jews."[26] Carpenter claims that Pound's comments to Laughlin were "a bluff" because Pound had already written a letter to Arthur Moore, his attorney in London, to discuss the charge against him.[27] But the contradictory behavior and inconsistent comments Carpenter cites may not have been so calculated. Pound's rational communication with Moore is privileged by Carpenter as evidence of his sanity, although individuals who recalled Pound's strange and disturbing pronouncements never believed that his passionate exhortations were a pose. In fact, Pound's sudden shifts in conversation from rational to irrational topics were seen by some doctors as indicators of his mental deterioration.

Williams also was concerned about Pound's delusional thinking; he wrote in his *Autobiography* that "Ezra is convinced that after twenty minutes' instruction in the Georgian dialect, if at the beginning of our difficulties with Russia, Stalin would have given him a five-minute interview, he could have shown the man the error in his thinking, made him see, comprehend and act on it, and all the subsequent confusion and disaster could have been avoided."[28] Charles Olson, who thought Pound seemed normal when he first visited him, changed his mind after Pound asked him: "Does anyone know Westbrook Pegler?" Olson says that he "must have froze" [*sic*] when Pound brought up this name; Pound said that Pegler was "the best man they've got." Olson explains: "Pound's praise of him reveals his utter incomprehension of what is going on, and what has happened to himself. . . . What a collapse. I wondered then how long more I can hold out my hand to him as a poet and a man."[29]

Westbrook Pegler was a popular right-wing columnist for the New York *World Telegram* who had a reputation for harshly criticizing writers and politicians. As Frank Luther Mott explains, "[Pegler] gained a reputation as a devastating crusader, and to be 'peglerized' was to be annihilated by exposure."[30] Pound was unaware that Pegler had a close but unstable relationship with the FBI and frequently received information from them for his attacks. In 1953, Quentin Reynolds, a friend of the FBI who had published a children's book approved by Hoover titled *The FBI*, won a libel suit against Pegler, who had written in a typical smear that when he was a war correspondent, Reynolds was "pro-Communist, immoral, and a coward."[31] As Bennett Cerf recalls: "Here was Pegler smearing Quentin Reynolds, who had lived through the London Blitz, gone with the expedition to Dieppe, and was shelled by Nazi batteries while on a boat one hundred yards from shore!"[32] During the trial, Reynolds' lawyer read a passage to Pegler and asked if he thought it sounded like something that a Communist would write. Pegler said, "It certainly is. That's typical Communist propaganda." When the lawyer revealed that the paragraph was written by Pegler himself and had appeared in one of his columns, Reynolds's victory was assured.

Pegler fell out of favor briefly with the FBI when he called FBI agents "trigger men" in an article. Hoover wrote him a letter explaining that "They have never been instructed to 'shoot to kill,'" but apart from this incident Pegler's point of view was respected by Hoover. His negative commentaries about writers were often clipped and saved in FBI files; the one article about Hemingway's death in his FBI file was a representative example of Pegler's style. "It has been my stubborn opinion," Pegler wrote, "that Ernest Hemingway was actually one of the worst writers in the English language during his time."[33] The FBI also saved an attack on Carl Sandburg by Pegler in his file. Even more damaging, Archibald MacLeish reports that Malcolm Cowley resigned from the Office of Facts and Figures as a result of articles written by Pegler that accused him of Communist leanings.[34] Pegler probably had gotten his information about Cowley indirectly from the FBI through the notorious Congressman Martin Dies, organizer of a special committee to investigate un-American activities in 1938.[35]

Pound's high opinion of Pegler seems to have changed when Pound found himself the subject of Pegler's column. In 1947 Douglas Larsen interviewed Pound for a sardonic article that appeared in the *Washington News*: "Ezra Pound, Accused Traitor, makes St. Elizabeth's [*sic*] Here a Mecca for the Literati."[36] Under the subtitle "He's Libeled!" Larsen quotes Pound: "You know, you reporters are always putting my name in the newspapers. I see Westbrook Pegler mentioned me the other day. And I think I have a libel suit against him because he linked my name with Henry Wallace. Wallace is just a soft-shelled dummy from the Mid West, who always believes the last man he talked to." Pegler discussed Pound again in one of his columns on September 16, 1955; the article was clipped and saved in Pound's FBI file. Clearly making an argument that had not been fed to him by Hoover, Pegler claimed that there was a government conspiracy to save Pound's life and that, as a result of pressure from the Department of Justice, the chief of Italian radio propaganda had been prepared to "say he thought Pound was crazy." Pegler also declared that Pound's radio broadcasts were "gibberish." Hoover wrote on the margin of the clipped article: "What about this?" Hoover received a response on September 20 from an agent:

> Recordings and transcripts of Pound's broadcasts were obtained during the course of our investigation, and furnished to the Criminal Division of the

> Department. These were used as the basis of Pound's indictment and the department, therefore, apparently did not consider them "gibberish." . . . the question of Pound's sanity was never an issue in our investigation.[37]

The FBI interviewed Dr. Overholser, Pound's psychiatrist at St. Elizabeths, on February 23, 1956, to check out Pegler's suggestions, but Overholser apparently did not suggest to them that Pound's diagnosis had been manipulated and the inquiry was not pursued further.[38]

Anyone reading through Pound's FBI file would immediately notice that the majority of his friends and acquaintances told agents that he was mentally unbalanced; but the FBI never considered these comments important, even when the issue was raised explicitly 10 years after his trial. Similarly, Pound scholars, whether defending or condemning him, have uniformly dismissed the significance of any comments or observations that suggest he might have been insane. In fact, some critics are forced into creative and surprising analyses to avoid the suggestion that Pound was mentally unstable. For example, in *The American Ezra Pound* Wendy Flory persuasively analyzes Pound's delusional thinking during World War II and shows that his misunderstanding of every country's motivation in the conflict begins with the false premise that Britain and the United States were initiating the war. Instead of arguing that this warped thinking is evidence of Pound's insanity, Flory claims that this "self-delusion and evasion [was] of such an extreme kind and of so prolonged an extent that his sanity could not help but be threatened."[39] This, of course, is a counterintuitive cause and effect relationship; Flory argues that Pound's sanity was threatened by his self-delusions, not that he was self-deluded because he was insane. But in the end, Flory excuses Pound altogether, arguing that there is a "separation between his basic personality (the 'real' Pound) and the psychotic state of mind into which he falls when the subject is his support of Mussolini."[40]

Some argue that Pound's thought processes after the war appeared consistent with the ideas he expressed in the late 1930s; therefore, he was not crazy. Before T. S. Eliot saw Pound at St. Elizabeths, he had heard reports from Julien Cornell and Dorothy Pound of his condition, and wrote to Arthur Moore on December 3, 1945 that:

> There is a curious similarity between Mrs. Pound's and Mr. Cornell's account of him in some respects and a complete difference of interpretation. One would suspect that Pound seems to his wife much more normal than he is, and to Mr. Cornell, meeting him for the first time, he seems much more unbalanced than he is. A good deal of what Cornell says about Pound's way of talking seems to me very much what I would expect of him at any time.[41]

Or, to put it another way, Pound was not any more irrational than usual. Eliot does suggest that Pound was not quite "normal" if he believes that Dorothy Pound might have thought him "more normal than he is." As Eliot points out, a person who knew him well may have normalized and thus excused Pound, unable to recognize the symptoms of his mental disintegration. It is not clear, however, why a person who was unfamiliar with Pound's erratic behavior would offer a similarly inaccurate mental diagnosis.

Pound seemed perfectly reasonable some of the time. Critics who admire Pound's work but dislike his political or economic positions often characterize his irrational, conspiratorial views as mistakes, but not fundamental lapses from sanity. His passion to change the world was certainly appealing, they suggest, even if his fervor was misdirected. In 1939, Pound did travel to the United States to meet with politicians, believing that he could alter governmental policy and prevent war. Was it crazy for Pound to believe he could change minds so quickly, and with such dramatic results? Or was his attempt both admirable and thrilling? Those who had seen or heard about the coexistence of the clear thinking Pound and the raving madman had the feeling that were "two Pounds," as Flory argues, including the psychiatrists who examined him at St. Elizabeths; some felt that this inconsistency proved that he was faking or playing up his craziness at times to save himself. In fact, as critics have repeatedly pointed out, some of the doctors at St. Elizabeths did not believe Pound was legally insane.

Pound's confidence in his ability to convince world leaders of his ideas was considered by the psychiatrists who testified during his trial to be delusional. It was not just that Pound thought his ideas were correct; he also believed that any world leader would immediately see the wisdom of his propositions. As Dr. Wendell Muncie pointed out during his testimony, Pound felt that he had "the key to the peace of the world through the writings of Confucius, which he translated into Italian and into English, and that if this book had been given proper circulation the Axis would not have been formed, we would be at peace now, and a great deal of trouble could have been avoided in the past . . . [and] that with himself as leader, a group of intellectuals could have gotten together in different countries, like Japan, for instance, where he is well thought of, to work for world order."[42]

Following this line of argument, Overholser stated that he thought that Pound suffered from "both delusions of grandeur and delusions of persecution, both of which are characteristic of what we call the paranoid condition," while King explained that, in his opinion, his mental condition would "fall in the category of paranoid states, sometimes called paranoid conditions . . . part way between so-called paranoid schizophrenia or dementia praecox, paranoid type, and true paranoia."[43] This testimony is rejected by Carpenter, who argues that "This was little more than a display of jargon to impress the jury, and not even very accurate psychiatric jargon (it is not at all clear what King meant to convey by these distinctions, which are not found in psychiatric textbooks)."[44]

Carpenter should have been able to find these terms, which were widely used in the United States in the 1940s. After Zelda Fitzgerald was diagnosed with schizophrenia and hospitalized, she wrote to Scott that if she were released, "We will have all the children we can, and call them Dementia Praecox Fitzgerald—Dear, how gruesome!"[45] And a doctor in Mary McCarthy's *The Group* (1963) observes that "We've noticed that now that we no longer speak of dementia praecox, we get fewer dementia praecox patients."[46] In fact, a useful series on "Insanity" was published in *Scientific American* in 1941; the first article was titled "Just What is Insanity?: Essentially it is Simply a Lack of Proper Adjustment to Environment and Society"; the next installment was "Paranoia; Dementia Praecox, or Schizophrenia; Paresis; Senile Dementia; Toxic Insanity."[47] According to *Scientific American*, in childhood the paranoid individual was "said to have been queer, taciturn, morose, avoiding other children and associating with older persons." In the second stage, he or she suffers from "delusions of persecution and corresponding hallucinations." Finally, in the last stage, "the subject [who] has suspected that people were cold and aloof to him . . . knows it. . . . [He may believe that] people are poisoning his food, are trying to gas him or to injure him with electricity." The description of a person who suffers from Dementia Praecox, or schizophrenia, exhibits other symptoms; he or she may be "unusually bright" and has "two or more trains of thought traveling together simultaneously. . . . A question may bring a totally unrelated answer, a command may bring an opposite action, or no action at all. All this is due to his twin or double train of thought. This also accounts for the incoherence of speech found so regularly in these cases, and to the emotional deterioration. . . . It is from this class that hoboes, prostitutes, cranks, eccentrics, and criminals develop."[48]

Some of Pound's behavior certainly does correspond with aspects of these descriptions. In addition to symptoms already mentioned such as Pound's belief that he was being poisoned, Pound's difficulty fitting in with his peers in childhood and especially while in college, where he was the victim of numerous practical jokes, failed to join a fraternity, and was known as a social outcast, has been detailed with care by E. Fuller Torrey.[49] If *Scientific American*'s descriptions of paranoia and schizophrenia were accepted definitions at this historical moment, it is not surprising that a psychiatrist might categorize Pound's behavior as paranoid and delusional. Furthermore, Wendy Flory points out that his mental state also corresponds with current definitions of paranoid psychosis, or "Delusional Disorder," "Grandoise Type" and "Persecutory Type."[50]

Scientific American defined insanity as "simply a lack of proper adjustment to environment and society," and it is easy to show that Pound was ill adjusted to his surroundings, as he maintained a deluded idea that Jewish bankers, with the help of Roosevelt and Churchill, successfully orchestrated World War II. But Pound was certainly not the only person in the 1940s who believed this conspiracy theory. During the trial, Dr. Muncie was asked, "Do you think [Pound's] delusion [is] any different than some of these other European leaders had?" Muncie replied: "I haven't had a chance to examine them." He was asked again: "But what I am getting at is whether you think it might be similar?" Muncie answered: "It might be, but I have never examined them."[51] This brief exchange was a serious moment in the trial. If Hitler, Stalin, and Mussolini exhibited thinking or behavior similar to Pound's, couldn't they all have avoided punishment by using an insanity defense (if they had all survived the war, of course)? In this especially patriotic moment, to connect Pound with such figures was in itself damaging to him; but to insinuate that his plea of insanity was some kind of trick that could be used by any brutal dictator would have made his case offensive to Americans who were badly shaken by the destruction and violence perpetrated during the war. In fact, Nancy Cunard wrote a furious letter to Pound soon after he was confined to St. Elizabeths in which she said that if he was crazy, "Goering, Goebbels, Hitler, Streicher, the whole gang of criminals were just 'merely' insane. . . . Fascism is not insanity, unless evil itself, all evil, be insanity."[52] The idea that Hitler might be insane, of course, was not new. Margaret Mead explicitly contrasted the values of German Nazism with American ideals in order to highlight the human deficiency in Germany's ideological views. Susan Hegeman observes that, according to Mead, "German culture, the newly anointed other to Western 'democracy,' 'freedom,' and so on, was not comparable to the west; like its leader, it was *insane*."[53] But as the horrors of World War II became known, any willingness to forgive or excuse the architects of the war evaporated. Any American citizen who had supported the views of Hitler or Mussolini deserved punishment; there was no defense.

The day before Pound's trial, some of the "young doctors" on staff at St. Elizabeths told Overholser that they did not agree with the diagnosis that Pound was mentally unfit to stand trial. Cornell reports that "[t]hey thought Pound was merely eccentric, and wanted to see him tried and convicted. Overholser felt they were in error, perhaps their judgment was distorted by patriotism."[54] I have come across no critic that has taken Overholser's concerns about his colleagues' possible bias seriously. But, familiar as we are with the ways patriotic attitudes can warp the judgment of some Americans, it may be useful to rethink the pervasive idea that the only special treatment Pound experienced during his arrest, examination, and trial was favorable.

The paranoia that Pound and others suffered in the 1940s was disturbing to psychiatrists and psychologists who struggled to explain the increase in the number of individuals suffering from the disorder. In 1937, Ernst Harms argued in an article titled "Paranoid Tendencies in Social Behavior" in the *Journal of Abnormal and Social Psychology* that certain factors in a person's environment may lead to a paranoid condition in individuals who "are already abnormal in their neurobiological structure"; according to Harms, there are three aspects of "modern social life" that significantly contribute to a paranoid person's understanding of the world.[55] First, modern society is dominated by secret bureaucratic organizations; second, our social structures accept and encourage racial or "social" prejudice; and third, our society is filled with private groups who adhere to specific symbolic structures unknown to individuals outside of these groups.[56] These are "all disorientating and paranoiac factors." Harms adds: "The seriousness of this problem must not pass without emphasis."[57]

The paranoid, not to mention racist, impulses of many Americans in this period were certainly encouraged by one powerful, secret bureaucratic organization in the United States; the ubiquitous FBI made it clear to citizens that they might be watched at any time. The massive publicity campaign that Hoover orchestrated consistently emphasized his power and omnipotence. In addition to the numerous G-Men movies, such as "G-Men" (1935), "Border G-Men" (1938), "Dick Tracy's G-Men" (1939), "Junior G-Men" (1940), the documentary-style short "You Can't Get Away with It" (1936), comic strips like "Dick Tracy," "Secret Agent X-9," and "War on Crime," and radio shows like "The FBI in Peace and War," numerous articles appeared, some by Hoover himself, such as a 1937 article in *The Rotarian* titled: "Fingerprint Everybody? Yes—Says John Edgar Hoover."[58]

Hoover appeared on the cover of *Time* magazine twice, on August 5, 1935 and August 8, 1949. The *New Yorker* published a glowing three-part profile on Hoover in 1937 that explained that any individual who toured the FBI headquarters could be fingerprinted and receive a souvenir copy of his or her own prints, suitable for framing—for free! As a guide explains to tourists, it is useful to have your fingerprints on file in case you suffer from amnesia, are mutilated in an accident so severely that you are unrecognizable, or need to prove your identity in a dispute over a relative's will.[59] The 1949 *Time* magazine story also describes the FBI tour, but there is at least a suggestion that Hoover's surveillance of everyday American citizens was disturbing to some people. "But what no tourist will see is the bureau's investigative file covering thousands of ordinary U.S. citizens. . . . It was the existence of those files—important strands in the nation's gigantic net to catch a few disloyal citizens—which gave even the most ardent admirer of the FBI a slightly uneasy feeling. It was not that very many people objected to flushing out

Communists and potential saboteurs. But it was a suspicion that any such collection was bound to damn the innocent as well as the guilty."[60] The article concludes that since the trustworthy Hoover runs the organization, there is no danger: "Certainly, in other hands, the FBI was a potential danger to every free citizen. It had not proved to be so in the hands of John Edgar Hoover."[61] When the *New Yorker* asked Hoover about allegations that FBI agents followed reporters who researched stories about the FBI, Hoover claimed he "has never had any writer shadowed. When the subject is brought up, he makes a point of recalling that the morbid fear that one is being followed is a classic instance of pathological behavior."[62]

Living in this "panoptic" world that Foucault has described surely played a major part in exacerbating the fears of the unstable. But do we want to concede that Pound was "crazy," "a madman," a "crackpot," "mentally unbalanced," or "completely insane" (to repeat the words of those interviewed by the FBI in the 1940s)? If we classify Pound as mentally unstable, can we maintain that his poetry is still significant, even brilliant? Louis Sass points out that:

> The truly insane, it is nearly always assumed, are those who have failed to attain, or else have lapsed or retreated from, the higher levels of mental life. . . . Another possibility does suggest itself, however: . . . What if madness, in at least some of its forms, were to derive from a heightening rather than a dimming of conscious awareness, and an alienation not from reason but from the emotions, instincts, and the body?[63]

Indeed, Pound's poetry illuminates, rather than obscures, a culture of corruption, avarice, deceit, and secrecy. Certainly Pound's worldview was not rational; but it is also true that this isolated, distorted man was watched, arrested, nearly executed, and locked up for almost 13 years. In *Madness and Civilization*, Foucault suggests:

> Through madness, a work that seems to drown in the world, to reveal there its non-sense, and to transfigure itself with the features of pathology alone, actually engages within itself the world's time, masters it, and leads it; . . . through the mediation of madness, it is the world that becomes culpable (for the first time in the Western world) in relation to the world of art.[64]

Pound's inability to adjust to his environment and society allowed him to see that organizations might conspire together against the better interests of citizens as a whole; to believe that most people did not listen to warning signals around them; to suspect the motives of patriots; and to see that it was difficult to know who to trust.

As early as 1920 Pound began to explore in *Hugh Selwyn Mauberly* the dangers of dishonest governments whose lies devastate the lives of everyday citizens. He attempted to expose an economic conspiracy that he believed brought about modern war, lamenting soldiers who went to war

> believing in old men's lies, then unbelieving
> came home, home to a lie,
> home to many deceits,
> home to old lies and new infamy;
> usury age-old and age-thick
> and liars in public places.
>
> (IV ll. 74–79)

This theme is further elaborated throughout the *Cantos*, as in, for example, Pound's "Hell Cantos," which are inhabited by corrupt politicians who enabled war profiteering.

As a correction to this amoral, insidious economic norm in the world around him, Pound instead looked to the Confucian ideal of order that begins with a sincere heart and is directly opposed to traits that lead to corruption and greed, such as the desire for fame and power. The important balance in Confucian thought that Pound saw as essential for the maintenance of justice is the direct result of laws, not the whims of corrupt individuals. Pound also promoted John Adams as a principled role model and alternative to the destructive politicians he distrusted. In the "Adams Cantos" Pound teaches readers that Adams declared, even as he defended an unpopular position, that "bad law is the worst sort of tyranny" (62 / 343), that he honestly negotiated "with bankers in Amsterdam/ . . . a treaty of commerce, by no arts or disguises/ no flatteries, no corruptions" (62 / 346) and that Adams was shocked by "men of no character" who for "a guinea a day write pro or con anything" (62 / 347).

Although Pound is not directly concerned with the kind of surveillance conducted by Hoover's FBI in his poetry, the ideals of Confucius and Adams certainly clash with the invasive, illegal, and destructive policies that Hoover instituted while in power. Furthermore, Pound repeatedly demonstrates his fervent belief in the central importance of art and literature for the health of any nation in the *Cantos* by celebrating in the "Malatesta Cantos" Sigismundo Maltesta (1417–1468), Lord of Rimini, whose financial support of artists including Piero della Francesca is directly at odds with Hoover's aggressive attempt to intimidate artists in the modernist period. Hoover's paranoid cynicism about the corruptibility of human nature contributed to his power; Pound's Confucian belief in the inherent good nature of the human spirit instead led him to trust the most unlikely leaders, such as

Mussolini, and fail to see corruption when it mattered most. His paranoia was focused on a select few who were irrationally blamed for all of the world's problems, whereas Hoover, of course, trusted no one. The secret organization that controlled the United States was unlike that which Pound imagined and it had different aims. But he was right that a powerful organization was threatened by him; Hoover's FBI had no patience for his political meddling, and exercised its will to silence his dissident views.

In recent years, scientists have uncovered evidence that schizophrenia is linked to a disturbance in dopamine levels in the brain and deficiencies in the neurotransmitter glutamate. Instead of suggesting that the label "mentally ill" must be a negative and arbitrary label attached to the deviant, it is important to see that the real and consequential symptoms of the disease should not be minimized or ignored.[65] The critical discussion about Pound's instability opens up when we acknowledge that certain individuals may be predisposed to react in paranoid and irrational ways. It is certainly true that, as Ronald Laing has suggested, to classify Ezra Pound as insane is a political act, but the decision by Pound critics *not* to discuss the possibility that Pound was mentally unstable is also a political decision. R.W. Flint argued in a letter to *Commentary* in 1951 that "[Pound's] anti-Semitism seems to be a link with outright madness and paranoia and is hence a powerful object-lesson and witness against itself."[66] Pound would not be released from responsibility for his racist and Fascistic views if we consider the possibility that he was mentally unbalanced and that the culture of the 1930s and 1940s contributed to Pound's delusions. Instead, Pound's views can be examined and understood as symptomatic of his historical moment: a paranoid mind living in a paranoid age. Hoover's bureau exacerbated the anxieties of citizens, creating a culture of secrecy, fear, and suspicion. Pound's FBI file reminds us of this terrifying, oppressive environment, even if Pound's own misdirected paranoia prevented him from recognizing the actual threat to his freedom.

NOTES

1. For discussion of the E.B. White and Robert Frost files, see Herbert Mitgang, *Dangerous Dossiers: Exposing the Secret War against America's Greatest Authors* (New York: Donald I. Fine, Inc., 1988).
2. See Humphrey Carpenter, *A Serious Character: The Life of Ezra Pound* (Boston: Houghton Mifflin, 1988), pp. 689–91.
3. C. David Heymann has connected some names to interviews in *Ezra Pound: The Last Rower* (New York: Viking, 1976) that I was unable to recognize on my own, such as e.e. cummings, Louis Zukofsky, Ronald Duncan, Tibor Serly, John Dummond, John Slocum, Reynolds Packard, and James Angleton. Heymann also asserts that there is no FBI interview in Pound's file with

Hemingway or Eliot, a fact I would have been unable to determine, since many interviews are simply too vague to suggest the source.

4. Natalie Robins, *Alien Ink: The FBI's War on Freedom of Expression* (New York: William Morrow and Company, Inc., 1992), p. 201.
5. Although his name is blacked out, this interview is clearly with William Carlos Williams. Reference file no. 100–34099. Unless otherwise mentioned, the files number for further references remains the same. The dates within parenthesis refer to the interview dates and the report filing dates.
6. Although his name is blacked out, this interview is clearly with James Laughlin.
7. Although his name is blacked out, this interview is clearly with Theodore Spencer.
8. Louis Sass, *Madness and Modernism: Insanity in the Light of Modern Art, Literature, and Thought* (New York: Basic Books, 1992), p. 70.
9. Editorial, *The Nation*, January 5, 1946, p. 3.
10. "America's Poet Pound," Richmond *Times Dispatch*, February 24, 1949, editorial page.
11. "Poets and Ezra Pound," Philadelphia *Inquirer Public Ledger*, February 21, 1949, p. 18.
12. "Ezra Pound's Prize," *Washington Post*, February 24, 1949, p. 10. See also Ollie Crawford, "Ezra Pound gets Pretty Penny by Going from Bad to Verse": "This proves that you don't have to be crazy to write poetry, but it helps. You can write about spring and be just as balmy." Philadelphia *Inquirer Public Ledger*, February 22, 1949, p. 21.
13. E. Fuller Torrey, *The Roots of Treason: Ezra Pound and the Secret of St. Elizabeths* (New York: McGraw-Hill, 1984); See Natalie Robins, *Alien Ink: The FBI's War on Freedom of Expression* (New York: William Morrow and Company, Inc., 1992), p. 198; Robert Casillo, *A Genealogy of Demons: Anti-Semitism, Fascism, and the Myths of Ezra Pound* (Evanston, IL: Northwestern UP, 1988).
14. Alfred Kazin, "The Fascination and Terror of Ezra Pound," *New York Review of Books*, March 13, 1986, p. 23.
15. Robins, *Alien Ink*, p. 198.
16. Carpenter, *The Life of Ezra Pound*, p. 699.
17. Ibid., p. 503.
18. Torrey, *The Roots of Treason*, p. 183.
19. Carpenter, *The Life of Ezra Pound*, p. 503.
20. Ibid., p. 703.
21. William M. Chace, "'Insanity,' 'Treason,' and Care," *Critical Inquiry* (Autumn 1987): 134–41.
22. Julien Cornell, *The Trial of Ezra Pound: A Documented Account of the Treason Case by the Defendant's Lawyer* (New York: The John Day Company, 1966), pp. 41–42.
23. Carpenter, *The Life of Ezra Pound*, p. 585.
24. *The Correspondence of Ezra Pound and Senator William Borah*, ed. Sarah C. Holmes. Foreword Daniel Pearlman (Chicago: U of Illinois P, 2001), p. 81.

25. Wendy Flory, *The American Ezra Pound* (New Haven: Yale UP, 1989), p. 129.
26. Ibid., pp. 143–44.
27. Carpenter, *The Life of Ezra Pound*, p. 697.
28. Qtd. Flory, *The American Ezra Pound*, p. 144.
29. See Carpenter, *The Life of Ezra Pound*, pp. 736–37. Pound also insulted Olson directly: "I have as much or more of a quarrel with the Swedes and the Irish as with the Yids so you better watch out." Carpenter, *The Life of Ezra Pound*, p. 737. Torrey only quotes Olson's initial reaction to Pound: "his jumps in conversation are no more than I or any active mind would make," see p. 206.
30. Frank Luther Mott, *American Journalism, A History: 1690–1960* (New York: Macmillan, 1963), p. 693.
31. Robins, *Alien Ink*, pp. 135–36.
32. Bennett Cerf, *At Random* (New York: Random House, 1977), p. 168.
33. Mitgang, *Dangerous Dossiers*, p. 70.
34. MacLeish was Librarian of Congress from 1939–1944, director of the wartime Office of Facts of Figures, assistant director of the OWI, and assistant secretary of state from 1944–1945.
35. Mitgang, *Dangerous Dossiers*, p. 91; Robins, *Alien Ink*, pp. 78, 220–25.
36. Douglas Larsen, "Ezra Pound, Accused Traitor, Makes St. Elizabeth's [*sic*] Here a Mecca for the Literati." *Washington News*, October 24, 1947, p. 3.
37. Robins, *Alien Ink*, p. 198.
38. See Torrey, *The Roots of Treason*, p. 217.
39. Flory, *The American Ezra Pound*, p. 103.
40. Ibid., p. 166.
41. Carpenter, *The Life of Ezra Pound*, pp. 705–06.
42. Cornell, *The Trial of Ezra Pound*, pp. 157–59.
43. Ibid., p. 181.
44. Carpenter, *The Life of Ezra Pound*, p. 748.
45. Nancy Milford, *Zelda: A Biography* (New York: Harper and Row, 1970), p. 218.
46. Mary McCarthy, *The Group* (New York: Signet Books, 1963), p. 296. Of course, *The Group* takes place in the 1930s; McCarthy was mistaken about how early the term fell out of use.
47. L.J. Pankow, "Just What is Insanity? Essentially it is Simply a Lack of Proper Adjustment to Environment and Society," *Scientific American*, 165 (December 1941): 330–32; L.J. Pankow, "Insanity: Paranoia; Dementia Praecox, or Schizophrenia; Paresis; Senile Dementia; Toxic Insanity," *Scientific American*, 166 (January 1942): 9–11.
48. Pankow, "Insanity: Paranoia," p. 9.
49. See chapter 2 of *The Roots of Treason*, pp. 18–41.
50. See Wendy Flory, "Pound and Antisemitism," in Ira B. Nadel, ed., *The Cambridge Companion to Ezra Pound* (New York: Cambridge UP, 1999), p. 287. Flory's representation of Pound's mental condition in this article corresponds more closely to my conclusions than her earlier study, *The American Ezra Pound*. Here, she argues that "his medical records, letters, and the testimony of many visitors to St. Elizabeths show clear evidence of psychosis" (287).

51. Cornell, *The Trial of Ezra Pound*, p. 168.
52. Torrey, *The Roots of Treason*, p. 221.
53. Susan Hegeman, *Patterns of Culture: Modernism and the Concept of Culture* (Princeton: Princeton UP, 1999), p. 164.
54. Cornell, *The Trial of Ezra Pound*, p. 43.
55. Ernst Harms, "Paranoid Tendencies in Social Behavior," *Journal of Abnormal and Social Psychology* 32 (October 1937): 431–38.
56. Harms, "Paranoid Tendencies," pp. 434–34.
57. Ibid., p. 437.
58. J. Edgar Hoover, "Fingerprint Everybody? Yes—Says John Edgar Hoover," *The Rotarian* (January 1937): 16–17, 64, 66.
59. Jack Alexander, "Profiles: the Director—I," *New Yorker* (September 5, 1937): 20–25; "Profiles: The Director—II," *New Yorker* (October 2, 1937): 21–26; "Profiles: The Director—III," *New Yorker* (October 9, 1937): 22–27.
60. "Boards & Bureaus: The Watchful Eye," *Time*, August 8, 1949), p. 12.
61. Ibid., p. 13.
62. "The Director—II," p. 23.
63. Sass, *Madness and Modernism*, p. 4.
64. Michel Foucault, *Madness and Civilization: A History of Insanity in the Age of Reason*, Trans. Richard Howard (New York: Random House, 1965), p. 288.
65. In controversial works like *The Myth of Mental Illness, Ideology and Insanity*; *The Manufacture of Madness* (1961) and *Schizophrenia: The Scared Symbol of Psychiatry* (1976) Thomas Szasz has argued that "the phenomenon psychiatrists call 'schizophrenia' is not a demonstrable medical disease but the name of certain kinds of social deviance" (*Schizophrenia*, p. 67). Furthermore, Ronald Laing explained in 1964 that "I do not myself believe that there is any such 'condition' as 'schizophrenia.' Yet the label is a social fact. Indeed, this label as a social fact is a political event" (qtd. in Torrey and Miller, *The Invisible Plague: The Rise of Mental Illness from 1750 to the Present* [New Brunswick: Rutgers UP, 2001]), p. 305.
66. R.W. Flint, "Pound, Poetry and Politics," *Commentary*, 12 (July 1951): 86.

Works Cited

Alexander, Jack. "Profiles: the Director—I," *New Yorker* (September 25, 1937): 20–25.

———. "Profiles: The Director—II," *New Yorker* (October 2, 1937): 21–26.

———. "Profiles: The Director—III," *New Yorker* (October 9, 1937): 22–27.

"America's Poet Pound," Richmond *Times Dispatch* (February 24, 1949): editorial page.

"Boards & Bureaus: The Watchful Eye," *Time* (August 18, 1949): 12.

Carpenter, Humphrey. *A Serious Character: The Life of Ezra Pound.* Boston: Houghton Mifflin, 1988.

Casillo, Robert. *A Genealogy of Demons: Anti-Semitism, Fascism, and the Myths of Ezra Pound.* Evanston, IL: Northwestern UP, 1988.

Cerf, Bennett. *At Random: The Reminiscences of Bennett Cerf.* New York: Random House, 1977.

Chace, William M. "'Insanity,' 'Treason,' and Care," *Critical Inquiry* 14 (Autumn 1987): 134–41.

Cornell, Julien. *The Trial of Ezra Pound: A Documented Account of the Treason Case by the Defendant's Lawyer.* New York: The John Day Company, 1966.

Editorial, *The Nation* (January 5, 1946): 3.

"Ezra Pound's Prize," *Washington Post* (February 24, 1949): 10.

R.W. Flint, "Pound, Poetry and Politics," *Commentary* 12 (July 1951): 86.

Flory, Wendy. *The American Ezra Pound.* New Haven: Yale UP, 1989.

———. "Pound and Antisemitism," in *The Cambridge Companion to Ezra Pound,* Ira B. Nadel, ed., New York: Cambridge UP, 1999: 284–300.

Foucault, Michel. *Madness and Civilization: A History of Insanity in the Age of Reason.* Trans. Richard Howard. New York: Random House, 1965.

Harms, Ernst. "Paranoid Tendencies in Social Behavior," *Journal of Abnormal and Social Psychology* 32 (October 1937): 431–38.

Hegeman, Susan. *Patterns of Culture: Modernism and the Concept of Culture.* Princeton: Princeton UP, 1999.

Heymann, C. David. *Ezra Pound: The Last Rower.* New York: The Viking Press, 1976.

Holmes, Sarah C., ed. *The Correspondence of Ezra Pound and Senator William Borah.* Foreword Daniel Pearlman (Chicago: U of Illinois P, 2001).

Hoover, J. Edgar, "Fingerprint Everybody? Yes—Says John Edgar Hoover," *The Rotarian* (January 1937): 16–17, 64, 66.

Kazin, Alfred. "The Fascination and Terror of Ezra Pound," *New York Review of Books* 33 (March 13, 1986): 23.

Larsen, Douglas. "Ezra Pound, Accused Traitor, Makes St. Elizabeth's [*sic*] Here a Mecca for the Literati," *Washington News* (October 24, 1947): 3.

McCarthy, Mary. *The Group.* New York: Signet Books, 1963.

Milford, Nancy. *Zelda: A Biography.* New York: Harper and Row, 1970.

Mott, Frank Luther. *American Journalism, A History: 1690–1960.* New York: Macmillan, 1963.

L.J. Pankow, "Just what is Insanity? Essentially it is Simply a Lack of Proper Adjustment, to Environment and Society," *Scientific American* 165 (December 1941): 330–32.

———. "Insanity: Paranoia; Dementia Praecox, or Schizophrenia; Paresis; Senile Dementia; Toxic Insanity," *Scientific American* 166 (January 1942): 9–11.

"Poets and Ezra Pound," Philadelphia *Inquirer Public Ledger* (February 21, 1949): 18.

Robins, Natalie. *Alien Ink: The FBI's War on Freedom of Expression.* New York: William Morrow and Company, Inc., 1992.

Sass, Louis. *Madness and Modernism: Insanity in the Light of Modern Art, Literature, and Thought.* New York: Basic Books, 1992.

Torrey, E. Fuller. *The Roots of Treason: Ezra Pound and the Secret of St. Elizabeths.* New York: McGraw-Hill, 1984.

CHAPTER 6

Investigative Savagery: Figuring Hoover in Richard Wright's *Savage Holiday*

Andrew Strombeck

When David Schine, infamous consultant (and rumored lover) of Joseph McCarthy lieutenant Roy Cohn, stopped by Richard Wright's apartment in 1953 to question Wright, the event likely came as no surprise. As a key writer of the "Literary Left" to emerge from the 1930s, Richard Wright, like many of his peers, found himself the subject of official surveillance that lasted from at least 1943 until his death in 1960. His FBI file contains detailed notes on his books, letters from concerned citizens, and information relayed to the FBI from the American Embassy in Paris. As both Claire Culleton and Natalie Robins point out, Wright's case was hardly unusual. In his war against "subversive" forces in American culture, J. Edgar Hoover cast a wide net, and both Communists and intellectualism were particular targets. As a prominent African American, Wright faced special interest; his active antiracism is described in his file as dissatisfaction with America, which, in Hoover's view, was itself cause for suspicion. Wright's long association with Communism, and the public conflation of his early work with African American politics forced him to bear burdens that some of his Modernist peers evaded (many of whom, like Dos Passos, slipped quietly out of the political spotlight, whereas Wright occupied this spotlight until his death).

As Claire Culleton argues in *Joyce and the G-Men: J. Edgar Hoover's Manipulation of Modernism*, FBI surveillance shaped the emergence of

Modernism in the United States, in particular the movement's more political aims—primarily, for the purposes of this essay, antiracist and pro-worker campaigns. It seems inevitable, then, that investigation would emerge as a theme in some Modernists' writing. Talking to Schine, Wright might have recalled Erskine Fowler, the angry, sexually frustrated protagonist of Wright's 1953 *Savage Holiday*. This chapter reads Wright's seldom-read *Savage Holiday* as Wright's response to the investigators dogging him, a response galvanized by the particularly visible, Hoover-driven American paranoia of the postwar moment. In *Savage Holiday*, recently fired insurance investigator Erskine Fowler accidentally causes the death of his widowed neighbor's son. The remainder of the novel concerns Fowler's attempts to evade detection by pursuing and marrying his neighbor, Mabel Blake. If, as E. Lâle Demirtürk argues, and Wright himself explained, Wright is after "cultural whiteness" in his only novel without African Americans as central characters, Wright depicts something more than simply the universalism and cultural arrogance often ascribed to whiteness. Whiteness, as it emerges in *Savage Holiday* is, as it is for Hoover, both investigative and managerial in character. Erskine Fowler is comfortable only when in the investigator's position. When he loses the security of this position, his entire life unravels. Fowler echoes the real-world life of Hoover, whose identity was bound up in his files, and who seemed to need the security of the FBI to banish his own repressed desires.[1] Like Fowler, Hoover could never get over his mother, and so feared strong women (most prominently, Emma Goldman, Ethel Rosenberg, and Eleanor Roosevelt), that he persecuted them, as Fowler does his neighbor Mabel Blake, for perceived subversiveness. This connection, of course, is metaphorical; nothing suggests Wright was familiar with the details of Hoover's life (though much of it was public). But it does suggest that Wright was on to something in his depiction of Fowler's fragility. Written in the shadow of McCarthyism—a movement heavily supported both politically and materially by Hoover and the FBI—*Savage Holiday* foreshadows the unraveling of McCarthy, and eventually Hoover himself, as deeply flawed (white) men who needed their causes more than their causes needed them.[2]

In his 1950s work, Wright turns to questions of institutional power. Wright saw this power as both the product of the individuals making up an institution, but also as having a momentum of its own. Institutions provide a way for individuals to hide their personal repressions, but these repressions nevertheless emerge in the very foundations of the institution. Wright's reading here echoes, of course, a widely ranging post–World War II concern about institutional control, as located in both sociology—as in David Riesman's *The Lonely Crowd* and William Whyte's *The Organizational Man*—and literary postmodernism, particularly the novels of Thomas Pynchon and Ishmael Reed. At the same time, Wright singles out the investigative gaze as a key instrument of institutional evil. This gaze, especially in *Savage Holiday*, cannot be controlled once put in action. In *Savage Holiday*, then, Wright examines the power effects felt by Hoover's files. By positioning Fowler as a product of his former employer, insurance company Longevity Life, Wright supersedes the question of individual will—the evils of Hoover—and focuses on institutional power—the greater evil of Hoover's files. In doing so, he engages what might be called a "posthumanist" model of race relations, examining how institutional practices shape cultural conceptions of alterity.

Wright's FBI File

Wright's FBI file begins in 1942 when an anonymous white New Yorker writes to the Secretary of War, calling attention to a passage in *Twelve Million Black Voices* in which Wright describes the feelings of certain black nationalists: "There are others of us who feel the need of the protection of a strong nation so keenly that we admire the harsh and imperialistic policies of Japan and ardently hope that the Japanese will assume the leadership of the 'darker races'" (quoted in Rowley 275). As Hazel Rowley notes, this letter was forwarded to J. Edgar Hoover, who in turn wrote to the New York Special Agent in Charge (SAC), asking the office to examine *12 Million Black Voices* and Wright's other works to determine whether they are "given to the expression of statements having significance under the Sedition Statutes." The impetus for Wright's surveillance originates with a private citizen, but Hoover knows just what slot Wright might fill in the FBI's imaginary—the familiar, all-encompassing problem of sedition, a problem that had obsessed Hoover since his early days as A. Mitchell Palmer's right-hand man.[3] This letter initiates Wright's files. Eventually, Wright seems sufficiently subversive to the FBI to earn him a Security Index Card. Even though Wright had, by that time, disowned the Communist Party, there was enough "subversiveness" in his past to mark him for life (Wright's file repeats the fact of his party membership in nearly every formal entry.) The Security Index was Hoover's A-list of subversives, a descendant of the Custodial Detention List that Hoover created in 1939.[4] Wright's file mentions his membership in the Communist-supported League of American Writers, along with the organization he founded in Paris, the Franco-American Fellowship.

Of course, the most prominent reason for the FBI's interest in Wright lay with Wright's intense, decade-long association with the Communist Party, which, as Culleton observes, was in the 1930s "enjoying its greatest popularity and influence in literary circles" (37), including the nationwide establishment of John Reed clubs. Chicago's Reed Club, of course, played a key role in Wright's career, effectively providing the vehicle for his earliest successes, and publishing his first works, two poems in its journal *Left Front* (Rowley 77).[5] Unlike other noted writers on the Left in the 1930s, such as Dos Passos, Hemingway, and Dreiser, Wright, after all, actually joined the Communist Party during this period, which, as Natalie Robins notes, was not easy to get into: "Few major writers actually joined the Party, and for its part, the Party did not encourage them, at least in the early 1930s. At that time, the CP was suspicious of intellectuals, because it feared it could not control them." This made little difference to Hoover, though, as Robins points out; Hoover's files did not recognize a writer's depth of involvement with the Communist Party and other radical organizations, only the writer's association with the organization (72).[6]

The other major pole of "subversion" that emerges in Wright's file is Wright's antiracism—what the file calls his "obsession with the problem of the Negro": "It appeared from Subject's contacts with his local board that his interest in the problem of the Negro has become almost an obsession and it was said that he apparently overlooks the fact that his own success refutes many of his own statements regarding the impossibility of the Negro's improving his personal position." In his post-Communist years, this seems to have been Wright's biggest crime in the eyes of the FBI: that he refused to acquiesce on race issues. After Wright expatriated to Paris, the problem became one of public relations; as the Cold War heated up, race relations in the United States became one more area to defend against the Soviet Union. Even in the last year of his life, Wright continues to be considered dangerous. A note added to Wright's file on February 11, 1960 mentions that Wright is on a U.S. Army security list of "Possible Subversives Among US Personnel in France."

Ironically, many elements of Wright's experience with FBI surveillance echo Wright's experience with the Communist Party. Despite Wright's public break with the Communist Party, the problems with the organization continued to bother him, as *The Outsider* demonstrates. These concerns form part of a larger critique of the organization's impact on the individual. *The Outsider* features manipulative, power-hungry party members whose actions seem not only sanctioned, but even produced, by the party's institutional structures. The party's distrust of intellectuals is not the only way in which it resembles Hoover's FBI; both, it seems, were exactly the kind of organizations that Wright viewed as threatening Western civilization. Out of these organizations, Wright sensed, emerged greater evil—racism, colonialism, oppression—than the evil of individuals. This theme characterizes much of his post-party writing, leading Wright eventually to embrace the third world as a space of possibility untainted by either Western or Soviet bureaucracy.

In reading Wright's file, then, I want to attend to the ways it reflects the FBI as a bureaucratic, managerial institution. While Hoover's FBI often seems (and partly was) the product of a particularly driven individual, Wright's file attests to the ways in which bureau policy eventually superseded Hoover's personal vendettas. "In view of specific allegations as to certain writings of subject, it is desired that your office make inquiry of sources available to you for the purposes of determining whether the book entitled 'Twelve Million Black Voices' or other publications of subject are in fact given to the expression of statements having significance under the Sedition Statutes." So writes Hoover to the SAC of the New York office on December 9, 1942. The tortured, distant phrasing here emerges out of the monstrous bureaucracy Hoover had steadily built since the twenties. While Hoover sought to project an image of the FBI as heroic crime fighters, accounts of the agency's history, such as Curt Gentry's *J. Edgar Hoover: The Man and the Secrets*, inevitably emphasize the relentless growth of the bureau as an organization dedicated to process, with words like "sedition" only occasionally hinting at the private desires and prejudices that shaped the FBI's impact on American cultural life. It is the techniques of bureaucracy, surveillance, and investigation developed by Hoover's FBI that I focus on here, particularly in terms of their emergence in *Savage Holiday.*

THE INSTANCE OF SURVEILLANCE IN THE AUTHOR

While, as in the case of Schine's Paris visit, governmental surveillance occasionally reared up in front of Wright's eyes, for the most part his FBI file exhibits little evidence of direct confrontation between writer and bureau. (The contacts with the government that are listed generally involve either Wright's draft card or passport.) While the file at times hints at interviews, no such interviews appear in Wright's file. Regardless, Wright was not, as was Langston Hughes, called up before the House Committee on Un-American Activities (HUAC), nor was he, like Paul Robeson, denied a passport because of his Communist past. Indeed, Wright's lack of overt conflict with the government leads some to believe that Wright was working with the Feds.[7]

Nevertheless, Wright seems to have absorbed the dictates of the FBI's investigating gaze, as manifested by both a growing suspicion of both the FBI and CIA, to the point where fellow African American writers Chester Himes and Oliver Harrington feared Wright was becoming paranoid (Fabre, *Richard Wright* xvi).[8] Wright would reportedly call Himes or Harrington before going to the American hospital, in case he "didn't make it." When Wright convenes the Franco-American Fellowship, an organization with explicit race-based political goals, such as the hiring of more African Americans by U.S interests in Paris, he asks participants to arrive in pairs, Rowley reports, "to avoid arousing the interest of the CIA" (390), presumably since the spy agency would attend more closely to groups of antiracists than pairs. Wright also conducted something of his own investigations; in Fernando Pivano's notes on an interview held in Wright's apartment, she observed that Wright had a telescope "to see into the houses of other people" (170), an explanation presumably provided to her by Wright. Finally, Wright may well have acquiesced to the government, though to what degree is never clear. Questions of Wright's "collaboration" with the U.S. government have regularly circulated, notably in James Campbell's "Black Boys and the FBI." Campbell bases his assertions on a note in Wright's file indicating that Wright called the American embassy about the 1956 Présence Africaine conference, warning the State Department about the conference's plans to invite dedicated socialists Paul Robeson and W.E.B. Du Bois, and suggesting "more moderate" delegates.[9] The ambiguity around this question, though, merely indicates the degree of ambivalence Wright felt about both American and Communist organizations. Wright's actions, as Fabre points out, hardly betray his more left-wing friends.

Wright's awareness of his surveillance folds into his more general postwar concerns about the repressiveness of both the Soviet Union and the United States. In 1948, a letter from Wright to Dorothy Norman expresses what Wright's file calls his "plague on both your houses" attitude towards the Cold War. In the context of the HUAC hearings, the highlights of which were printed in *Les Temps Modernes*, a journal read regularly by Wright, he writes to Norman that "Russia has her cultural purges and so do we; only in Russia it is official, and with us it is the force and so-called moral power of the community. But the results in the end are the same, that is, the suppression of the individual" (quoted in Rowley 373). Wright publicly abandoned the Communist Party in part because of its stifling bureaucracy and antihumanism, but he recognized that the United States was equally repressive. Throughout the late 1940s and early 1950s, Wright became increasingly dismayed about the cultural turn taken in the United States. He refused to return to New York for the 1953 publication of *The Outsider*, for example, writing to Harper editor John Fischer that he feared he might himself become of interest to HUAC.

Wright's concern about "cultural purges" is validated by HUAC, but also by the activities of his fellow citizens. As Culleton argues, the FBI produced surveillance that exceeded the capabilities of its agents: "[T]he 'Red Scare' in America led regular law-abiding citizens to turn to the Bureau of Investigation for direction or counsel when they had questions about the appropriateness of a coworker's comment, a neighbor's activity, a teacher's instruction, a son's or daughter's reading material, or a writer's work" (98). Wright, she observes, raised particular concerns among several Americans who wrote to share their suspicions with Hoover and the bureau. For these Americans, Hoover reinforced a sense of self and community. Writing these letters seemed to give them a sense of importance, and a sense of connection with the FBI. One writer from Dallas denounces Wright's novel *Black Boy* as seditious propaganda, then ends his letter by addressing Hoover: "All loyal Americans, I feel sure, are grateful for all the splendid work done by the FBI in detecting and eradicating crime." The citizenry's role in Wright's file also surfaces in some of the sources quoted on Wright's potentially subversive activities in France. One note in the file concerns the niece of an informant, who attended a meeting of the Franco-American Fellowship and concluded that "despite its disavowal of Communism" the group "espoused the Party line as the girl had known it in the United States."

Even while unaware of the exact extent of his surveillance, then, Wright critiques the culture produced by Hoover's FBI files, and the organization that produced them. Wright was a relentlessly analytic writer, turning a scientific eye onto everything with which he came into contact. Inevitably, the issue of surveillance found its way into Wright's intellectual project. His concern with the power embedded in organizations like the FBI—surely influenced by his reading of Nietzsche—echoes that of Foucault, and demonstrates an evolution away from the viewpoint of *Native Son*, wherein racism is more a function of powerful individuals (and their influence on the media) than of organizational bureaucracy. By the fifties, influenced by both his experience with the Communist Party and his growing disgust with American paranoia, Wright can no longer see racism and colonialism as the products of individuals. He looks for broader psychological explanations in psychology, but also, I argue, in institutional critique. It is the latter that makes *Savage Holiday* interesting reading, pushing the book past what John Fischer saw as its "dated" elements (Fabre, *Unfinished Quest* 380). Fischer here seems to refer to the book's overt use of Freudian theory, that resulted in the book's dismissal by many Wright critics. But read in the context of Wright's file, and, in McCarthyism, the triumph of Hoover's antisubversive vision, *Savage Holiday* emerges as not looking backward, but looking forward, to writers such as Pynchon and Reed who deploy paranoia as a mechanism for blurring the line between individual and institution.

THE INVESTIGATIVE IMAGINARY IN *SAVAGE HOLIDAY*

Since the moment it was turned down by Harper, *Savage Holiday* has been widely ignored, starting with American reviewers who barely acknowledged the book's existence. At the very least, the book stands, along with the rest of Wright's work from the early 50s, as an example of how a certain modernist politics shifted from the 1930s to the 1950s, how the promise of widespread cultural transformation gave way to the censorship (self and otherwise) of the

McCarthy years. As Gerald Early notes, Wright's work from the 1950s is generally neglected in favor of his early work; critics seem much more comfortable with the Wright who emerges as literary spokesman against racial oppression than they do with the Wright who embraces existentialism, extends his Leftism beyond Communism, and widens his political range to include all colonized subjects. *Savage Holiday* is indicative of Wright's evolution as an artist, and, more importantly for this chapter, is an attempt to grapple with the political fallout from his literary celebrity. Both Michael Fabre and Gerald Early read *Savage Holiday* as an interesting work along these lines; Fabre links the book to *The Outsider* as part of Wright's attempt to settle accounts with his past. Early notes that the novel was intended by Wright as part of a trilogy critiquing the Western psyche, and views the book as "another expression [. . .] of his intense, lifelong, and unsentimental interest in exploring the human soul, the position of women in modern western culture, and the pathological aspects of various forms of repression" (*Unfinished Quest* 223).

The plot of *Savage Holiday*—as nearly all of its critics point out—is simple. Erskine Fowler has been forced into retirement from his job at the insurance company, Longevity Life; the book opens with a staged farewell banquet for Fowler. Disturbed by the loss of his job, which the 43-year-old Fowler had held for 30 years, Fowler returns home to his Manhattan apartment. The next morning, still dazed, Fowler steps out into the hallway in the nude to get his newspaper. As he steps out, his door locks behind him, trapping Fowler in the hallway. Distraught, he moves frantically around the building before remembering that he can reach his bathroom window from a balcony. But when he steps out onto the balcony, he frightens Tony, his neighbor's five-year-old child, who falls to his death. Instead of confessing, Fowler spends the rest of the novel covering up his crime, out of fear that others would believe he had been up to something "perverse" (72). As the child's mother, Mabel Blake, grows more and more suspicious, Fowler seeks to marry her, fighting his repulsion at her promiscuity. At the moment Mabel realizes the truth, Fowler brutally kills her, stabbing her with a knife "until his arm grew so tired that it began to ache" (215).

In interviews, Wright positioned the book as part of a larger critique of Western whites.[10] For Wright, *Savage Holiday* was an attempt, through an exploration of Fowler's psychology, to examine the forces shaping Western racism and colonialism. He tells Raymond Barthes in 1956, "Having left America and having been living for some time in France, I have become concerned about the historical roots and the emotional problems of Western whites which make them aggressive toward colored peoples" (167).[11] Wright viewed his depiction of Fowler as something like a case study, inspired, as Early notes, by Fredric Wertham's 1947 *Dark Legend: A Study in Murder*. True to his intentions, Wright couches Fowler's story in psychoanalytic explanations. Readers learn that Fowler's murder of Mabel has its roots in his childhood, when his prostitute mother's own promiscuity ("all the boys said his mother was bad" [216]) lead Fowler to harbor fantasies of murdering her. Most of *Savage Holiday's* critics, with some exceptions, focus on Wright's use of Freudian psychology to explain Fowler's actions. J.F. Gounard and Beverly Roberts Gounard, for example, agree with Fabre that "the focus is really on [Fowler's] mother and his relationship with her," (347), an assertion they see supported by Wright's earlier title choices for Savage Holiday, which include *The Queen Mother* and *Monument to Memory* (347). Similarly, John Reilly notes that "Fowler's love-hatred for Mabel becomes the premise and the source for the remainder of the plot. [. . .] As a child [Fowler] could only symbolize these repressed feelings toward his mother; now, on an enforced 'holiday' he has actually acted out these feelings and killed the maternal figure" (221).

But if Wright depicts Fowler on a "holiday" where his buried psyche can finally wreak its havoc, the institution that keeps such havoc at bay is equally important—especially in thinking about the FBI in relation to *Savage Holiday*. The unacceptable nature of Fowler's fantasies, Wright describes, is what lead to Fowler's early, busy employment as an insurance investigator:

> a daydream buried under the rigorous fiats of duty had been called forth from its thirty-six-year-old grave by a woman called Mabel Blake, and that that taunting dream had so overwhelmed him with a sense of guilt compounded of a reality which was strange and alien and which he loathed, but which, at the same time, was familiar to him: a guilty dream which he had wanted to disown and forget, but which he had had to reenact in order to make its memory and reality clear to him! (220)

Fowler's tangled emotional history is kept in check by "the rigorous fiats of duty." The "duties" of Fowler and his ilk, like the "duties" of Hoover and his ilk, serve to corral such emotions into productivity. If the book is about the unresolved emotions of Western whites, it is also about the institutions that keep these emotions in check. *Savage Holiday* is dedicated to Clinton Brewer, the imprisoned musician for whom Wright helped arrange parole, and who shortly afterward stabbed another woman to death. If, as Wright claims, the book is indeed about the emotional roots of aggressive whites, why dedicate it to an African American murderer? In the transformation of Brewer's story into *Savage Holiday*, Wright seems as fascinated with the prison's function in the Brewer case as he does the function of the unconscious. Fowler, after all, is freed from a kind of prison when he leaves Longevity Life. But because

Wright sees such institutions as problematic, he encounters a paradox. Longevity Life keeps Fowler's traumatic drives repressed. At the same time, if Longevity Life can absorb the errant desires of men like Fowler, it must itself be contiguous with the sickness of these drives' repression.

"You've been tracking me down like a detective," Mabel tells Fowler (192), and with good reason: Fowler has been eavesdropping on her telephone conversations, grilling her about acquaintances, and in general, treating his neighbor like a fraudulent holder of a Longevity Life insurance policy. Fowler's job as an insurance investigator required that he collect clues, and maintain a heavy dose of the detective's cynicism. Reilly calls *Savage Holiday* "a parodic detective story" (221), and while, unless Fowler is investigating his own crime, this model does not really work, *Savage Holiday* is nevertheless concerned with the investigative mindset gone awry. Wright finds in Fowler's need to investigate a fascinating sickness, an idea that surely drew on the plague of Hoover-driven investigative paranoia that infected the postwar United States. If Fowler is meant to figure for a certain Western type, his occupation forms part of this type, especially because Wright blurs the boundaries between Fowler's personal and professional identities. Of course, this is, to some degree, Wright's overt point, as he tells Barthes: "Until [Fowler is expelled] he had been capable of forgetting, we can even say repressing, his feeling of guilt through his acquisition of material wealth. And now he finds himself suddenly deprived of his job and work" (168). But Wright's comments could apply equally to any job held by Fowler. Why, then, give Fowler the particular role of insurance investigator? It is here—through the narrative trope of the investigator who must know all—that Wright exhibits the influence of the FBI on his work. This is the instance of the investigator in the artist. What emerges in *Savage Holiday* is a reflexive relationship between Wright's file and his work, between Hoover and the FBI, and between Erskine Fowler and Longevity Life. A classic bureaucrat, Hoover develops these procedures out of his personal desires, but eventually the organization shapes him as much as he shapes the organization. In *Savage Holiday*, Wright shows how the knee-jerk racism of the crowds amassed outside Bigger Thomas's courtroom can transform into ordinary procedures, those embedded in insurance. In *Savage Holiday*, insurance becomes a technology of Otherness, functioning much like Hoover's files. Insurance, which works to mediate risk, mediates a risk determined by the signifiers of class, race, and ethnicity—akin to the set of practices recently described as profiling.

Fowler's description of his insured clients reveals a deep distrust—what might be called a fear of subversion—that, for Fowler, solidifies his place in the world. Immediately after he has marched out of the Longevity Life building—on the verge of his two-day descent into madness—Fowler thinks:

> Insurance was life itself; insurance was human nature in the raw trying to hide itself; insurance was instinctively and intuitively knowing that man was essentially a venal, deluded, and greedy animal . . . .
>
> Yes; insurance was a shifty-eyed, timid, sensual, sluttish woman trying, with all of her revolting, nauseating sexiness, to make you believe that she'd been maimed for life in an automobile accident [. . .] insurance was a small-time, stupid, greasy-faced Italian grocery-store keeper who had amateurishly set his dingy, garlic-reeking place ablaze hoping that he'd collect enough insurance money to start all over again under another name and in another state [. . .] insurance was an old, sweet-looking woman of seventy-odd who'd insured her new daughter-in-law for a huge amount of money and then had, with a stout hatchet, killed her one night in her bed and had told a seemingly plausible tale of having awakened from her sleep and having seen a tall, dark man. (28–29)

Sluttish woman, Italian grocer, violent elderly. Like Hoover, Fowler collects examples of humanity gone wrong, proofs of the "subversion" lurking everywhere. The insurance investigator, like the FBI agent, must be on guard, for everyone who walks into the office is a potential defrauder. Predictably, these defrauders are Others: nonwhite, ethnic, female, elderly. The collection of such stories—the surveillance of his clientele—has provided a bulwark against emptiness for Fowler. Unlike Cross Damon of *The Outsider*, who relishes freedom but eventually finds himself destroyed by it, Fowler fears his postsurveillance life.

Fowler's masculine identity is reinforced by his management of these Others. His satisfaction with his "superb, practical knowledge of insurance" solidifies him. When, then, Fowler finds himself helpless, it is natural that he feels himself the subject of surveillance: "He became dismayingly conscious of his nudity; a sense of hot panic flooded him; he felt as though *a huge x-ray eye* was glaring into his very soul" (43, emphasis mine). The reversal here, and the trauma it causes Fowler, is bound into the investigator's position. The investigator, defined by his position, breaks apart when the gaze is turned on him. The rest of *Savage Holiday* revolves similarly around themes of surveillance. In stepping out of his apartment Fowler encounters his worst nightmare, a situation in which he himself becomes the object of (perceived) surveillance. Doubtless, his anxiety with his own nakedness is, as Demirtürk asserts, part of a "Puritan disgust with his own body" and reflects Fowler's privileged whiteness, set against a savagery associated with nakedness (133). But I would argue that Wright takes particular pleasure in locating this investigator in a position where the mechanisms of surveillance have completely reversed.

The idea of an "x-ray eye" applies neatly to the FBI's cultural position, as Wright indicates in the second and third stanzas of his 1949 "FB Eye Blues":

> Woke up this morning
> FB eye under my bed
> Said I woke up this morning
> FE eye under by bed
> Told me all I dreamed last night, every word I said.
> Everywhere I look, Lord
> I see FB eyes [. . .]
> I'm getting sick and tired of gover'ment spies.
> (641)

This short poem, some 45 lines, is perhaps Wright's most straightforward acknowledgment of the investigators haunting him. The mindset it describes is exactly what seems to be operating in Fowler. For years, Fowler himself operated the x-ray. Now he cannot escape it, just as Wright must have felt he could not escape the Federal government's surveillance. Trapped outside his apartment, Fowler fears a gaze that comes from everywhere—the elevator, the windows, the stairs—he cannot escape it, just as the "stupid, greasy-faced Italian grocery-store keeper" and "shifty-eyed, sluttish woman" could not escape Fowler's own gaze. The reversal here, and the trauma it causes Fowler, is bound into the investigator's position. The investigator, defined by his position, breaks apart when the gaze is turned on him, just as Hoover fervently resisted anything that smacked of "investigating" the FBI. As Curt Gentry reports, Hoover worked to suppress publication of *The Federal Bureau of Investigation*, a book critical of the bureau, by a former Truman aide named Max Lowenthal (386). (Among the U.S. presidents under whom he served, Truman seems to have liked Hoover the least, or found him the least useful.) When suppression failed, Hoover worked to discredit both book and author, engaging in a smear campaign against the writer.

The Problem of the Organization

While Fowler acts alone, his personality seems far from unique, and Wright in fact hints at greater evil amongst his superiors at Longevity Life. Wright ties the violence latent within Fowler to the organization from which he has recently emerged, and while this organization ostensibly covers the rot within, the organization itself seethes with the same violence that later destroys Fowler, and Wright positions Fowler's superiors as "fouler" still. Prior to his termination, Fowler requests a meeting with his superiors, to unveil what Fowler sees as their ulterior motives for firing him. In this meeting, his superiors emerge as cold, calculating men, men who are of the same cultural stock as Fowler, but who represent the perfection of the type:

> Ricky's thin lips had been shut tight, like a trap; and Warren's China-blue eyes had gleamed as cold and blue as twin icebergs. And at that moment the nervous, discordant sounds of the musicians' instruments being tuned up in the banquet room had come to him. Erskine trembled. Ricky had reached out suddenly clutched hold of Erskine's arm and had pushed him roughly against a wall [. . .] Do you want to fight Longevity Life? [Ricky had said]. (27)

Fowler is sick; these men are sinister. So while Wright spends much of *Savage Holiday* constructing a psychological framework for Fowler's actions, he here indicates that the problem he is after in *Savage Holiday*, what he calls "the emotional problems of Western whites which make them aggressive toward colored peoples" is as much a disease of groups as a disease of individuals. Fowler is as much a function of Longevity Life as he is his tortured past. If Western white men are pathological, this pathology becomes codified in their institutions. Longevity Life, like the FBI, both feeds on and engenders "loathsome" behavior.

Power, of course, is the key to these institutional problems. *Savage Holiday* exemplifies the Foucauldian maxim that "power relations are rooted in the whole network of the social" (345). Subject to the government of the management at Longevity Life, Fowler in turn wields power over first his clients and then his neighbor. Again, the Wright of the 1950s is overtly concerned with power exercised on a "micro" level, as in the following passage from *The Outsider:*

> [T]his system of sensualization of the concept of power wasn't restricted to the Communist or Fascist worlds; the Communists had merely rationalized it, brought it nakedly into the open. Cross began to see that this systematization of the sensuality of power prevailed, though in a different form, in the so-called capitalistic bourgeois world; it was everywhere, in religion as well as in government, and in all art that was worthy of the name. And bourgeois rulers, along with the men of the church, had forged through time and tradition methods of concealing these systems of sensual power under thick layers of legal, institutionalized, ritualized, ideological, and religious trappings. But at the very heart of this system were the knowing and conscious men who wielded power, saying little or nothing of the real nature of the black art they practiced, the nameless religion by which they lived. (201)

Wright uses Damon Cross to voice a Nietzschean critique of the sedimented power of organizations.[12] If Wright draws on his personal experience with the Communist Party to articulate this power, his ideas apply equally to the emerging national culture of managerialism in the United States—a culture in which the FBI, led by a lifelong bureaucrat who praised order and despised individuality—flourished. As Gentry and others show, Hoover was a master of these power relations, understanding this managerial culture on a seemingly intuitive level. Like the FBI, Longevity Life is not just any organization, but one devoted in purpose to promoting conformity. Like Hoover's FBI, Longevity Life is, at least in part, an investigative organization, one devoted to ferreting out subversiveness amongst its clients. Insurance, like Hoover's files, serves as a bulwark against moral weakness. In each case, of course, the opposite is true; the investigators themselves become the real source of corruption.

I see *Savage Holiday*, then, as a fascinating work in the way that it evidences Wright's own governmental persecution. In so doing, Wright foreshadows the widespread paranoia that invades both literature and culture in the 60s onward. The control systems so apparent in the immediate postwar period, systems both epitomized and powered by Hoover's FBI, serve a disciplinary purpose for both observer and observed. Fowler, cast out of the observer's role, feels both empty and exposed. The surveillance culture in which Fowler participates so joyfully functions not just out of "security" or "necessity" but to forestall the gaping uncertainty faced by Fowler, an uncertainty that also seems to have eaten at Hoover himself. In his overlooked "little book," Wright attacked what he saw as the key problems facing the Western world, a tendency to repress—the inability of power to relate to itself—that produced control systems which wreak havoc on the disempowered. As the FBI's (and CIA's) early-twentieth-century activities continue to be revealed, and as new instruments of surveillance are created (such as the USA PATRIOT Act), Wright's response to his own surveillance continues to be important. Because, as *Savage Holiday* demonstrates, the problem of J. Edgar Hoover did not disappear when he died, or when his infamous secret files vanished. Hoover's pathologies live on in the institutional methods he created.

NOTES

1. This is attested to by the frequent use of the word "secret" in the titles of Hoover's recent biographies: Curt Gentry, *J. Edgar Hoover: The Man and the Secrets* (New York: Norton, 1991); Anthony Summers, *Official and Confidential: The Secret Life of J. Edgar Hoover* (New York, NY: G.P. Putnam's Sons, 1993); Richard Hack, *Puppetmaster: The Secret Life of J. Edgar Hoover* (Beverly Hills, CA: New Millennium P, 2004); Richard Gid Powers, *Secrecy and Power: The Life Of J. Edgar Hoover* (New York: Free Press, 1987).
2. In many ways, McCarthyism represented the public apex of Hoover's campaign against subversives. Not only was McCarthy's campaign entirely

consistent with Hoover's anti-Communist work since the Palmer raids, the Wisconsin senator's efforts would have quickly fallen flat without Hoover's support. Along with behind-the-scenes political support, Hoover provided the names McCarthy needed to flesh out his imaginary list. Curtis Gentry derives this account from a conversation with former FBI assistant to the director William Sullivan. According to Gentry, from McCarthy's election in 1946 until the collapse of McCarthyism in the mid-1950s, Hoover and McCarthy maintained close professional and personal ties. Gentry writes, "(T)he pair seemed to hit it off immediately, since it wasn't long before McCarthy was seen dining with Hoover and [Hoover second in command Clyde] Tolson at Harvey's or accompanying them to the track. As early as 1948 Hoover extended McCarthy the honor or letting him address the graduating class of the FBI National Academy." Characteristically, Gentry adds, "even though Hoover already had extensive files on the senator, including allegations which, if made public, could have ended McCarthy's career" (378).

3. The Red Scare of the teens began officially with the bombing of Attorney General Palmer's house on June 2, 1919. The events of this bombing led directly to the official organization of the General Intelligence Division (GID) of the Justice Department some two months later. Gentry writes, "As his first project, the former librarian set up a card index system listing every radical leader, organization, and publication in the United States. Finding it just as easy to categorize people as he once did books—a simplification he'd follow for the rest of his life—within three months he had amassed 150,000 names and by 1921 some 450,000" (79).
4. In a sign of the autonomy Hoover developed for the FBI, Hoover developed the list on his own initiative, without Congressional or Presidential order. "Hoover also . . . without any statutory authority—set up a Custodial Detention list of persons to be rounded up and imprisoned in concentration camps, should the need arise" (Gentry 213).
5. Rowley calls the Reed Club Wright's "university," and it seems hard to overestimate the importance it played in his life.
6. Wright himself experiences the Party's ambivalent feelings toward intellectuals, as he recounts in his famous (or infamous) "I Tried to Be a Communist": "In trying to grasp why Communists hated intellectuals, my mind was led back again to the accounts I had read of the Russian Revolution. There had existed in Old Russia millions of poorer, ignorant people who were exploited by a few educated, arrogant noblemen, and it became natural for the Russian Communists to associate betrayal with intellectualism" (Wright, *Atlantic Monthly* 53). Wright became an important figure to the Party, as exhibited by Robert Minor's question in the *Daily Worker* after Wright's well-publicized break with the Party: "Can we do without Richard Wright?"
7. Robins quotes Kay Boyle: "There is a story, a rumor, about you that is going about [. . .] that you are known to be working with the State Department, or the FBI, I don't know which, and that you give information about other Americans in order to keep your own passport and be able to travel" (285).

8. Wright exhibits evidence of a deeper, more conspiracy-minded cynicism as well: "Most revolutionary movements are government sponsored," Wright would write in "The Position of the Negro Artist and Intellectual in American Society" (qtd. in Fabre, *Books and Writers* 28).
9. Wright's file notes: "On his own initiative, Mr. Wright called at the Embassy to express certain concern over the leftist tendencies of the Executive Committee for the Congress. He believed the members of the Committee were liberal thinkers and he thought there was a distinct danger that the Communists might exploit the Congress to their own ends. [. . .] To counteract such a tendency, Mr. Wright wondered if the Embassy could assist him in suggesting possible American Negro delegates who are relatively well-known for their cultural achievements and who could combat the leftist tendencies of the Congress. Mr. Wright, the Department will recall, was himself formerly a member of the Communist Party. He indicated that he was originally on the Committee of the *Presence Africaine*, but that he had been dropped recently because of his present anti-Communist principles."
10. Gerald Early points out that while Wright pushed his writerly capabilities by taking on white characters, in this respect he was far from unique among African American writers: "Zora Neale Hurston, Ann Petry, Chester Himes, William Attaway, Willard Motley, and Frank Yerby had all written 'white' novels that predated Wright's book" (227).
11. In the same interview, Wright also explains the significance of Fowler's name: "Fowler brings to one's mind the notion of being 'foul,' of defiling, of not behaving according to social rules" (167).
12. Wright was far from alone in voicing these fears, of course, with books like *The Organization Man* by William H. Whyte (1956) fretting about the effects of organizations on the American character, and, by implication, the ability to resist Communism.

Works Cited

Campbell, James. "Black Boys and the FBI," *Times Literary Supplement* November 30, 1990, pp. 1290–91.

Conversations with Richard Wright. Ed. Michel Fabre and Keneth Kinnamon. Jackson, MI: U of Mississippi P, 1993.

Culleton, Claire A. *Joyce and the G-Men*. New York: Palgrave Macmillan, 2004.

Demirtürk, Lâle. "Mapping the Terrain of Whiteness: Richard Wright's *Savage Holiday*." *Melus* 24, 1 (1999): 129–40.

Early, Gerald. "Afterword." *Savage Holiday*. By Richard Wright. Jackson, MI: U of Mississippi P, 1994, pp. 223–35.

Fabre, Michel. *Richard Wright: Books and Writers*. Jackson, MI: U of Mississippi P, 1990.

———. *The Unfinished Quest of Richard Wright*. 2nd Edition. Chicago: U of Illinois P, 1993.

Foucault, Michel. "The Subject and Power," In *Essential Works of Foucault 1954–1984*, James D. Faubion, ed., New York: The New Press, 1994.

Gentry, Curt. *J. Edgar Hoover: The Man and the Secrets*. New York: Norton, 1991.

Gounard, J. F., and Beverley Roberts Gounard. "Richard Wright's *Savage Holiday*: Use Or Abuse of Psychoanalysis?" *College Language Association Journal* 22 (1979): 344–49.

Hack, Richard. *Puppetmaster: The Secret Life of J. Edgar Hoover*. Beverly Hills, CA: New Millennium P, 2004.

Minor, Robert, "Mr. Wright Didn't Discover It," *Daily Worker*, August 15, 1944, p. 6.

Powers, Richard Gid. *Secrecy and Power: The Life of J. Edgar Hoover*. New York: Free Press, 1987.

Reilly, John M. "Richard Wright's Curious Thriller, *Savage Holiday*." *College Language Association Journal* 21 (1977): 218–23.

Robins, Natalie. *Alien Ink: The FBI's War on Freedom of Expression*. New York: William Morrow, 1992.

Rowley, Hazel. *Richard Wright: The Life and Times*. New York: Henry Holt, 2001.

Summers, Anthony. *Official and Confidential: The Secret Life of J. Edgar Hoover*. New York: G.P. Putnam's Sons, 1993.

Wright, Richard. FBI File. Two sections, approximately 190 pages.

———. "I Tried to Be a Communist." *Atlantic Monthly* (September 1944): 48–56.

———. *Savage Holiday*. Jackson, MI: U of Mississippi P, 1994.

———. *The Outsider*. New York: Perennial, 1953.

———. "The FB Eye Blues," in *American Poetry: The Twentieth Century*, Robert Hass, John Hollander, Carolyn Kizer, Nathaniel Mackey, and Marjorie Perloff, eds., New York: Library of America, 2000, pp. 641–42.

CHAPTER 7

"POETESS PROBED AS RED": MURIEL RUKEYSER AND THE FBI

JEANNE PERREAULT

UNDER THE SEAL OF THE DEPARTMENT OF JUSTICE AND THE FEDERAL Bureau of Investigation (FBI), a Freedom of Information Act (FOIA) cover page informed American poet Muriel Rukeyser in 1978 that her bureau file consisted of 118 pages.[1] This cover document asserted that

> Muriel Rukeyser, author, poet, and editorial free lance writer, came to the attention of the FBI when a background investigation for suitability was initiated in 1943 in conjunction with her government employment as a copywriter with the Office for emergency Management.

Within the file itself, however, a different reality appeared. On October 31, 1942, Geo. J. Gould, Chief, Investigations Office, wrote to the director of the FBI requesting a "summary of the information in your files concerning Miss Muriel Rukeyser." This letter is stamped with the first appearance of Rukeyser's case number, 77-27812. On November 4, J. Edgar Hoover responded with a cover letter: "For your information there is attached hereto a separate memorandum setting forth a summary of the pertinent information pertaining to Miss Muriel Rukeyser as reflected in the files of this Bureau." The next documents in the file include a copy of Rukeyser's notarized application (October 16, 1942) to work for the Office of Emergency Management (a federal umbrella agency to the domestic propaganda agency, the Office of War Information [OWI] where Rukeyser was employed) and an account of

Special Agent Ronald A. Reed's interview with Rukeyser, dated February 18, 1943.[2] These documents set the stage for an examination of Rukeyser's history as a leftist activist and poet and the ways the FBI associated Rukeyser's antifascism so readily with anti-Americanism. Muriel Rukeyser was in fact a passionate and idealistic American, too given to humanist values to be considered anything but bourgeois by doctrinaire Marxists. She allied herself consistently with the forces of resistance to economic, militaristic, or social tyranny and worked throughout her life against fascism in whatever form it took. Her thinking was imagistic, idealistic, and polemic rather than ideological, and she saw in poetry a vital and necessary force for and expression of human connection. This chapter will read Rukeyser's poetry and essays against both the FBI's accounting of her and the treatment her work received by the left.

Although Rukeyser has been gaining critical attention in recent years, no biography, no collection of letters, no collection of her whole body of writing yet exist, so discussion of her life is necessarily piecemeal.[3] Rukeyser, whose grandfather was an immigrant from Prague, was born in 1913 to a prosperous secular Jewish family in New York. Her father was a businessman, cofounder of a large construction supply firm, whose work building the skyscrapers of New York excited Rukeyser's imagination. In *The Life of Poetry* in which she gives fragmentary accounts of her becoming a poet, she says, "You are a part of the city. New York is a part of you. For your father is in the building business, and the skyscrapers are going up. Your father can climb these skeletons, he laughs with the men who are the bravest" (205). Her awareness of the damage to people and land on which her family's prosperity was based also developed young, as an early poem describing a visit to one of her father's developments shows:

> "Look," he said, "this quarry means rows of little houses,
> stucco and a new bracelet for you are buried there;"
> but I remembered the ruined patches, and I saw the land ruined,
> exploded, burned away, and the fiery marshes bare.
>
> ("Sand-Quarry with Moving Figures"
> *Collected Poems* 15)

The will to remember the "ruined patches" is part of Rukeyser's willingness to count the costs; that is, for her, one part of a dynamic does not cancel out the other. Even as a youngster, she did not simplify reality and wanted to know what things meant. She was a protected child, "blindfolded," she says, but found her way to connect: "The maids and nurses and chauffeurs, those who most talk to you, who give you books to read" (*Life* 220, 206). Rukeyser remembers getting a new set of portrait stamps for her album, all of men with flowing beards. "Do their faces frighten you? You are told to be frightened.

They are Bolsheviki. What are Bolsheviki?" (208). She registers the tension in her home: "I imagine the farthest intimacy in terms of perfectly open talk at the dinner-table" (214) and grasps its cause: "There is deep estrangement in all the houses I know. Money is seen as the estranger" (214). Rukeyser threads her awareness of the larger world through her childhood memories, some fixing themselves, it seems, as moments that must be held, others that simply blur into the accretion of everydayness. As she puzzles about the difficulties in her family, she also internalizes the anomalies that later form the basis of her activism and her art. Rukeyser attended Vassar and Columbia University, but left at the age of 19 without taking her degree when her father lost his fortune. By then her hunger for experience, understanding, and poetry was established. She remembered the death of Nicola Sacco and Bartolomeo Vanzetti (Italian anarchists, suspiciously convicted of robbery and murder, electrocuted in 1927), saying, "Sacco and Vanzetti are dead and something is signified by this that cannot be put aside" (214).[4] One of her earliest published poems, "Poem Out of Childhood" contains the enigmatic line "Sacco not Sappho," suggesting that she found it necessary to choose between a classical poetics that requires remoteness from the present and an ethically engaged life (CP 3). From the beginning of her writing career, Rukeyser seems to fit Daniel Aaron's acute description of "fellow travelers": although not members of the Communist Party, they sympathized with the objectives of the party, wrote for the party press, participated in groups sponsored by the party (ix). Aaron asserts that for these writers the "the Communist Party had far less influence . . . than the *idea* of communism or the image of the Soviet Union" (ix). Rukeyser spent her life refusing to "put aside" injustice and seeking an understanding of what is signified by decisions of the powerful against the weak.

While Rukeyser was pushing against the constraints of her life, absorbing its lessons, and learning her craft, political anxiety about immigration, labor unrest, and international revolutionary anarchists was intensifying. The social and political context in which Rukeyser's consciousness was developing had produced an extremist atmosphere. Curt Gentry lists the Espionage Act (1917), the Sedition Act (1918), and the Alien Deportation Act (1918) as instrumental in creating a climate in which "pacifism became disloyalty, [and] complaints about wages or working conditions were called 'seditious utterances'" (70). J. Edgar Hoover was appointed director of the FBI on December 10, 1924, his lifetime habits of compiling secret files, disregard for the law—especially those protecting civil liberties, and hostility to activists of any hue—firmly established.[5] Within a few years, Natalie Robins notes, Hoover expanded his list of suspect persons to include many writers, though few were actual members of the Communist Party.

The exact date on which Muriel Rukeyser's file was opened is not clear from the file itself. Her application to the Office of Emergency Management is dated October 16, 1942, and is the earliest dated document in the file, although many references to earlier reports appear in subsequent materials. Rukeyser had been active in progressive causes and published in leftist venues since she was a young woman. The earliest of her known radical activities was to go to Decatur, Alabama at the age of 21 to work with the International Labor Defense (ILD) on the Scottsboro trial, a leftist, almost certainly Communist group that organized the fight against the convictions of nine young black men sentenced to death for the rape of two white women.[6] Her file records that "Applicant states under arrest record 'Held on March 31, 1933, in Decatur, Alabama. Released the following day without trial or formal charges.'" (Rukeyser FBI file; Apr. 12, 1943). Later information reveals that she was picked up by the police for instigating negro insurrection, based on her having made phone calls to an African American man. No other reference to the Scottsboro case appears in Rukeyser's file, nor can I find reference to the bureau's interest elsewhere, despite the well-known conflict between the ILD and the National Association for the Advancement of Colored People over control of the trial.[7]

Rukeyser's disclosure of her arrest in her application for the position of "Copywriter CAF 12" indicates that the poet was inclined to be open and transparent about her activities, and not inclined to hide matters from the government. However, she omits and elides some important particulars.[8] In a note amended to her application, Rukeyser explains that her freelance writing accounts for her erratic work record. She mentions that she was on assignment for *Life and Letters Today* in London (1935–1936), but does not say that she was in Europe in order to attend the antifascist Olympic Games in Madrid, organized to counter the showcasing of Hitler at the 1936 Berlin Olympics. As Rukeyser's train was arriving in Spain, the anti-Franco Republican forces clashed with the fascist forces of the Nationalists. Tim Dayton says that "Rukeyser emphasizes the exhilaration felt by those for whom open conflict with the forces of reaction was preferable to the long period of tension that followed the series of right-wing victories in [Europe]" (9). Although Rukeyser was excited by the United Front she saw in Catalonia, in which "socialists, anarchists, Communists, trade unions and gypsies were together" (qtd. in Dayton 11), Dayton also argues that by 1937, Rukeyser's awareness of the complexities of the Spanish conflict had gone far beyond the simple clash of reactionary and progressive forces. Cary Nelson describes the division among the Left in the Civil War: "Stalin's secret police collaborated with the Spanish Communist Party in suppressing the revolutionary Marxist POUM (*Partido Obrero de Unifacación Marxista*) and the Spanish anarchists in May 1937" (*Revolutionary Memory* 188). By "suppressing," Nelson means killing the POUM leadership and destroying resistance to a hierarchically organized and centrally controlled army (188).[9] Although

Dayton does not claim that Rukeyser was aware of Communist Party perfidities in the Spanish Civil War, certainly all evidence suggests that Dayton is correct when he asserts that Rukeyser was not "one of those for whom the Communist party *was* the Left" (12).

The FBI's April 12, 1943 report makes clear that the fact her Spanish Civil War poem "Mediterranean" was published in the *New Masses* was more important than its content. Louise Kertesz sees in this poem the roots of much of Rukeyser's later work (123–24), and Nelson argues that her keen awareness of the betrayal of the Popular Front makes her one of those poets of the Left who "took with them this contradictory experience of international solidarity and subsequent disaster" (224). By the time "Mediterranean" appeared, Rukeyser was already a recognized poet, both by the mainstream (she won the Yale Younger Poets' Award for her first collection, *Theory of Flight* in 1935) and by leftist authors. The complexity of that volume, with its integration of her lifelong interest in science, physics, and flight, her treatment of the experiences of childhood and the city, and her belief in the fight for justice, solidly indicates how resistant she was to any aesthetic or political convention. Allen Guttman argues, perhaps too unequivocally, that for Marxist poets "'correct' political position" was essential and demanded "almost the same degree of consensus on poetic forms" (254–55). Form was not dismissed, but if the poems were to reach their intended audience, the working class, poetry would have to be simple. Obscurity, the profound flaw of modernist (bourgeois) poetry, was to be eschewed. Guttman says the argument was based on the view that just as Copernican thought superseded Ptolemaic astronomy, so does "Marxism simplif[y] the world and ma[ke] complexity unnecessary" (255). Rukeyser speaks quite directly to the attacks on obscurity. She critiques the attacks on obscurity and makes a distinction between the "intentionally obscure" and the "necessarily complex." The "intentionally obscure," she argued—obviously a phrase in common critical parlance—were part of a group whose aim was to set themselves apart from an audience upon which they looked with contempt. She calls this "the product of corruption of consciousness" (*Life* 55), and asserts that "The charge of obscurity . . . must be looked at very closely . . . which tells us, at first, very much about the audience and nothing about the poem" (56). Emphatically, in italics, she declares: "*Nothing has yet been said about the poem*" (56). She concludes that the charge of obscurity requires us to "inquire into the consciousness of the challenger" and asks whether this is "merely another way of disowning imaginative experience" (56). For Rukeyser to disown that is to negate life itself.

Rukeyser's great poem "The Book of the Dead" is said to "rank with the milestones of high modernism in complexity, accomplishment, and aesthetic bravery" (Thurston 61). This long, 44-page poem set in Gauley Bridge, West

Virginia, is a meditation, a narrative, a lament, and an accusation in which she gives voice to among others the workers who died of silicosis drilling a tunnel for a hydroelectric project (CP 73–111). This poem has been given extensive treatment by critics, and my mention of it here is to suggest that it, more than any of her other works, demonstrates her ability and her willingness to incorporate emerging strategies of modernism into her works, including the integration of Egyptian mythology with contemporary life, and the consolidation of documents such as court records, medical reports, personal letters, transcripts, interviews, and individuals' voices. Michael Thurston sees it as a manifestation of Popular Front poetics (59). Shoshana Wechsler claims it engages with the questions that preoccupy postmodernity—the problem of objectivity (121), and Tim Dayton dedicates a whole monograph to analyzing the poem and its significance to support his argument that its importance lies in its (Marxist) "vision of history" (131). Contemporary scholarship is in its own way reiterating the debates of the 1930s, still working to fix the poet in place, despite her own best examples of how and why that should not be done.

The summary of her file requested by the Office of Emergency Management (OEM) dated June 14, 1943 mentions her 1937 publications the *New Masses* and her 1938 participation in the John Reed Club as indicated by a Dies Committee report. The John Reed Clubs were founded, Alan Wald explains, "as organizations of workers and proletarianized intellectuals who were openly anticapitalist and partisans of the Soviet Union" (Wald, *New York Intellectuals* 80). Under the guidance, if not the control, of the Soviet Communist Party, the groups aimed to develop proletariat cultural consciousness. Members debated correct literary forms for socialist literature, for example, but also provided an education in Marxism and urged other members to "take up activity in the Communist movement" (Wald, *Exiles* 74). Rukeyser participated half-heartedly, but with the reaction against Stalin's pact with Hitler, the John Reed Clubs lost their cachet among leftists and the party dissolved the clubs and encouraged the formation of groups that "had a wider appeal to the liberals among the academics, commercial authors and literati" (Wald, *New York Intellectuals* 80–81). The League of American Writers (LAW) was one of these groups. Franklin Folsom's memoir of the seven years of the LAW's existence (1935–1942) opens with the perhaps disingenuous assertion that "before [he] read the FBI file on the League, [he] had not seen proof that this country's political police attached great importance to the organization" (ix), an unlikely surprising piece of proof since Folsom later asserts that "the FBI and other agencies kept close watch on many (perhaps all) League members who were United States citizens" (148). Again, Rukeyser seems not to have participated extensively in the League's activities. Since her primary concern, consistently, was antifascism, and since the League's executive and others in its "Keep America Out of War Committee," including Lillian Hellman and Dashiell Hammett, had other priorities, she may have wished to keep her distance. She was however, actively involved in translating the League's publication of Spanish poems and ballads: *. . . and Spain Sings: Fifty Loyalist Ballads* (Folsom 334).[10]

Each paragraph of the summary Memorandum is followed by a parenthetical citation, presumably a record of the original location of the information such as the following: "(Dies Committee Report, Walter Steele, Vol. I. page 256.)" or simply "(61-9182-IX p. 5, 19, 28.; 61-901-37X p. 18)." An October 31, 1942, request from the OEM asked Hoover to provide a "summary of the information in [bureau] files concerning Miss Muriel Rukeyser." With his usual alacrity, Hoover responded on November 4, and indicated that Rukeyser had been a subject of interest since 1937 when she published articles, all detailed in the FBI report, in the *New Masses* and the *Nation*. The FBI cites the Dies Committee as the source of information: she "was reported in 1938" as being a member of the John Reed Club, was signatory to a letter dated January 11, 1939, that "defend[ed] the work of the WPA Federal Arts Project," and was organizing a mass letter writing protest against the dismissal of 1526 Project workers. She was a member of the LAW, "said to possess Communistic tendencies and . . . to closely follow the Communist Party line." Further, the FBI reports, she spoke against the embargo on Spain at the American Student Union, "an alleged Communist front organization." This summary of her activities was alarming enough to provoke a request from the OEM for a full-bodied FBI investigation. The only direct method of obtaining information was to approach Rukeyser herself. She was interviewed February 18, 1943 by Special Agent in Charge (SAC), Ronald A. Reed. George Gould, then Chief of the Investigations Office, specified the following questions:

1. To determine Miss Rukeyser's present connection with the League of American Writers, and
2. Whether in her own thinking about economics, she favored a collective security as late as 1939 and what changes, if any, have occurred in her thinking with respect to collective security and fascism since 1940.

The three-page, single-spaced document that paraphrases Rukeyser's responses is instructive, not only for Rukeyser's answers, which are a model of precise obfuscation, but because it keenly demonstrates her unwillingness to fuel anticommunist agendas. When questioned about her activity in the LAW, Rukeyser said that as a freelance writer she wished for a group of others with whom she could discuss the craft; SAC Reed added, "Her other reason was the preservation of free speech by the elimination of fascism. With other writers, she shared a hatred for fascism and because she regarded this movement as an immediate and powerful menace, she wished to lend her efforts in combating its progress in the United States." Clearly, some care was taken to provide an accurate rendering of Rukeyser's words. Rukeyser noted that she lost interest in the group in 1938 or 1939: "Her chief objections to the 'League' were the failure of the organization to clarify its aims and the overemphasis placed on money raising projects." Evidently following protocol, the agent pressed Rukeyser to elaborate and asked her to discuss, in particular, the presence of Communists in the League, which she admitted with "some reluctance." She insisted on fully articulating her view of the issue:

> With some reluctance, Miss Rukeyser admitted the presence of some Communistic influences . . . which she was disinclined to regard as a serious or important matter on the basis that she felt the purpose of [this group and others like it] was to combine all forces in the fight against fascism. In the same manner that Russia, today, is an ally of ours, fighting on our side, so was Communism likely to be found working as one of the combined forces of these organizations.

Although no quotation marks are used, the statement is Rukeyser's, marked by the use of the pronoun "ours" in referring to Russia as an ally. Despite the government's efforts to portray Russia as "Our Friend," few conservatives forgot that the USSR was Red. Asked about her objections to fascism, Rukeyser explained that they were "based upon the fact that it was intent upon the destruction of democratic government; that under it, freedom of thought and speech could not survive and that because of its rapidly moving progress, America was imminently in danger of its threat." Using the passive voice, the agent seems to play devil's advocate: "When it was pointed out that her interest in preserving freedom and democracy would probably produce in her a similar reaction against other 'isms,' Miss Rukeyser denied the existence of any other force sufficiently powerful to be considered a menace . . . but she stated that she would naturally be opposed to any movement where freedom of speech and the democratic way of life were denied." Rukeyser asserted that "we should feel strong enough to work along with other movements and nations without fear of losing our identity as a free person or as a democratic nation." The fine line Rukeyser walks in this interview suggest that she is able to maintain her integrity by insisting on her fundamental beliefs about fascism (though she does not feel it necessary to mention that fascism within the United States is probably the source of her immediate sense of its menace), democracy, and Communism.

Following the interview, a "Memorandum to the Director" interprets Rukeyser's demeanor, saying that she "attempted to create the impression" that she "had little knowledge or interest in Communism" and that she answered questions on Communism with "hesitancy and vagueness"; she "declined to make any statement relative to the advantages of Communism"; she also resisted (it must have been a temptation) to comment on "the part capital is playing in the fight against fascism," and she refused to articulate her own vision of what would solve America's problems, saying she did not have the answers. In a final effort to draw her out, the agent asked about the Dies Committee: "Miss Rukeyser assumed a disinterested attitude . . . merely remarking that our real enemy was fascism and that it was not well to lose sight of or divert our attention from the fight against fascism." I elaborate on this single document because it offers insights into the kind of demeanor SACs such as the well-informed Ronald Reed were expected to present. The questions, predetermined to elicit very specific answers and to flavor the conversation, the philosophical discussion, and the intellectual debate—however clumsily handled—indicate the relentless circuity of the typical SAC's approach. When direct questions about Communism do not provide satisfactory answers, the agent then asks about capitalism, government responsibility (he asks "whether complete government control of industry would be necessary to safeguard the worker's interests"), then turns to the general issues of America's problems. Rukeyser with some discomfort (if we are to believe that she was hesitant and vague) stays focused and will not be drawn into a discussion. She does not forget that she is talking to an FBI agent and her repetition of the word "fascism" might suggest she is embedding a message of her own in the document. The pretext for the February interview, a position at the Office of War Information (OWI), took place when Rukeyser had already been there for about two months and suffered, along with Archibald MacLeish and others with like minds, ongoing virulent attention.

While Rukeyser worked in the OWI, the domestic right wing kept up a constant barrage of attacks, with anti-Soviet feeling increasing after revelations that Russia had slaughtered 15,000 Polish Army officers during the Nazi-Soviet conquest of Poland in 1939. Clayton Laurie cites congressional charges that the OWI was "pro-Communist," that it sheltered "aliens, radicals, and subversives," and that "the agency harboured radicals, and Communists, and was heavily influenced by 'international Jewry'" (175). The anti-Semitism of Republican congressmen was buttressed by the statements of members of the Office of Security Services who argued that the problem was not that Communists were spies within the OWI but that it was "full of international left-wing Jews'" and that its "Jewish saturation makes its voice un-American in the Western ear" (175). Rukeyser as a Jew and fully aware of Nazi anti-Semitism would have found these attacks not only repellent but also ironic given the similarity of these views to Nazi thought.

The accusations of a communist presence in the OWI were met directly by its director Elmer Davis, who announced that after exhaustive investigation of the 2,000 employees of the OWI, only six Communists had been found. Neither Congress nor the FBI was satisfied with this. Hoover undertook an enthusiastic investigation of the OWI, and Muriel Rukeyser, already listed in bureau files as a leftist, inevitably became one of its suspects. The *New York Times* found Rukeyser among the most interesting of the 1,300 New York City OWI employees, and reported the story as "Poetess in OWI Here Probed by U.S. as Red" (May 7, 1943). The column refers to her as a "well-know young poetess . . . alleged to have mixed considerable left-wing politics with her iambic pentameters" and describes her writings in the *New Masses* as "violently partisan." One of the ironies of Rukeyser's file is that by the time the FBI's documents were fully organized, she had, along with others, given up on the hope of being able to influence the direction of American propaganda toward democratic ideals of equality and freedom from fascism, which her OWI posters emphasized.

As demonstrated in her own writings, however, Rukeyser was hardly a partisan of any rigid ideology and held constitutional American ideals as central to her beliefs. The document of resignation simply states that she was leaving for "policy reasons." However, the FBI chose to record a different source: FBI File No. 100-27, dated December 21, 1944 cites The University of California's "Current Biography" published in 1943: "On May 1, 1943 she resigned from the Classification Division, Office of War Information six months after she had been engaged to plan poster campaigns because she said most of the posters had been rejected through a policy of down with the world or through fear of these issues" (6).[11] The readable (that is unexcised) sections of Rukeyser's FBI file do not indicate further speculation or information about her reasons for leaving the OWI. Later, in *The Life of Poetry* (1949), Rukeyser articulates her frustration with the lost opportunity to make American propaganda meaningful; her reasons for leaving are clear:

> During the war, an attempt was made to use writing with the work of some of the painters. . . . Advertising men came in, telling the administration that ideas were their field, that the government needed their techniques. The advertising men made it clear that there were two ways of looking at ideas in a war against fascism. Those of us who were working on the project believed ideas were to be fought for; the advertising men believed they were to be sold. The audience, those at home in wartime, were not "citizens" or "people." They were "customers." No such ideas as ours were to be executed. The advertising men won, with those who decided that this was not a war against fascism, that it was a war to be won, and the meaning worked out afterward. (145)[12]

Although the ostensible reason for the investigation, the position at the OWI, was no longer relevant, Rukeyser's file continued to fatten. The pre-1944 documentation is relatively free from excision or blackout, with only identifying notes on informants removed. Some of these notes show extensive investigation of her father's business, her family's neighbourhood, and so forth. In 1978, Rukeyser remarked after perusing her file that "'They knew more about the circumstances of my father's bankruptcy than I did'" (qtd. in Kertesz 273). More distressing is the list of "Confidential Informants," 25 of them between 1943 and 1952. The petitions she signed, the company she kept (about 30 people attended her housewarming party, the file notes), and the demeanor of her visitors—all of this is captured and documented in bureau files. Moreover, the file notes that Rukeyser averaged about five guests a week, "not people of fashion, but people plainly dressed and seem to be people of good solid American stock"[13] Voting lists declare that she registered to vote in 1936, with no party affiliation, but that in 1942 she registered with the American Labor party. Later documents, from 1944 onward, are more heavily censored. Rukeyser moved to San Francisco and the FBI office there picked up her case. Perhaps because the information becomes increasingly personal and the investigation clearly more intrusive, or maybe just because so much of it is disappeared under layers of black ink, this segment of the file is more chilling. It reiterates the New York information (repetition seems characteristic of bureau files), but it also reports on a letter Rukeyser wrote to Ludwig Renn in Mexico, a member of the Abraham Lincoln Brigade in the Spanish Civil War. Rukeyser was asking about the fate of Otto Boch, her lover who had joined the International Brigade against Franco's forces.[14] Between the blacked-out sections the file reports that Rukeyser got Renn's address from Jack Bjoze, and there follows a full paragraph on Bjoze's history. The file blends accounts of trivia and nonsense with its menacing reach into people's lives. It mentions, for example, that "an unknown person at the University of California sent MURIEL RUKEYSER to Mrs. BARBARA COWLES to sub-lease the COWLES apartment while Mrs. COWLES was east for an operation." When Rukeyser is helped by Dr. Herbert Evans to get a library card at the University of California, Evans gets "preliminary investigation" treatment, and two pages of blackout follow the information that he has donated to an antifascist group. Hotel employees report when she registered and left, what phone calls she made ("not pertinent to the investigation"), and her teaching at the California Labor School. What the FBI does not mention, Kertesz reports, is that "Communists there at first argued against hiring her because she had been attacked by New York Communists for defending Horace Gregory and for being what they called a nationalist" (369).[15] Rukeyser gave a series of workshops at the CLS that later formed the basis of 1949 book *The Life of Poetry.* How far Rukeyser is from anyone's party line is apparent in her discussion there of "the Resistances" to poetry:

> This is not a real choice [purity or corruption], between an absolute positive and an absolute negative, with only one moment to choose. In a world of growth, the moment of choice may come as long as there is life. There is process: man can change and he can go on changing; at any moment he can do the work of re-creation on himself, and purify his consciousness. (*Life* 54–55)

Rukeyser does not disdain "purity"; but she sees it as a horizon, a process. Her refusal to demonize with absolute judgment or make a final decision about any thing is what, she argues, keeps the imagination, the life, and thus the poetry dynamic and that is the responsibility of the poet.

While the FBI provided a thorough accounting of the newspapers Rukeyser wrote for, the speeches she gave, and the company she kept, Rukeyser was not overtly harassed or blacklisted, so far as we know. The FBI closed its file on Rukeyser on November 1, 1949, but after the infamous ex-Communist Luis Bundez named her as one of the "400 Concealed Communists," on December 20, 1950, her file was reopened. She was not called before the House Committee on Un-American Activities (HUAC), but she was, in 1951, listed as being the "subject of a Communist Index card." Later notes indicate that "MURIEL RUKEYSER sponsored or was a member of numerous organizations which had been cited by HUAC as Communist Front organizations" (April 22, 1952). Busy work and repetition characterize the file until September 1955, when a SAC informed Hoover that Rukeyser did not "meet the standards [of the Security Index]" and that no "extremist activity" was taking place. The SAC recommended that Rukeyser's file be closed.[16] In November 1963, the FBI asked the SAC in New York to locate someone named "ROKEYSEE" at 790 Riverside Drive, New York City. SAC reported that agents could not find "ROKEYSEE" at 790 Riverside Drive "or anywhere else in Manhattan." They did however find a listing in the telephone book for a MURIEL RUKEYSER at that address. The only other new document is a provocative memorandum from the New York City SAC to the FBI, dated August 20, 1973, captioned "WOUNDED KNEE." It is entirely blacked out. Clearly a "closed" file does not mean the FBI forgets a subject.

Rukeyser got access to her file in 1978, though she had already suffered a stroke. Brief marginal notes, sometime her initials, appear on a few of the latter pages. One might speculate that had Rukeyser been well, she would have provided an extensive gloss on the information the FBI gathered. As it is, she corrects addresses, names, even dates. She adds "YES" to the information that "William Rukeyser" is her son. Next to the assertion that she is a member of the Communist Party, a large X and "NO" are written in bold ink.

Jan Levi, who has edited Rukeyser's collected poems, suggests that "a subtle form of blacklisting" may have prevented some of Rukeyser's many projects from reaching fruition (192). Although I found no explicit complaints in Rukeyser's files at the Library of Congress or the Berg Special Collections at the New York Public Library, Kertesz sees in the poetry of the Cold War era, "the suffering of one aware of spirit-splitting isolation and suspicion" (273). Arnold Mesches, a contemporary artist and activist whose bureau file was released to him after a long struggle, makes quite vivid the experience of being under FBI surveillance, especially the difficulty of reading reports citing information supplied by people one knows: "a student who joined you for a beer and pizza after class, a close neighbour whose children played with yours, . . . a confidant whose life's torments were deeply intertwined with your own, a trusted friend who had sat next to you at a funeral. A lover or two" (288).[17] These anxieties would have tormented Rukeyser as well, and the malevolent effect of betrayal must have exerted its costs. She did not join the Party; she did not submit her art, her beliefs, or her activism to external authority; and she showed by her work in the OWI that she was a nationalist and an individualist in the most complex ways. Despite the forces arrayed against her and her values, Muriel Rukeyser never retreated into simplicity, never lost her will to connect. Neither the FBI's vision of America nor the Left's vision of the world could contain or control her. Their constricted images of America and the world never intercepted her music.

NOTES

Research for this essay was supported by the Humanities and Social Sciences Research Council of Canada. The author gratefully acknowledges its assistance and the help of librarians at The Library of Congress archives and The Henry W. and Albert A. Berg Collection of the New York Public Library.

1. All quotations unless otherwise cited are from the holdings of Muriel Rukeyser's papers at The Library of Congress. Rukeyser's FBI file, with her marginal notes, is part of those holdings.
2. See Perreault, "Muriel Rukeyser: Egodocuments and the Ethics of Propaganda" for an extended examination of Rukeyser's work at the OWI.
3. Kaufman and Herzog edited an informative edition of Rukeyser's poems in 2005. All quotations of poems are from this volume.
4. See Gentry for a concise statement of the case, 104–05.
5. See Claire Culleton's detailed account of the early days of Hoover's career (18–29).
6. Kertesz reports that Rukeyser had driven south to cover the trial for the leftist *Student Review* and that she was arrested for talking with black reporters (22). See also Alan Wald's account (*Exiles* 299).
7. Several sources mention Hoover's 1956 speech in which he warned of communist infiltration of the NAACP. See Ungar 408. Until his well-documented aggression

against Martin Luther King and the civil rights movement, Hoover (and thus the FBI) seems largely indifferent to African American political activities (see Robins on Langston Hughes and Richard Wright, 279–87).

8. The form itself attempts to cover all possibilities: Question 17 asks, "Do you advocate or have you ever advocated, or are you now or have you ever been a member of any organization that advocates the overthrow of the Government of the United States by force or violence? If so give complete details under Item 45." Rukeyser checked X in the "No" column. Rukeyser was hired to work in the Graphics division of the OWI.
9. Nelson's presentation of this event is rather ambiguous. He indicates that the "independent militia" had been highly successful in urban attacks but would probably have been less so against Franco's army in the open field. He adds the understatement, "Yet a negotiated, rather than murderous, solution to differences on the Spanish Left would have benefited everyone" (188).
10. See Cary Nelson's *Revolutionary Memory* for further discussion of Spanish Civil War poetry.
11. The inconsistency of dates is typical of materials in this FBI file. A later file indicates she resigned on May 17, 1943.
12. Rukeyser here reiterates the grievous loss of the poster series: "In a workshop where Shahn, Perlin, Koerner were among the painters, I served as writer and many artists were called in; work was commissioned and planned. Welders by Shahn were to be used to remind us of our mixed birth; a head by Shimin, the head of a young Negro boy; . . . the starving children of Käthe Kollwitz. None of these was ever used" (145).
13. "American stock" must be code for white, not evidently foreign. This same informant considers her "an excellent tenant and a loyal American." (document dated May 5, 1943).
14. Apparently Boch was killed early in the fighting. His presence haunts many of Rukeyser's poems, and the fact that she had no knowledge of his fate shows something of the chaos following the defeat of the Loyalists.
15. Wald mentions that Rukeyser and Gregory had been "courted" by the party (*Revolutionary Imagination* 87), but that Gregory had been attacked in the *New Masses*, possibly for resisting party orthodoxy in his poetics (*Exiles* 123–24).
16. Considering that Rukeyser was active in the antiwar movement and traveled to Hanoi, it may be that other files exist elsewhere.
17. An artist, Mesches recreated his file in *Public Culture* (2003). Moved to transform the file pages into "contemporary illuminated manuscripts," Mesches comments in his project on "the sheer aesthetic beauty of the pages themselves—the bold, black, slashing eradicating strokes" (293).

WORKS CITED

Aaron, Daniel. *Episodes in American Literary Communism*. New York: Harcourt, Brace & World, Inc., 1961.

Culleton, Claire A. *Joyce and the G-Men: J. Edgar Hoover's Manipulation of Modernism*. New York: Palgrave Macmillan, 2004.

Dayton, Tim. *Muriel Rukeyser's The Book of the Dead.* Columbia MS.: U of Missouri P, 2003.

Folsom, Franklin. *Days of Anger, Days of Hope: A Memoir of the League of American Writers, 1937–1942.* Niwot, CO: U P of Colorado, 1994.

Gentry, Curt. *J. Edgar Hoover: The Man and the Secrets.* New York, London: Norton, 1991.

Guttman, Allen. "The Brief Embattled Course of Proletarian Poetry" in *Proletarian Writers of the Thirties,* David Madden, ed., Carbondale: Southern Illinois P, 1968. pp. 252–269.

Kertesz, Louise. *The Poetic Vision of Muriel Rukeyser.* Baton Rouge: Louisiana State U P, 1980.

Laurie, Clayton D. *The Propaganda Warriors: America's Crusade against Nazi Germany.* Lawrence, Kansas: U P of Kansas, 1996.

Levi, Jan Heller. Ed. *A Muriel Rukeyser Reader.* New York: Norton, 1994.

Mesches, Arnold. "The FBI Files." *Public Culture* 15, 2 (2003): 287–94.

Nelson, Cary. *Repression and Recovery: Modern American Poetry and the Politics of Cultural Memory, 1910–1945.* Madison, Wisconsin: U of Wisconsin P, 1989.

———. *Revolutionary Memory: Recovering the Poetry of the American Left.* New York: Routledge, 2001.

Perreault, Jeanne. "Muriel Rukeyser: Egodocuments and the Ethics of Propaganda." *Tracing the Autobiographical,* Marlene Kadar et al., eds., London, Ontario: Wilfrid Laurier U P, 2005, pp. 143–64.

"Poetess in OWI Here Probed by U.S. as Red," *New York Times,* May 7, 1943, p. 4.

Robins, Natalie. *Alien Ink: The F.B.I.'s War on Freedom of Expression.* New York: William Morrow and Company, Ltd.1992.

Rukeyser, Muriel. *The Collected Poems of Muriel Rukeyser.* Eds. Janet E. Kaufman and Anne F. Herzog. Pittsburg: U of Pittsburg P, 2005.

———. *The Life of Poetry.* New York: A.A. Wyn, 1949.

Thurston, Michael. "Documentary Modernism as Popular Front Poetics: Muriel Rukeyser's 'Book of the Dead,'" *Modern Language Quarterly* 60, 1 (March 1999): 59–83.

Ungar, Sanford J. *FBI.* New York: Little, Brown and Company, 1975.

Wald, Alan M. *Exiles from a Future Time: The Forging of the Mid-Twentieth Century Left.* Chapel Hill: U of North Carolina P, 2002.

———. *The New York Intellectuals: The Rise and Decline of the Anti-Stalinist Left from the 1930s to the 1980s.* Chapel Hill: U of North Carolina P, 1987.

———. *The Revolutionary Imagination: The Poetry and Politics of John Wheelwright and Sherry Mangan.* Chapel Hill: U of North Carolina P, 1983.

Wechsler, Shoshana. "A Mat(t)er of Fact and Vision: The Objectivity Question and Muriel Rukeyser's 'The Book of the Dead,'" *Twentieth Century Literature* 45, 2 (Summer 1999): 121–38.

PART II

THE FBI AND THE ARTS

CHAPTER 8

An Archive of the (Political) Unconscious: Jean Renoir at the FBI

Christopher Faulkner

> The theory of psychoanalysis, then, becomes a theory of the archive and not only a theory of memory. (Derrida 19)

Archive Works

This chapter has two objectives. It is first of all about a certain kind of unintended archive or, let us say, a certain institution that I shall choose to think of as an archive, an institution that seems to me paradigmatic of all archives. It is paradigmatic because an analysis of its practices must rely upon the insights included by psychoanalysis, which, as Derrida insists, "aspires to be a general science of the archive, of everything that can happen to the economy of memory and to its substrates, traces, documents, in their supposedly psychical or technoprosthetic forms . . ." (Derrida 34). Not only is the unconscious an archive, but archives can be said to function like the unconscious. I hope this relationship between the one and the other will prove to be something more than a conceit.

In the simplest terms, the purpose of the archive, any archive, like the unconscious itself, is to serve as an operating system for both remembering and forgetting. Forgetting, as we are often reminded, is the verso of remembering, of archiving. Forgetting is that equal and relational activity to which memory is bound—as the leaves of manuscripts, incunabula, books are tightly bound; but also bound in the sense of a direction or destination—and which thus enables it. What I am trying to get at is that the deposits of an archive should not be thought of as merely existing in a passive state; they are always already meaningful by virtue of their dynamic relation with that which has had to be forgotten. Remembering or saving, and forgetting or discarding, are active movements, mental or physical, that belong to the economy of the archive, in either its "psychical or technoprosthetic forms" (Derrida 34).

In that economy of hoarding and expenditure lies the ethical-political function of the archive. Of course, it can only serve that function when we act to excavate it, when we activate its meanings. The archaeological work we do will force us to consider the uses of the past and the necessities we might want it to serve. In this chapter, I want to activate some of the meanings of my unintended archive as a formal system, and thereby speak to its ethical and political function, as well as analyze the specific content of what it remembers. Not surprisingly, it will prove to be difficult to do justice to the analysis if one does not reflect on the workings of the system.

My interests are in what I would broadly call the social function of cinema. To that end, a lot of my work—books, articles—has been devoted to French cinema of the 1930s and more particularly to the career of Jean Renoir (1894–1979), who directed some 40 films over 45 years in France, the United States, Italy, and India. My research has been largely historical and critical and has depended significantly on archival resources in Paris, Los Angeles, New York, London, and Montreal. This research continues, albeit somewhat obsessively (as years have passed, I find that I have actually written twice about two of Renoir's films). What I want to address here is a new research undertaking, research that is still in progress, around Renoir's American career and the wartime and postwar French émigré community in the United States. My second objective, therefore, will be to claim that the unexpected rewards of an unintended archive must completely rearrange our thinking of what Renoir was up to personally and professionally in the United States.

About 10 years ago I had the inspired idea of writing to the Federal Bureau of Investigation to inquire whether their multitudinous files included a dossier on Jean Renoir. This was an idea that ran contrary to all expectations, because I am not an American citizen and I did not know whether I had the right to request the release of documents under the US Freedom of Information Act (FOIA). Two years passed—and I had long forgotten my initial inquiry—before I received a response from the FBI. The response came in the form of a large, brown envelope with a discreetly marked return address. (This felt a little like being invited to partake of a guilty pleasure.) An accompanying letter advised me that the FBI did not have a main file on Jean

Renoir, but did have 95 cross-references to Renoir in files on other subjects. The present envelope contained 20 cross-references amounting to some 83 pages. I was advised that 75 cross-references were currently unavailable for review and were to be placed on something called "special locate" before being released. In brief, I could expect more material. The 80 pages of documentation I had in hand were already tantalizing. As I suggested above, part of what I want to do is to explain how this (FBI) archive works—or better, because more active in design—explain how it can be made to work, how it can be made to *do* work, in relation to my subject Jean Renoir.

AN AMERICAN POPULAR FRONT

On December 31, 1940, when Renoir landed at New York in full flight from Vichy and Occupied France, he was one among a stream of refugees, German mostly, but French too, and Austrian, Hungarian, Czech, and so on, refugees with very considerable artistic and/or intellectual attainments, who sought sanctuary from European fascism in the United States. Because of their politics (radical, Communist; liberal, socialist), their heritage (often Jewish), or both, many of these refugees were distressed exiles from their homelands, not just relieved immigrants to a newfound land. Their cultural or professional identities and their political identities were not things apart, whether these men and women were novelists, playwrights, film directors, academics, poets, painters, musicians, research scientists, or what have you. If they brought their talents with them to America and continued to practice their professions, they necessarily brought their various (mostly left-wing) politics and continued the old arguments on new shores. Two things followed from this European tradition of the inseparability of professional from political or social life. The first was that many of these émigrés predictably became involved in social or political causes in America. Occasionally these were American causes (Scottsboro and antilynching, the Sleepy Lagoon case and minority rights), but more often they were European causes (relief for Republican Spain or Mother Russia, various anti-Nazi organizations). The inevitable corollary to these sorts of commitment was the pall of suspicion cast over many of them by certain investigative bodies during the first years of the Cold War as to their involvement in so-called "subversive" activities. To have had a political past in Europe ("premature anti-fascism": Ceplair and Englund 55) or to have been active in liberal, social causes in the United States (with alleged communist front organizations) did not help one's chances of eluding investigation.

In a frustrated effort at making his way in the Hollywood film industry, Renoir made five commercial features in the United States between 1941 and 1947. Only one of these films alludes specifically to political events. *This*

Land Is Mine (1943) is a melodramatic tale of Occupation and Resistance in which a location "Somewhere in Europe" is a thin screen for collaborationist France. The film does inveigh against a number of policies and practices synonymous with Vichy, such as anti-Semitism, the break up of unions, and the suppression of women's rights. Apart from this film, Renoir struggled rather unsuccessfully with and against the conventions of the American genre system until he went to India in 1949–1950 to make *The River*, thereby opening up his return to Europe in the 1950s and a new career as a postnational filmmaker.

In the 1930s, however, in France, Renoir's name was synonymous with the popular causes of the decade, with workers' rights and antifascism. At the time of the Popular Front he was French cinema's most celebrated man of the left. He directed the anarcho-syndicalist political comedy, *Le Crime de Monsieur Lange* in 1935, made *La Vie est à nous* for the French Communist Party in 1936, and wrote regularly and widely for Party papers and journals in the latter half of the decade. (He even stood as godfather to the son of Maurice Thorez, the Party's Secretary-General). At the end of the decade, at the time of the release of *La Grande Illusion* (1937), *La Bête humaine* (1938), and *La Règle du jeu* (1939), Renoir was consistently excoriated by his enemies on the right as "politically of the same persuasion as the Judeo-democratic lineage of Zola" (Vinneuil 256). In short, when Jean Renoir disembarked at New York on December 31, 1940, he came ashore carrying a great deal of political baggage not easily disposed of. In other words, there was every reason to think he might have been put on file by the FBI and that he might have had to deal with the consequences.

Congressional interest in American Communists in the arts, their fellow travelers, and foreign associates dates from the formation of the first House Committee on Un-American Activities (HUAC) in 1938. The Dies Committee, as it was then known, actually cited Renoir because of two articles that he had written in France for the Communist youth magazine, *Les Cahiers de la jeunesse*, in February and July 1938 ("Hearings before a Special Committee . . .," 1938).[1] But it was the prospect of the Cold War that brought about that period of political-juridical and extrajuridical notoriety with which we are most generally familiar, and whose repercussions continue to make the news these 50-odd years later. The death of Roosevelt in April 1945 spelled the end of progressivist legislation and a progressivist climate in the public realm. (Renoir: "I love Mr. Roosevelt . . ." [in Thompson and LoBianco 128]). With the Truman Doctrine of 1946 and the desire to limit the sphere of Soviet influence, the Cold War began in earnest. This was the period of renewed application of the Smith Alien Registration Act, the introduction of the Taft-Hartley Bill in 1947 and various other loyalty oaths, the investigation of the Hollywood Ten of 1947, the McCarran *Internal Security*

Act of 1950, Joseph McCarthy's red-baiting tactics and the ensuing witchhunts, and the second round of House Committee hearings on Hollywood between 1951 and 1953. All of these public institutions of inquiry and regulation relied, of course, on the secret investigations of the FBI for their (mis)information.

There were those among Renoir's close friends and coworkers in the United States, both American citizens and foreign nationals, whose personal liberties and professional careers were directly affected by this postwar regime of discipline and punishment represented by bodies like HUAC. Bertolt Brecht, whom Renoir had known since the early 1930s, and with whom he socialized in Hollywood, was the "eleventh" of the Hollywood Ten, and fled the day after his HUAC hearing on October 30, 1947. The composer, Hanns Eisler, who wrote the music for Renoir's *The Woman On the Beach* (1947), was denounced by his sister, Ruth Fischer, and after a year-long investigation "voluntarily" deported to East Germany in February 1948. Irving Pichel was the dialogue director on *Swamp Water* (1941), Renoir's first American film. He was one of the original "nineteen" subpoenaed in 1947, a member of the Hollywood Democratic Committee and a signatory of the famous "Open Letter" in the *Hollywood Reporter* in October 1947, which denounced HUAC's violation of First Amendment rights, its attack on cultural freedoms, and its attempt to control the film industry. Renoir had an enduring friendship and planned numerous projects with Clifford Odets, who confessed his Communist Party membership and named names to the HUAC in May 1952. The blacklisted Hugo Butler, a Communist and twice vicepresident of the Screen Writer's Guild, who went underground to avoid a hearing, was the writer on Renoir's belated New Deal-influenced *The Southerner* in 1945, as well as for two films by the blacklisted director John Berry. His partner, Jean Rouverol, recently published an account of their 12-year exile in Mexico. Additional research will bring to light more friends and coworkers who suffered similar fates.[2]

In the 1940s Renoir was a frequent visitor to the homes of members of the German émigré community in Santa Monica and on Sunday afternoons at Salka Viertel's where everyone talked "film and politics." Here one could find her husband Berthold, along with Lion Feuchtwanger, Hanns Eisler, the brothers Thomas and Heinrich Mann, Arnold Schoenberg, Emil Ludwig, Bruno Frank, Franz Werfel, and Alma Mahler, among others. A handful of British émigrés and sympathetic American friends also attended (Viertel 259). At this time, Renoir spoke German almost as fluently as he spoke French, and certainly a great deal better than he spoke English. Many among this crowd had honorable left-wing credentials, and many among this crowd—little did they know it at the time (or do they know it to this day?)—were under more or less constant surveillance by the FBI, who provided their files to HUAC.[3]

In other words, there is no question that Renoir had a close and ongoing personal and professional relationship with the kinds of people, both foreigners and U.S. nationals, who were actively trying to change the course of European and American political and social history. But it is important to remember one crucial fact: film criticism and film history have always reliably reported that in the United States Renoir was not involved in politics. Renoir seems to have made this disavowal of political life clear himself by his complete silence on the matter in his autobiography, *My Life and My Films*, published in 1974, many years after the period in question. Was Renoir's disavowal of his involvement in politics in the United States a matter of forgetfulness? Or, to open a different meaning, did he choose to reject from *My Life and My Films* the inclusion of any memory that he was involved?

Célia Bertin, Renoir's biographer, has insisted that, "In California, Jean Renoir was careful to stay away from political activity of any kind. He wasn't even tempted to indulge during the war . . . Accordingly, no one even dreamed of adding Jean's name to those of suspected Communists" (Bertin 273). Certainly, Renoir was never denounced to HUAC, and he had not done anything especially reprehensible in the United States. However, if HUAC was primarily interested in certifiable Communist Party members during the two stages of the hearings into Hollywood, in 1947 and again from 1951 to 1953, there were other agencies interested in fellow travelers, progressives, and liberals who belonged to alleged CPUSA cultural front organizations or organizations with international connections.[4] And it appears that on this score, Renoir was more than a little worried about something in 1947–1948. When his son Alain was a student at the University of California, Santa Barbara, "his hair and his political opinions—the one as red as the other," as Renoir said to Robert Flaherty at the end of 1946 (in Thompson & LoBianco 201), Renoir wrote with concern to his son:

> Don't go and get yourself kicked out. That would really be a shame, after all the trouble you've taken to learn. On another front, a little scandal in my family wouldn't help my own business. Hollywood movie people are even more conservative than the suburban middle class in Paris. The latest thing is that Hanns Eisler is being insulted in the papers because he's a foreigner and, it seems, a Communist. The same thing could happen to me, even though I stay away from politics, not out of fear, but from boredom. There's nothing more boring than an American Communist. (Bertin 234–35)

That Renoir wished to distance himself from "boring" American Communists is not altogether surprising. Many liberals who espoused reformist causes, people like Philip Dunne and Melvyn Douglas, for example, were determinedly anti-Communist, especially after the end of the War, when the CPUSA returned to a Stalinist hardline. Guilt by association, however, was a very real force. And certainly Renoir had reason to worry. The American papers were preoccupied with the Eisler affair for an entire year, beginning in February 1947, through Eisler's HUAC testimony in May, right up to the moment of his "voluntary" deportation from the United States on February 16, 1948. The Eisler affair actually extended before and after the furor that broke out around the Hollywood Ten between September and December 1947, which suggests that the course and outcome of the two investigations (one into domestic communism, the other into a foreign communist presence) were deliberately interrelated (at the very least with a thought to the publicity value that each would accrue for the other). Following his work for Losey, Lang, Odets, and Chaplin, Eisler finished the music for Renoir's *The Woman On the Beach*, his last American film, just months before he was subpoenaed.

The Hermencutics of the FBI Files

Sixteen months went by before I received my next (similarly plain) brown paper envelope from the FBI, this time with another 40 cross-referenced files amounting to 105 pages. Fifteen months after that, 7 more pages came from the State Department, followed by 3 pages from the Department of the Navy six months later, and finally 32 cross-references or 63 pages again from the FBI more than 3 years further on. That was in 1998. I have been promised 3 outstanding cross-referenced files. I am still waiting. After 10 years and a total of 261 pages of material, this is an archive whose intermittent rewards require that one exhibit a monastic patience.

What are the rewards? What does the material look like? There are numerous pages that offer little help. In fact, the FBI has reached the limit-case of archival scrupulousness. Documentation received under the FOIA comes with a reader's guide that explains (justifies) the erasures. With FBI material, ongoing concerns about national security still remain paramount.

This ongoing production of secrecy can be seen as a continuation of the Cold War by other means. For the past 60 years that war has been a war waged by agencies of the state against its own citizens as much as it has been a war against foreign powers. Although it may be illegible (not the same thing as unintelligible), the unconscious of an earlier period makes its presence felt in the blacked-out pages of these documents. What has been repressed still awaits its return.

The erasures on the pages of the files signify the very *raison d'être* of the FBI as an archive. These blackings out testify to its power and authority, to its "hermeneutic right and competence" (Derrida 2), a right and competence that applies definitionally to all archives. Part of the FBI's interpretive competence here involves designating certain utterances as unsayable, as to be repressed, and in this very prohibition creating the (political) unconscious of the archive, or rather signifying in this bold way that this archive (like all archives) has an unconscious. At the same time, however—literally, at the same moment—that it blacks out, it unwittingly calls its authority and its hermeneutic competence into question. It undermines itself. The admission that there is the unsayable, the repressed, that there is an unconscious of the archive, makes room for the heterogeneous, the unassimilable, the incommensurable, for the possibility of meanings that are beyond control, that are left over and open. I need hardly underline the political and ethical importance of such a possibility with regard to an institution like the FBI, which is charged with nothing less than the responsibility of securing the meaning of (and for) the nation-state.

There isn't space to present a detailed account of the extent to which Renoir was evidently caught up in ongoing FBI surveillance, involving the interception of mail, pursuits by car or on foot, stakeouts on street corners, or conversations in person or on the telephone as recorded by informants, all of which appear in reports filed to the office of J. Edgar Hoover. One has the impression of a thick cloak and dagger world populated by secret agents, spies, and informers; in short, all the ingredients of espionage fiction are here. Make no mistake, the world of the documents is constructed, interpretive, mediative, which is why it invites the language of metafictional analysis (which is also always the discourse of psychoanalysis). The omniscient narrator, one might say, of this constructed world, is none other than J. Edgar Hoover himself, Hoover, that hand-washing, germ-obsessed, anti-Semite and homophobe—every "subversive" a pollutant, all of them disease-carrying vermin—drawn so carefully in Don DeLillo's brilliant *Underworld* (1997), itself a novel about the *Niederschriften* of the 50 years of the Cold Postwar.

Once so many whispers have been overheard, conversations recorded, meetings, affairs, encounters noted in so many rooms, and the reports submitted that accumulate in the FBI archives—reports that become the archive as they accumulate—what has been confirmed is the evidence of the passage of so many lives from the private to the public sphere, of the now forever inescapable interrelation between the two. Institutional memory has become personalized; private memory has become publicized. This is a convergence of some importance that needs to be pursued. However, a first reaction of the disinterested researcher might be frustration or disappointment at the incompleteness of the material because of its erasures (both pages blacked out and pages withheld). These FBI documents (familiar enough in their appearance to anyone who has worked with restricted material) immediately raise questions about the limits of knowledge and the problem of evidence. After all, recognition of the evidence provided by this body of material depends upon the acknowledgment of a lack. What can I hope to know, the inquisitive researcher asks, given what I have to acknowledge is lacking? The documents are incomplete, partial, unsatisfying. What can they tell me? In the files, the blacked out passages (apparently) situate the object of desire, full knowledge, as founded on an absence. "Is not . . . mass communications defined by its limits, the energy with which it excludes, its *censorship*?" Barthes once famously said (158). But Barthes' remark represents a prohibitionist view of the problem of limits.

Let me revise what I just wrote about the incompleteness of these documents. "Incompleteness" supposes the (im)possibility of completeness. When did a researcher ever think an archive or a set of documents was *complete*? What does that mean? That can only be a necessary illusion (of coherence) that we may have to tell ourselves, in order to get the job done. If I don't begin to write something, if I wait, always in the expectation of more files, I shall never write anything. The supply of files is, after all, potentially inexhaustible. But it is a necessary illusion for another reason, too, because without a fiction of completeness the security and authority of one's own subject position is endangered. As Joan Copjec cleverly argues (in quite a different context), all totalities are, in truth, incomplete, either because they lack something (something is excluded, the prohibitionist view) or because they lack nothing (everything is included) (253–55). In other words, a surfeit makes the formation of a totality as impossible as a deficit. A totality—one can only imagine such a thing—would be a body, any body, which is ordered, coherent, delimited. That is, confronted with our archival material, we are always reminded of that which is inaccessible, on the one hand, and of that which exceeds, on the other. Not all meaning(s) can be recovered; there is no secure (in the sense of inviolable, transcendent, omniscient) reading position. Archival research is about compensating for the incommensurable; that is a first condition of the research.

But what of those under investigation? All those secrets that the FBI documents create (yes, create: does the unconscious *not* create secrets?), all those plots, real and imagined, that they reveal, do they not operate, as has been suggested, at the unstable borders between the public and private, between the individual and the state, and even "between oneself and oneself" (Derrida 90)? In blurring those borders more than is usual, how could one's sense of identity not be troubled, how could one not wonder where one's subjectivity intersects with the authority of the public interest? One's otherness as a suspect under investigation is to the state as the otherness of one's unconscious is to oneself (Kristeva 21). Given the "technoprosthetic" and psychic circumstances, one might understandably have a sense of one's relation as *unheimlich*, as not at home, so to speak, both with respect to the state and to one's self. One can therefore understand the difficulty of writing about all of this, about the need to defer writing about all of this, for Renoir, as for so many others.

The question to be begged is not that Renoir should find himself a character in this world of the FBI files. Guilt by association with all those others, who are in turn guilty by virtue of their associations, has ensured that. It is not within his, or their, power to declare oneself not guilty. The point is that Renoir is indeed a character in this world, but he is not the agent of its narrative. To be under surveillance, to be the object of someone else's look, attention, knowledge, is to be deprived of agency. The power to drive this narrative history of incrimination and guilt lies somewhere else. To suffer the fate of the guilty object, or to play the part of the bad object (thereby doubling the burden of guilt), as Renoir did by disavowing his political involvement in the United States, is to invite the punishment of having to relinquish one's agency. This is the punishment that is appropriate to the refusal of recollection, to talking it out, to taking the cure. To have gone to jail for contempt (the fate of the Hollywood Ten), to have been blacklisted (perhaps 300–400 hundred people), or graylisted (how many more hundreds?), were (unmistakably) serious material consequences for having been found guilty. But in themselves they are no substitute for (re)visiting and making public the archive of the private unconscious.

However, the paradox faced by all these people, including Renoir, is that since power cannot lie with the (not-)guilty, each must assume the position of a guilt-laden, scapegoated figure in order to (re)claim his or her agency. Hence, all those memoirs written by all those who were surveyed and punished (most of the Hollywood Ten, for example), memoirs that continue to appear to the present moment (by Gordon for example, and Rouverol and even the children of the punished in McGilligan), the personal archive that has to be searched, recorded, talked out, to (dis)burden oneself with guilt even as one talks. Only in this way can private memory contest the authority of the public record; in this way institutional memory can be altered by personal recollection.

I could say that with this project I am taking on the task of restoring Renoir's forgotten memory to public history. I have already established that such a project is not just a matter of restoring the facts. No archival work is ever simply that. Perhaps a better explanation of what I am doing would be to say that I am returning (political) agency to Renoir.[5] The repressed that awaits its return in the material of the FBI documents is not just some hidden knowledge; it is also the agency of the actors involved. In being granted agency, Renoir is being permitted to take up a subject position with respect to his political self in America; this period of his life can be entered into the record of the Symbolic order. The fact that everyone who is implicated has to write about this period emphasizes first of all the singularity of every experience of that period, but also the specific singularity of every being, of every particular existence altogether. We would have to think of the former as a political move, just as the latter is an ethical move. In so many ways, John Howard Lawson, Dalton Trumbo, Samuel Ornitz, Adrian Scott, and so many others were right to draw a (psychical) analogy between these events, their repercussions, and the excoriation of Jews in Germany after 1933 or the long history of systematic racism in the United States (Kahn 76, 84, 99, 106–07). In fact, that (analogy) was the very condition of any continuing engagement between the FBI, HUAC, the American (too often Republican) right—and its suspects: their heterogeneity, their unassimilability, their otherness. Politically, ethically, the meaning of the files is that they sustain the evidence of the other and of the continuing war with otherness; they therefore keep the potential for political disturbance open. Reading the archive becomes an experience of the uncanny. It will always be an *unheimlich* world, within and without.

Renoir and the Hollywood Left

What kind of character does Renoir make in this *unheimlich* world of espionage and double-dealing? The FBI files offer evidence that Renoir was an active participant in the affairs of at least three organizations that were named as "subversive" by the Department of Justice, pursuant to Executive Order No. 9835, issued by Truman in March 1947, because they were alleged to be cultural front organizations for the Communist Party. Witnesses who appeared before HUAC were routinely asked if they had ever been associated with or were ever members of one or more of these three organizations.

Renoir was first of all a supporter of the People's Educational Association (to whom he gave money) from 1943 to 1945. The PEA was an experiment in education for working people that grew out of a 1943 writers' congress held at UCLA on the theme of "unconscious fascism." Although it survived until 1948, this organization was condemned in the 1945 Tenney Report (the state of California equivalent of HUAC) because it had been directed by some members of the Hollywood Writers Mobilization, who were also members of the Screen Writers Guild, and of the defunct League of American Writers (LAW). The blacklisted writer Ben Barzman, for example, was told that he lost his U.S. passport because he had worked for the People's Educational Center in Los Angeles, which offered courses "in history, in culture, and in the problems of various ethnic groupings within the community, such as blacks, Chicanos, and Jews, in addition to courses in the arts, which included writing workshops . . ." (Schwartz 219, 203). Prior affiliation with the LAW was in itself condemnable. On April 23, 1943, Renoir delivered an address to the LAW, just a month before the release of *This Land Is Mine*, and many of his remarks about workers' rights and antifascism in that talk are to be found in the dialogue of the film (Faulkner 165–66). According to Larry

Ceplair and Steven Englund, among those few groups who really played "crucial" parts in the struggle against fascism, two were the LAW and the Joint Anti-Fascist Refugee Committee (100). To the American right, their antifascism was synonymous with pro-communism.

The Joint Anti-Fascist Refugee Committee (JAFRC) was frequently cited in the HUAC hearings as an anti-Catholic communist front, "master-minded by Jews" (Schwartz 239). Along with people like John Garfield, Dorothy Parker, Irving Pichel, Frank Tuttle, and others no less well known or well connected on the left, Renoir was an active member from 1941 through until at least 1948. In fact, he was, for a time, codirector with Dorothy Parker of the motion picture committee, and then honorary chairman of the Los Angeles branch in 1946 and 1947. (Before Renoir's turn as honorary chairman of the JAFRC, Philip Merivale had preceded him in the position. In a fortuitous bit of casting, Merivale was the actor who had played the role of Professor Sorel in *This Land Is Mine*, the editor of the pro-worker, antifascist underground resistance newspaper who is executed by the Nazis after having been denounced). The JAFRC was a coalition of groups like the American Committee to Save Refugees, the LAW and the United Spanish Aid Committee, all of which had previously been cited as subversive by the Dies Committee. To raise money for medical supplies, ambulances, hospitals, orphanages, and the like on behalf of refugees from European fascism, the JAFRC sponsored a number of events in the 1940s with which Renoir's name (and many another name) is repeatedly linked in the FBI files. One such event infiltrated by FBI informants was a gathering called the "Free People's Benefit Dinner" at the Beverly Hills Hotel on July 2, 1942. The entire guest list is in the FBI files. A letter written to Burgess Meredith on October 27, 1945, gives every indication that Renoir was actively collecting funds in support of JAFRC programs: "The Varsovie Hospital people are hanging on the phone to proclaim their enthusiasm about your name and Paulette's name printed on the mail paper. I feel the same and hope that we will very soon get the necessary money to help these Spanish Partisans who, in the real beginning of the war, were the first defenders of our liberties" (Thompson & LoBianco 167–68). With this last sentence, Renoir seems to be recalling the defeated antifascist Popular Front governments of the 1930s in both France and Spain, causes to which he had willingly devoted his energies in film and print. Later, in March 1948, Renoir was the committee head for a fund-raiser chaired by Edward Dmytryk and attended by Edward Barsky, the national chairman of the JAFRC, who had earlier been cited for contempt of Congress along with 16 other executive members (Schwartz 239). The main speeches at this gathering were about the fate of refugees loyal to the Spanish Republic and the subject of "Atomic Energy for Peace."

The third important, targeted organization with which Renoir was connected in the 1940s was the National Council of American-Soviet Friendship. It was as a member of this group that Renoir made occasional visits to the Soviet Consulate and, with Hanns Eisler, attended a reception for the Soviet filmmaker, Mikhail Kalatozov (who later directed *I Am Cuba*, 1962), at the Mocambo Cafe in Hollywood on August 12, 1943. (Kalatozov became Soviet Consul in Los Angeles). On behalf of this group Renoir broadcast an address—still unpublished—to the women of the Soviet Union on March 8, 1944, that begins: "Women of Russia, I send you my best wishes. Although these greetings are coming to you from the United States of America, they are those of a Frenchman, a Frenchman among so many others, who has not forgotten that in Red Square, beside Lenin's Tomb, there rests a tri-colored flag, the standard of the Paris Commune."[6]

Renoir's most important role on behalf of the National Council of American-Soviet Friendship was his membership on the committee of administration for the cinema. His most interesting service on the committee's behalf, and far and away his most interesting political engagement during this entire period, was his stage direction of a spectacle whose existence has until now been entirely forgotten. Renoir took responsibility for mounting an elaborate political rally held at the Shrine Auditorium in Los Angeles on November 16, 1943, to commemorate the 10th anniversary of diplomatic relations between the Soviet Union and the United States. Thanks to the diligence of the FBI, I can report the discovery of a "new" work by Renoir and reproduce the program of the event.

Many details about this rally are still wanting, but recognizable among the names on the program is that of Eugène Lourié as the art director, Renoir's close collaborator since the mid-1930s and the art director on *This Land Is Mine*. Earl Robinson, the composer of the cantata "Song of a Free People," was interrogated by HUAC on April 11, 1957, on the subject of this music and about his role on the musicians' committee of the National Council of American-Soviet Friendship (a question, incidentally, he declined to answer). Another highlight of the rally was the screening of extracts from American and Soviet films. An invitation to the event, found in the Renoir correspondence files at UCLA, reads as follows: "The climax will be a spectacular film presentation, arranged by Jean Renoir, showing the parallelisms between the American and Soviet people at war and at peace."[7] There is also an unpublished letter of thanks to Renoir for his contribution to the rally from the Los Angeles office of the Council: "Your ideas, and Mr. Lourié's, turned what might have been just another stuffy meeting into something which at moments was genuinely exciting—and we are really grateful. I still hope that we can work out your two-screen film idea for a meeting some day. It's too good an idea to give up."[8]

There is no question that all of this activity on Renoir's part in the People's Educational Association, the LAW, the JAFRC, and the NCASF qualifies as political. Renoir was a partisan of the Hollywood left during the American Popular Front of the 1940s for the same reasons that he got caught up in the French Popular Front of the 1930s. To many people, the taking of sides did not seem a particularly complicated matter in those days. Against the isolationist politics and cultural nationalism of the American right, against the forces of antilabor, racism and anti-Semitism, there wasn't much doubt about the stand someone of Renoir's background and convictions would adopt. This is also a way of saying that there is not quite the hiatus or break or rupture between Renoir's career in France in the 1930s and his career in America in the 1940s that is usually supposed.

The information revealed by the FBI files suggests the necessity for new research on Renoir's activities in the United States that may encourage us to rethink the meanings of his American films. For example, one could look at *This Land Is Mine* as a film that is interested in the ethics of naming names before it became a fact of American life. Concerned with a right-wing assault against the working-class, against women, and against Jews, the film was implicated as subversive in the files of the FBI along with other pro-labor, antifascist resistance films from 1943 such as Fritz Lang's *Hangmen Also Die*, written by John Wexley from a script by Bertolt Brecht; *Hostages*, directed by Frank Tuttle from a script by Lester Cole; and Irving Pichel's *The Moon Is Down*, from the John Steinbeck story. The point is that *This Land Is Mine* belongs to a minor genre of films from the early 1940s that engaged a number of left-wing film personnel on a body of related subject-matter and that this is the political and cinematic context within which it should be situated and understood. In the guise of a European story, then, *This Land Is Mine* is interested in a subject-matter and its dilemmas that may have been nearer to the American consciousness than the French.

Was Renoir "graylisted" for his films, for his friendships, for his activism? The "graylist" was devised to dispose of liberals and fellowtravelers who were not subpoenaed by HUAC:

> The graylists never enjoyed the publicity or effectiveness of the blacklists, but they touched many more people. [A number of reactionary organizations] culled HUAC and Tenney Committee reports, appendices, and hearing transcripts, back issues of the *Daily Worker*, letterheads of defunct Popular Front organizations [like the JAFRC], etc., to compile a list of people who could not be accused of "communism" but who had, at one time or another, dallied with liberal politics or causes. . . . No studio was without a full set of these blacklists and graylists; no studio failed to "honor" these judgements from without; no studio was without its "executive vice-president in charge of clearance." (Ceplair and Englund 387–88)

The reactionary organizations that compiled these lists included groups like American Business Consultants, the American Legion, the Wage Earners Committee, and Aware, Inc. Certainly, after Howard Hughes took over RKO Pictures in 1948, one cannot imagine Renoir working there again.

With its theatrical release in June, 1947, in a form never intended by Renoir, *The Woman On the Beach* marked the end of his American career. Despite his frustrations with Hollywood production methods and studio practices, Renoir did endeavor to undertake new projects but all of his efforts were stymied. In view, therefore, of the total collapse of his Hollywood career at the end of the 1940s, notwithstanding the commercial and critical failure of *The Woman On the Beach*, and in view of the two-and-a-half years he was without work until the opportunity presented by *The River* in late 1949, one might be forgiven for speculating about Renoir's fate. But the evidence that Renoir was graylisted is not yet conclusive.

There is one more tantalizing detail, however, just to add fuel to the speculation. After the disaster of *The Woman On the Beach*, Renoir returned to his old dream of an independent production company. Now he wanted to create a company called The Film Group (obviously an homage to the left-wing Group Theater). In a letter to Clifford Odets, dated October 1, 1948, he wrote:

> My independent production is a complete failure. After months (I should say years) of useless talks, after having found the private guarantees asked by the bank, the same bank decided to reject my bid for a loan. No money, no pictures. My partners and I are going to have a meeting very soon to decide whether we dissolve the corporation or not. . . . I don't feel unhappy. The reason given by the bank is that they act according to the new policy recommended to the Federal Reserve by the Congress. But I believe that even without this contrary circumstance there was a worm in the nut, and that I will some day find a better way to put on the screen one of your works. (Thompson & LoBianco 213)

One day we may even find the worm in the nut.

If we are forced to remap Renoir's American career in the 1940s, and to rethink the meanings of his American films in light of the knowledge revealed by the FBI files, we will also have to look again at the transition from this decade to the international coproductions and humanist philosophy of the 1950s. The new worldview offered up in *The River* says a great deal about the psychology of forgetting on the part of many former social activists. Whereas his Popular Front films (both French and American) left room for the agency of individuals and groups in the face of injustice, Renoir's new, conservative humanism after 1950 depicted worldly problems as cyclical, and personal struggle as pointless. In the face of social violence and personal tragedy, the message of *The River* is to "consent." Renoir's first post-American film (which happens to star Thomas Breen, son of the infamous Joseph Breen of the censorious Production Code Administration), is quite possibly a more profound mea culpa for his past convictions than any public denial or personal repression of his political life could ever be.

NOTES

Some of the empirical evidence in this article was first presented in an earlier version as a paper by Charles Tepperman and myself at the annual conference of the Society for Cinema Studies in 1999 in Chicago. I have to thank Charles for his permission to allow me to develop this material after a different fashion. To Barbara Gabriel I owe a debt of gratitude for some productive exchanges on the subject of psychoanalysis and the archive.

1. "Hearings Before a Special Committee on Un-American Activities," *Congressional Record*, 75th Congress of the United States, 3rd Session, August 1938, p. 17. Cited in Célia Bertin, 1991, p. 148. A third article for *Les Cahiers de la jeunesse* appeared in December, 1938.
2. One of the most coincidental of associations is with the blacklisted writers Ben and Norma Barzman. In the 1950s, they uprooted to France, where they had a son, Paul, who (by chance?) became Renoir's private secretary in the 1970s.
3. It has been reported that in the first nine years of its existence alone (from 1938 to 1947), HUAC had accumulated files on over one million people whom it claimed were subversive or Un-American (Kahn 174).
4. In a letter that he wrote to Dudley Nichols on January 12, 1954, Renoir advised his old friend and colleague that his name had appeared in a report of the Joint Fact-Finding Committee on Un-American Activities of the California Legislature, otherwise known as the Tenney Committee: "probably my 'activity,'" Renoir said, "is the article I wrote about Chaplin's *Monsieur Verdoux* in *The Screen Writers Magazine* [*sic*] in 1947" (in Thompson and LoBianco 314). The article was "Chaplin among the Immortals," which appeared in *Screen Writer* for July 1947, not a good month in a good year, or in a good venue on a good subject, for anyone who might want to keep a low political profile.
5. "There is no political power without control of the archive, if not of memory" (Derrida 4, note 1).
6. Unpublished typescript. UCLA Library, Special Collections, Renoir Collection.
7. Unpublished letter of November 3, 1943, to Renoir from the Los Angeles Council of American-Soviet Friendship. UCLA Library, Special Collections, Renoir Collection, Correspondence Files.
8. Unpublished letter of November 22, 1943, to Renoir from the Los Angeles Council of American-Soviet Friendship. UCLA Library, Special Collections, Renoir Collection, Correspondence Files.

Works Cited

Barthes, Roland. *Image-Music-Text*. London: Fontana, 1977.
Bertin, Célia. *Jean Renoir*. Paris: Perrin. Trans. 1991. *Jean Renoir: A Life in Pictures*. Baltimore: Johns Hopkins U P, 1986.
Ceplair, Larry and Steven Englund. *The Inquisition in Hollywood*. Garden City: Anchor Press/Doubleday, 1980.
Copjec, Joan. "More! From Melodrama to Magnitude," in *Endless Night: Cinema and Psychoanalysis, Parallel Histories*, Janet Bergstrom, ed., Berkeley: U of California P, 1999, pp. 249–72.
DeLillo, Don. *Underworld*. New York: Scribner, 1997.
Derrida, Jacques. *Archive Fever: A Freudian Impression*. Chicago: U of Chicago P, 1996.
Faulkner, Christopher. "Jean Renoir Addresses the League of American Writers," *Film History* 8, 1 (1996): 64–71.
Gordon, Bernard. *Hollywood Exile, or How I Learned to Love the Blacklist*. Austin: U of Texas P, 1999.
Kahn, Gordon. *Hollywood on Trial*. New York: Boni & Gaer, 1948.
Kristeva, Julia. *Nations without Nationalism*. New York: Columbia U P, 1993.
McGilligan, Patrick. *Tender Comrades*. New York: St. Martin's Press, 1997.
Renoir, Jean. *My Life and My Films*. New York: Atheneum, 1974.
Rouverol, Jean. *Refugees From Hollywood*. Albuquerque: U of New Mexico P, 2000.
Schwartz, Nancy. *The Hollywood Writers' Wars*. New York: Knopf, 1982.
Thompson, David and Lorraine LoBianco. Eds. *Jean Renoir: Letters*. London: Faber and Faber, 1994.
Viertel, Salka. *The Kindness of Strangers*. New York: Holt, Rinehart and Winston, 1969.
Vinneuil, François. "Screen of the Week: *La Bête humaine*," in *French Film Theory and Criticism, 1907–1939*, Richard Abel, ed., Vol. II: 1929–1939. Princeton: Princeton U P, 1988, pp. 256–59.

Archival Sources

UCLA Arts Library Special Collections—Jean Renoir Collection
U.S. Department of Justice, Federal Bureau of Investigation
U.S. Department of State
U.S. Department of the Navy, Naval Criminal Investigative Service

CHAPTER 9

New Information from the FBI, CNDI LA-BB-1: The Surveillance of Bertolt Brecht's Telephone in Los Angeles

Alexander Stephan
translated by Emily Banwell

On the FBI's homepage, http://www.fbi.gov/, there is a link that reads "Freedom of Information Act. Frequently requested FBI files." Clicking on this spot leads to a file that, much like "America's Most Wanted," contains information on dozens of prominent "subjects" about whom the FBI has collected material. Delving deeper into this electronic reading room's table of contents, under the heading "Famous Persons"—alongside people like "Machine Gun Kelly," Bonnie and Clyde, and Pretty Boy Floyd—one finds the name of Bertolt Brecht. Another double-click finally opens up access to materials that have long been inaccessible, kept under lock and key both in the FBI archive in Washington, D.C. and in the Brecht archive in Berlin, known only to a small group of initiated Brecht researchers. This is the 369-page FBI file on Bertolt Brecht, who after Thomas Mann was the most famous exiled German author in the United States.

A secret service can hardly be expected to do more to appease public curiosity. All questions as to whether the Brecht file contained 369, 427 or even 1,100 documents seem to have been cleared up.[1] Any suspicion that the FBI could use the malleable paragraphs of the Freedom of Information Act (FOIA), which allow research into U.S. government documents, for its own benefit seems to have been laid to rest.

Far from it. As we have recently learned, the material the FBI makes available to everyone on their Web site represents only a fragment of what is stored in the cellars of America's secret police. Besides the approximately 400 pages that have been made available to date, years of research—occasionally met with downright brusque refusals and warnings—have turned up more than 1,500 new, previously unknown documents. Of the documents I had already accessed—15,000 pages concerning the surveillance of German exiles in the United States and Mexico—the majority of these new Brecht documents are something novel: transcribed recordings of approximately 2,250 telephone calls from and to Brecht's house in Santa Monica, California, during the time from April 18 to November 3, 1945.

More than 800 of these conversations were summarized or transcribed (in English translation) by the FBI's special agents. Of these conversations, approximately 50 were personally conducted by Brecht. Helene Weigel, Barbara Brecht and others are responsible for the rest of the phone calls. In nearly 200 of the recorded calls, no one picks up; 91 calls are met with a busy signal. On June 6, the file reports "children playing with phone." For other days, the reports are incomplete or entirely lacking. The telephone-surveillance transcripts are supplemented by a new, expanded version of Brecht's main file from the FBI headquarters in Washington, and by 350 pages of correspondence from the FBI office in Los Angeles, which was responsible for Brecht's case. In addition to the previously unknown documents, these contain a number of items that are also in the Web-accessible Brecht file—though with significantly fewer censored passages.

Now, one might assume that the FBI's archivists simply overlooked the bundle of documents—small in comparison to the files on "Adolph" [*sic*] Hitler, Frank Sinatra, and Elvis Presley—regarding a playwright who was never particularly successful in the United States. After all, the Freedom of Information-Privacy Acts Section of the FBI has received more than 6,000 requests for the release of around 1.6 million documents. But here, too, the first impression is deceptive. The FBI organizes its files clearly by proper names and sorts them according to a complex card-catalog system of file numbers and cross-references. Numerous references in Brecht's main file from the period in question, along with the placing of toll calls, for example, from August 16 to October 2, 1944, prove that Brecht's phone was tapped even earlier. However, transcripts and recordings from this time have yet to be found in the FBI archives in either Washington or Los Angeles. In addition, the Brecht file is mentioned in dozens of reports on other suspicious "subjects" from the same milieu; in Brecht's case, this means primarily the German exiles, but also Americans like Charles Laughton. For nearly 30 years, a small army of Brecht scholars, whose correspondence with the FBI is—ironically—included in the documents now before me, has campaigned for the release of all of Brecht's files. And as early as October 20, 1987, the Special Agent in Charge (SAC) of the FBI branch in Los Angeles personally and urgently requested, via Airtel, that the FBI director in Washington, D.C. preserve the Brecht file for posterity: "Do not destroy, historical value, National Archives."[2]

It is not worth speculating whether the Brecht case was caught up in the bureaucratic struggle between the FBI—which wants to protect its files from public access—and the U.S. National Archives, which is pushing for greater openness; or whether larger politics played a role. As we know, politics under conservative and liberal presidents can have very different influences on the practices of making government documents available, particularly FBI material. It is also not productive to spend too much time wondering whether the FBI branch in New York, for instance, which also focused intensively on Brecht and has yet to respond to my repeated requests for information, has further material mildewing away on its shelves. And certainly it would be pointless to put off an analysis of the documents from the Los Angeles FBI field office until the recordings of the 1945 conversations have turned up—assuming they even still exist. The only thing we know for certain is that J. Edgar Hoover and his successors, like the secret service in other countries and at other times, have trouble finding a middle road. They are constantly trapped between the desire to collect as much material as possible; and the fear that illegal or semi-legal surveillance methods like wiretapping could show their agency in a bad light when it is scrutinized by lawmakers and judges, by the public, and by future generations.

Following similarly contradictory logic, the FBI concealed its activities concerning Brecht's telephone by using a code name: LACNDI-BB-1, where CNDI stands for Confidential National Defense Informant and BB for Bertolt Brecht. Various abbreviations are used whenever mail belonging to Brecht or other suspicious "subjects" is opened; when spies' observations are entered into an FBI report; and in the evaluation of documents from agencies, banks, and hospitals. Even in their internal correspondence, the special agents adhere to this code of secrecy. When the director of the FBI branch in Los Angeles complains to Washington headquarters that the technically complicated wiretapping is growing too expensive, he refers to LACNDI-BB-1 ("Advise by return tel if this check should be continued, inasmuch as it entails considerable amount of agent time" [February 16, 1945][3]). The formulation LACNDI-BB-1 can also be found in J. Edgar Hoover's correspondence when he asks his superior in the Department of Justice for an extension of the surveillance time ("through this technical surveillance it has been ascertained that Brecht is in frequent contact of individuals suspected of espionage activities on behalf of the Soviet Union" [Los Angeles, October 3, 1945]).

The transcripts I recently obtained of Brecht's telephone calls are interesting for three reasons. First, and this is the core of the new Brecht file, the transcribed conversations grant us insight into the exiles' reactions to political events during the fateful year of 1945—the news of Hitler's death, the Potsdam Conference, the Nuremberg Trials, and the dropping of the atomic bomb on Hiroshima. A second point of interest in the surveillance of Brecht's long-distance calls has to do with his literary projects during that time, including the largely unsuccessful staging of *The Private Life of the Master Race* in New York. And finally, the transcripts are a particularly rare type of text that—in the vein of George Orwell, "Big Brother" and films like *The Truman Show* and *The Matrix*—leads us to a better understanding of the Brecht family's daily life and surroundings. It is more effective than autobiographical memoirs, *roman à clef*, diaries, letters, and retrospective interviews, which—as with Thomas Mann, Brecht's neighbor in Los Angeles—are often produced with posterity in mind. As such, these are all subject to a degree of self-censorship. On the other hand, however, even without resorting to an in-depth discourse analysis, we know that the wiretap's authenticity is limited by a number of factors. Telephone conversations, even when they are seamlessly recorded, portray only a small fraction of the Brechts' everyday life. Underlined passages in the transcripts indicate that the FBI brought certain expectations to the shadowing of the "subject" "Bertolt Eugen Friedrich Brecht, was, Internal Security—R,"[4] and that the personal experiences of special agents—and the stated goals of their superiors in the field offices and FBI headquarters—played a role in deciding which conversations would be summarized and which would be reported verbatim. Additionally, over and over again, translators in the FBI visibly struggled with German language, history, and culture.

Let us look first at the original recordings emanating from Brecht's house on the subject of serious politics. Even where politically minded people like Brecht and Helene Weigel are concerned, politics are quickly overtaken by everyday problems: the love triangle between Brecht, Weigel, and Ruth Berlau; the nitpicky gossip among the colony of exiles in Santa Monica and Pacific Palisades; or simply the trivial but necessary business of day-to-day life. Thus, the news of Hitler's death, for example, which filters through to Los Angeles at the beginning of May 1945, is hardly acknowledged. In a conversation with his doctor, Brecht devotes half a sentence to the event—"You have heard that Hitler is dead" (May 1, 1945). Lion Feuchtwanger lets Helene Weigel know he has been "so sunk in work" (May 1, 1945) that he cannot meet with Brecht for an exchange of ideas until the following week. Weigel, for her part, complains to an acquaintance about being interrupted while sunbathing, and discusses with another woman whether a Martini or a White Lady makes for a worse hangover (April 30, 1945). And someone named Gina, whom the FBI identifies as the Austrian writer Gina Kaus, jokes: "Hitler is dead . . . It is a pity that it did not come off on the first of May, that would have been a great thing for Mayday" (May 1, 1945).

A few days later, Brecht does know precisely when General Keitel will sign the notice of capitulation ("it will take place this afternoon between 12 and 1 p.m." [May 8, 1945]), but is otherwise preoccupied with his work ("I am very busy with my work" [May 8, 1945]) and by an invitation to visit the director Wilhelm Dieterle and his wife Charlotte (May 9, 1945). And the dropping of the atomic bombs over Hiroshima and Nagasaki are all but subsumed in the daily minutiae of family business, even though Brecht and Charles Laughton are at this time working intensely on the scientific drama about the life of Galilei. When an unknown man asks on August 8, "What do you think of the Bomb?" Brecht responds, as the translator expressly notes, "in monosyllables." Otherwise, the 60 conversations, which take up 40 pages in the file, recorded during those days in which the history of the war and of humanity was being rewritten, deal simply with the usual day-to-day events: a duck that Helene Weigel buys for $3.20; a dinner at the Brechts' with friends in front of the fire; and a restless night because the milkman has forgotten to lock the door.

More informative on the subject of Brecht's political position just after the war, and on relations within the exile community, are the conversation transcripts that deal with the Nuremberg Trials. In "German Cut #2" from October 3, 1945, the FBI demonstrates interest in the following exchange: "Brecht to man. I just got an idea, I think that is the *principal* point why you should go over there and attend the anti-Nazi proceedings. It is the most important thing that has happened to Germany since the Peasant War. (Note: he means in Luther's time). It will be very important to note down what precisely these criminals say in their defense. That in itself would make it worthwhile to go over there." And, added in the handwriting of the special agent on duty: "The principal point is that they are trying to *whitewash* fascism and the fascists" (October 3, 1945). The identity of this man Brecht would like to see as a witness in Nuremberg becomes clear from another telephone report from the same day: "Mrs. Brecht to woman . . . maybe I could have a talk with the doctor. Doctor comes and has many arguments against doing what they wish him to do . . . Mrs. Brecht . . . you are the only man in sight who can do it . . . My personal interest in the matter is, that you take Brecht along as your secretary . . . Please, talk to Brecht about the matter, and please, I say please, do it." Brecht is trying to convince not just

"Doctor" Lion Feuchtwanger, but also Heinrich Mann, the FBI believes, to testify at the trials of the Nazi leaders: "Who would there be otherwise"—an agent or translator identified as DvHL transcribes from a recording of a conversation between Brecht and an unknown woman—"Ludwig might be, and is that the fellow to do it? Look at the book he wrote, superficial and terrible. This meeting of the nations in their wrath will be more valuable and more interesting than 20 culture-congresses" (October 3, 1945).

Brecht's conversations about Hitler and the Nuremberg Trials did not receive the FBI's full attention, but notice was taken of the conversations held with acquaintances in the summer of 1945, around the time of the Potsdam Conference, about the future of Germany and Europe. The reason for this is clear. For Brecht as well as for the FBI, for other U.S. secret services and for the American government, this period just before and just after the end of World War II meant thinking less about concluded events like Hitler's death or the end of World War II, and more about another topic: the cultural and political reconstruction of Germany and the role that the exiles would play in this new Germany.

Brecht's interest in returning to Germany as soon as possible was clearly formulated even in the poems written during his exile in Denmark. Years later in the United States, as a member of the Council for a Democratic Germany and under the watchful eye of the Office of Strategic Services,[5] he took part in the debates surrounding the future German postwar politics. And, of course, Brecht attentively observed the policies of the Free Germany movements that had been called into being by his friends and comrades in Moscow, Mexico, and London.

Conversely, U.S. secret services were interested in harvesting as much information as possible from the exiles' colonies on the country's West and East Coasts. They wanted to find out how these refugees from Hitler pictured their country's future; who would play which roles in the work of rebuilding; and how all this fit in with the ideas that Washington had about the new world order. Agencies like the Foreign Nationalities Branch of the Office of Strategic Services (OSS), which soon after was integrated into the CIA, had been trying since 1941/1942 to put together analyses of exiled authors' views on Germany—Brecht, the Mann brothers, and Emil Ludwig were all scrutinized. The OSS skillfully integrated exiles into the Department of Research and Analysis, which compiled a deluge of position reports for political decisionmakers in the U.S. government. At the end of 1945, a good half-dozen interview transcripts were submitted to the State Department, of interviews OSS employees had conducted with prominent exiles like Thomas Mann, Lion Feuchtwanger, Alfred Döblin, and Emil Ludwig, although not Brecht.[6] And the FBI made a note of even the slightest indication that an exile wanted to leave the United States for Europe.

No wonder, then, that the special agents listening in to the telephone connection at Santa Monica 5-4943 grew especially alert when Brecht commented on the results of the Potsdam Conference, when Helene Weigel talked about the elections in Austria, and when a group of exiles came together to listen to radio broadcasts about Germany. When Stalin, Churchill, and Truman met on those July days in the former Hohenzollern castle to decide the future of Central Europe, special agents excerpted not just long passages from a conversation by "Helen Weigel" about the best way to cook chicken in Mexican clay pots (August 4, 1945),[7] but also—seeking evidence of the political untrustworthiness of Brecht and his wife—comments like: "The big thing is whether the Germans—and there still are 80 million of them—will get rid of the capitalistic exploitation, to which the people were submitted. The military, which was the power for the capitalistic exploitation, has gone underground now . . . Things do not look so bad. It would have been much worse if the black forces had succeeded in returning a Bruening to power, and reinstalling a 'black' Reichswehr (defense army of the Reich)" (August 2, 1945). The following exchange develops when a conversation partner identified as "Man (Doctor)," once again probably Lion Feuchtwanger, wants to know from Brecht whether he has any news from Germany: "Brecht. Yes, doctor, very bad news. Germany will be broken up, and not retain its unity as a Cultural State. The greatest part of it is going to the Soviet. Man. That is not so bad, it will quicken its development" (August 2, 1945). At one point Helene Weigel complains to a woman that she cannot get used to American thermometers, which use Fahrenheit. Just afterward, Brecht has a conversation in which he develops the following scenario, which—though he could not have known it in 1945—turns out to be fairly accurate, at least for the Western occupied zones: After reparations have been paid, the country will take about two and a half years to get back on its feet, set up a democracy according to the Allies' standards, and reclaim its place "among the nations"—"This means that in 1948 everything will be settled" (August 2, 1945). A woman's voice, plainly that of Helene Weigel, sounds pleased with the election results in Austria: "2 Social-democrats, 2 Communiests [!], 2 Partyless, 2 Liberals" (April 30, 1945). The FBI men are just as interested in what Brecht and Weigel have to say about the elections in England as they are in the couple's commentary on the U.N. conference in San Francisco, and on the political development of Yugoslavia. And, again and again, the FBI agents suspiciously note that Brecht and his fellow exiles are receiving information about Germany via radio broadcasts: "Man to Brecht. I listened in to news from London over KHJ but it came through very poorly, it was about the Soviet . . . Brecht. Did you give a transcript to Marion . . . Man. Yes, as far as I could get it. You better listen in at 4 p.m. over KNX . . ." (August 2, 1945). Or: "Mrs. Brecht and woman.

Both are already in bed. Brecht is very tired. Have a long talk about Radio news etc, but inconsequential" (May 3, 1945). Yes, even where cultural topics are concerned the special agents take notes, as long as there is anything to do with the rebirth of Germany after the war. The FBI pricks up its ears when the name of "Ilya Ehrenbourg" [!] (April 19, 1945) is mentioned in a phone conversation, in connection with the debate over the difference between Germans and Nazis. Internal conflicts among the exiles' community, surrounding a project to send care packages to needy actors in Austria, are considered just as worthy of inclusion in the file as the discussion about the best way to feed the hunger for spiritual food in war-torn Europe: "Man to Mrs. Brecht. They have written to me that they need material, poems, songs, chansons, not only in Germany but outside of Germany as well, and, as your husband is one of the recognized great authors, we want to have as much as possible from him. Mrs. Brecht. Of course we have plenty of material here, the only trouble is with copying etc." (September 11, 1945). And Cut 4 from August 18, 1945, transcribes a phone conversation labeled "Man to Man—German" in which Brecht responds curtly to the news that Thomas Mann is being sent to Germany as an American: "Yes, and I am going with him . . . as *a German.*"

No question, then: Brecht, Thomas Mann, and other prominent members of the exiles' colony in Los Angeles captured the FBI's attention most often whenever the subject was the United States' role in postwar Germany. Analyzing the exiles' literary works, on the other hand, was not a strength of the FBI agents. This does not mean that what Brecht produced at his writing desk left no trace in the files. People who tend to ignore the slight difference between reality and fiction, like Hoover and his G-Men, can easily take everything in a novel or a play to be absolute truth. Thus the poem "Abbau des Schiffes Oskawa durch die Mannschaft" ("The Dismantling of the Ship Oskawa by its Crew") becomes an attack on the U.S. economic system. The FBI and House Un-American Activities Committee commission several independent translations of Brecht's play *The Measures Taken* because, unlike the similarly structured but unheeded pieces *He Who Says Yes* and *He Who Says No*, it uses a concrete political conflict in China as its inspiration. And the Hollywood-produced film *Hangmen Also Die* stirs up the FBI because in it Brecht and Fritz Lang glorify an illegal underground organization's fight against government violence.

It follows that Brecht's political views, his contact with native artists, and (subliminally at least) his un-American criticism of U.S. culture are the main focus of the surveillance transcripts in which he talks about the staging of *The Private Life of the Master Race*, the play with which he—unsuccessfully—tries to gain a foothold in the New York theater scene in the summer of 1945. A special agent drily transcribes a conversation between Hanns Eisler and

Helene Weigel in which Eisler cites a letter from one "Rot" (probably the stage designer Wolfgang Roth, with whom Brecht had met in New York in 1943): "the whole thing has been a failure," "enscenering [*sic*] was bad . . ., the execution poor, the acting was mediocre . . . the translation was too academic" (June 16, 1945). "Reactionary critics" (June 16, 1945) had panned the staging, and many people had gone home in the middle of the piece, even though—as passages underlined in the summary of another conversation emphasize—the theater was full of union members ("filled with the Unions" [June 20, 1945]). Brecht and his colleagues, continue the G-Men, do not blame themselves for this miserable failure; instead, they blame it on Americans' inability to conduct the theater profession. ". . . You know how plays are being put up in America," the FBI cites from one of Brecht's conversations on April 14, 1945; "it is all makeshift business." "Mrs. Brecht" complains bitterly that her husband is forced to work with "dilletants" (June 4, 1945). And in an exchange between "Mrs. Brecht and Man (Hanns?)," it simply says: "In London one of his things has been quite a success . . . But that is with these people in Hollywood, they are no real experts" (June 20, 1945).

The FBI's text continues more or less in this fashion. Charles Laughton, who during the summer of 1945 often called Brecht several times a day to talk about the production of *Galileo*, startles the sleepyheaded agents when he asks the left-leaning exile for advice on how to deal with a strike in the film studio ("Laughton to Brecht . . . He wanted to get some idea of what to do in case he was called to work . . ." [undated, around October 12, 1945]). Another time, the FBI takes notes when Laughton, Brecht, and Helene Weigel wonder aloud on the phone whether one Norman Cohen has the right political background for putting on *Galileo*: "Norman Cohen is a number one patriotic American . . . it takes away any sort of business of the church, of Brecht in Russia and everything . . . it means an absolutely clean bill of health" (August 23, 1945). And, finally, Laughton awakens the agents' interest when, after Brecht's death in August 1956, he worriedly asks whether it would be appropriate to send a sympathy telegram to East Berlin (Los Angeles, August 18, 1956).

Other recordings that J. Edgar Hoover's agency made regarding Brecht's artistic work are of a more sporadic nature. In one, Helene Weigel and Erna Budzislawski discuss the quality of a translation of the "Lied vom Weib und dem Soldaten" ("Ballad of the Wise Woman and the Soldier")—and the FBI listens closely because the poem mentions Russia (May 16 and May 18, 1945). When Brecht requests of an unknown person: "You are getting around quite a bit, and I want you to look out for poems, or ballads or songs in which you find some 'social note' expressed" (August 28, 1945), the special agents suspicously take notes. A fight between Brecht and his translator

Eric Bentley is immortalized on the records ("he refused to accept" [April 21, 1945]). And occasionally an FBI man smuggles a personal opinion into the dry transcripts: "Mrs. Brecht and Hanns discuss with German enthusiasm a poem from Klopstock . . ." (June 15, 1945).

But phone calls about political and literary themes, as indicated previously, play a subordinated role in the conversations that the FBI recorded in the Brecht household. By far the largest part of the now-public file is devoted to the author's private life; in this section, in turn, the most attention is given to his difficult relationship with Ruth Berlau, who lived in New York. For, as R.B. Hood, SAC, noted in various memoranda to the FBI director, the "immoral Association of Brecht with Ruth Berlau" (e.g., Los Angeles, February 24, 1948) could play an important role in initiating a deportation case against Brecht, who was suspected of being a "fellow traveler" of the Communists.

Brecht, who seemed to have no suspicion of either the surveillance or a possible deportation, had other problems to deal with anyway: torn between Berlau and his wife Helene Weigel, he tries to maintain as much freedom in each relationship as possible. This is why, in the summer of 1945, while staying as usual with Ruth Berlau after the performance of *The Private Life of the Master Race* in New York, he defers Weigel's repeated plea, "please, please, come soon . . ." (June 27, 1945). And when he is back in Santa Monica shortly thereafter and Ruth Berlau asks, in one of the secret midnight phone calls that particularly interested the FBI, "when are you coming," his irritated response is: "I do not know yet, I do not have the date yet . . ." (October 24, 1945).

But their next meeting is not the only subject of these long-distance calls between Los Angeles and New York. Brecht is also worried about Berlau's health, since after losing Brecht's child she is very weak both emotionally and physically. His concern is not, of course, without thought for himself: "And how is your health-condition? Is everything under control? And if I come, are you all right then? Or is there some trouble yet?" (October 24, 1945). Ruth Berlau, for her part, asks over the phone for a small part in Brecht's play—without receiving a clear answer: "I will have to think over it" (May 12, 1945). And imagine the impression that the FBI agent on duty (and his secretary, typing the notes) must have gotten of Brecht's relationship with his lover when listening to the following exchange: "Woman (Berlau) . . . I wrote yesterday a beautiful thing about you. Brecht. Certainly. I will write you, don't worry. But tell me, is everything all right . . . no trouble with . . . you get me . . . Ruth Berlau. No, nothing at all don't worry. Are you alone at home now? Brecht. Yes, Ute, I am alone in the house, don't worry" (October 3, 1945).

But, as we have learned from the release of the telephone transcripts and the now equally accessible dossier of the Los Angeles Field Office—which in comparison with Brecht's main file is much less blacked out—the secret agents' interest in Brecht's personal life did not end with their surveillance of the romantic whispers between Los Angeles and New York. Emotionlessly, an agent notes in his report to the immigration office that Helene Weigel, of all people, received the telephone message from the Cedar of Lebanon Hospital that Brecht's child with Ruth Berlau had died during labor. Shamelessly, special agents trained to catch dangerous criminals spend the late summer of 1944 perusing "Book No. 461 on 'deaths'" in the city health department's files, noting: "Berlau . . . was delivered of a seven and one-half month male child by Caesarian section, . . . child, one day old, . . . died September 4, 1944 . . . of . . . prematurity (asphyxia)." Berlau's loneliness in the days before the birth ("a few nights previously she had called police department for assistance") is coldly registered in the files, along with her fear of being exposed before the bureaucracy: "The alleged father, Mechel Berlau, was described as 39 years of age, born in Denmark, usual occupation soldier"; and "Berlau listed 'Mr. Brecht, Santa Monica 5-4943' as 'friend and husband'" (Los Angeles, June 30, 1945). And even the doctors who treated Ruth Berlau—according to the Cedar of Lebanon hospital files, which the FBI investigated as well—did not come away unscathed: "Dr. Gordon Rosenblum is known to have been a member of the Communist Party in recent years" (Los Angeles, May 20, 1946).

The FBI grows pettier still where Brecht and Berlau are concerned. For years, Hoover and his men have the Security-First National Bank in Santa Barbara inform them of all activity in Brecht's accounts, and they record, in dollars and cents, exactly when the writer sends just how much money to his lover: "Berlau . . . is payee of three checks drawn on Brecht account since 3/25/45 totaling $1100" (Los Angeles, June 30, 1945). Or: "Brecht's bank account reflects $500.00 check dated 7-12-45 payable to Ruth Berlau" (Los Angeles, October 24, 1945). The FBI is recording the conversation when Weigel, with gallows humor, complains to a female friend about her husband's affair with "that girl" and calls the whole thing "a piggishness" (April 24, 1945). And when a woman reports on the phone that Lou Eisler is "crazy about Ruth" and blames her, Helene Weigel, for the complications, Weigel listens—as the FBI remarks—"without showing much enthusiasm in the tale" (August 3, 1945).

Another aspect of the wiretapping of Brecht's telephone that still needs evaluating is a quantitatively negligible, but qualitatively relevant part of the surveillance, the part that deals with everyday life in exile, including the minor and not-so-minor rivalries and injured vanities among the writers and their wives who had fled Hitler. With tireless zeal, the FBI reports that Helene Weigel doesn't feel like wishing Lion Feuchtwanger a happy birthday ("Why? Well, there are reasons and reasons"). In the same conversation with an unknown woman, she admits to an antipathy for the Jews ("I do not care so much for them" [July 8, 1945]). An FBI agent's vigorous underlining emphasizes "Mrs. Brecht's" comment that her family has money in Switzerland (October 20, 1945), and that Brecht is looking for his daughter Hanna, "from his first marriage" (September 11, 1945), in Germany. "Marital trouble" seems to have been a constant topic of discussion among the exiles—now between Salka and Berthold Viertel ("he is a very unreliable character, . . . she is not to blame" [April 25, 1945]), now between Lou and Hanns Eisler ("you see it may be that Lou has plans for a divorce" [June 21, 1945]); and, throughout the whole period of surveillance, in the home of Maria and Ludwig Donath, until the FBI men are able to determine—no doubt breathing a sigh of relief—that at least the refrigerator orphaned by the break-up has found a new home with William Dieterle (July 26, 1945), the director of such romantic films as *Love Letters*. And when Helene Weigel comments on the press report that Gustav Gründgens (here spelled "Gruentchen,") has been castrated in a Danish prison camp, the FBI agent on duty—clearly oblivious of the significance this report has for the family of Brechts' close enemy Thomas Mann—emotionlessly records Weigel's conciliatory remarks: "Well, I think that all the people over there will have to clear themselves, but on the whole I think, from what I know, that the actors have been among the best and the most courageous against the Nazis" (June 24, 1945).

For one reason or another, the FBI abandoned the Gründgens case, even though this, too, was relevant to the rebuilding of German culture. On the other hand, the special agents—following the principle that secret services should initially note down every bit of information they receive—immortalize even the smallest triviality of the Brecht household in their wiretapping transcripts. The G-Men, highly trained at following bank robbers and kidnappers, listen carefully on April 18, 1945, at precisely 19:20, as two girls complain that their mothers won't let them go out any more; an hour later, at 20:20, they are still listening as the conversation, "girl to girl," turns to a lost lipstick (April 18, 1945). The connection between sunbathing, puritanism, and modernism is a leitmotiv in the Brecht file: "Mrs. Brecht . . . thinks that she is quite 'modern' doing such undressing stunts" (June 13, 1945). Other conversations deal with the Brechts' tuning of their "grand piano" (August 16, 1945), their lack of money for a new motor for their Dodge (October 6, 1945), and the fact—which no doubt pleased the special agent on duty—that they liked the FBI film "Dillinger, Public Enemy No. 1" (August 16, 1945). On May 13, the G-Men transcribe—word for word—a conversation in which a woman, probably Helene Weigel, berates her employee like a good capitalist: "I am not satisfied with the way you do your job . . . if you serve your clients, you have to serve them properly or else." Hoover's agents do not omit the fact that Mrs. Brecht uses her husband's absence, while staying in New York with Ruth Berlau, to give the linoleum in Brecht's room "a new gloss" (May 25, 1945). The saga of Helene Weigel's failed attempts to learn to drive is a recurring theme throughout the FBI file: "Mrs. Brecht says that she did not go in for the test for her driver's license. She does not quite trust herself, and as long as Brecht does not get bored trying to teach her, she would rather exercise a bit more" (August 17, 1945). Any gourmets among Brecht's researchers will appreciate the information that Weigel, known to be an excellent chef, calls an acquaintance at 10:15 am on August 26, 1945, and asks her to bring a salad to a potluck dinner "but not a Gurkensalat [cucumber salad], please" (August 26, 1945). With a variety of conversation partners, she not only exchanges uninhibited thoughts on the roast chicken mentioned above, but also (without any consideration for the agents, who are accustomed to American fast food) talks about "Potato-goulash," (June 20, 1945) "boysenberry tart" (June 30,1945) and preserving apricots (July 14, 1945)—not to mention an order, shocking to puritan sensibilities, placed at the "liquor store" for "1 case of beer, wine, and soda" (October 3, 1945). Less clear is whether U.S. domestic security is compromised by the fact that "Helen Brecht," in a conversation with an unidentified man, shrilly calls Lou Eisler a "cow" (June 20, 1945), and that she rebukes Lion Feuchtwanger for always wanting to speak English to her on the phone (June 14, 1945). A careful review of the files confirms, however, that Hoover's men, whose job was to record, not interpret, the plain facts, remain neutral both in divorce cases and in discussions of cooking recipes.

The surveillance transcripts threaten to devolve into pure comedy when the FBI agents and translators are crossed by foreign languages, German culture, and their own recording technology. The Russian playwright Anton Chekhov becomes, phonetically, "C. Hekoff" (October 23, 1945). Formulations like "He has had a heavy time" (July 17, 1945) for "Er hatte eine schwere Zeit [He had a hard time]" and "It is out now" (May 1, 1945) for "Es ist jetzt aus [It is over now]" evoke Karl Heinrich Lübke's English. When Brecht begins a telephone conversation with "Grüß Gott," the translator wordily explains: "The south-German greeting before 'Heil Hittler' [!] was introduced was: 'let us Salute God', the emigrees still often use it among themselves" (August 6, 1945). At the bottom edge of the FBI photos of Brecht's house, as in bad detective films, we see the window frame of the car from which the agents took their pictures (Los Angeles, undated). On September 25, 1945, one of J. Edgar Hoover's men in Los Angeles concludes a recorded phone conversation with Hanns Eisler in a colleague's observation report: "On this date Brecht & wife in Brecht car, & Eisler & 2 men in 4T9909 were tailed by Cohid + Van Loon to Marquis Theatre, Melrose & Doheny where there was a special showing of a German color film entitled 'Lady of My Dreams'"

(September 5, 1945).[8] It is unclear whether the FBI men were allowed to watch the movie, presumably Maria Rökk's 1944 music film called *Die Frau meiner Träume*, or whether they had to wait outside for the five "subjects." The quest for an apartment near Brecht, one in which the complicated recording devices could be set up—in secret service jargon, a "technical plant"—is threatened with failure because the seekers only have $75 available for the monthly rent (Los Angeles, April 26, 1945). Entries in the file like "blank—defective needle" (October 2, 1945) or "can't completely understand because of interference" (September 16, 1945) indicate that even the FBI occasionally has technical problems. Long after Brecht had left the United States, the Los Angeles FBI office filed a "Complaint Form" from an informant. He reports that the buyer of Brecht's house complained about Brecht's insurance agent because the agent had defended the suspicious foreigner's "radical connections" (Los Angeles, February 18, 1948). And even in 1969, 22 years after Brecht's departure from the United States and 13 years after his death, special agents make a note in his file when the writer's name comes up at a meeting of the Students For a Democratic Society, or when one of his works is cited by an opponent of the Vietnam War (Los Angeles, March 17, 1969).

Enough of these details, though. Ultimately it is more important to ask whether, in a time as difficult as the months before and after the end of World War II, it was really worth recording and transcribing the phone conversations of a German exile who was practically unknown in the United States, and whose works found almost no resonance there. The answer, without hesitation, must be a resounding "Yes." For us—living after the dramatist in a time that is hardly less dark, flooded by the deluge of these and other secret-service files—the notes and summaries of the conversations in the Brecht household do not necessarily give an earth-shattering view into the life and work of the great playwright (unless we take the FBI's notes at face value). And the lengths to which the Los Angeles office went cannot have been much more useful to the decision makers in Washington. However, the special agents provide us with information that, in the style of reality shows like "Big Brother" and "Survivor," cannot be obtained any other way—information about the relationship between everyday life and politics in the exiles' colony in Los Angeles, and, for those who are interested in such things, information about the way America's famous secret service works and what its goals have been. Fifty years later, in my television documentary *Im Visier des FBI (In the FBI's Line of Sight)*, Elmer F. "Lindy" Linberg—who along with his colleague Ernest J. van Loon took part in the surveillance of German exiles—reminisces about this period: "Looking back, you could ask: Was it all worth it? I think so. Because we uncovered the Communist network in the USA. And the last proof that our work was meaningful is the collapse of the Soviet Union and the survival of our democracy."[9]

NOTES

1. The cover sheet of the Brecht file I obtained from the Freedom of Information Act Department in 1990 mentions 369 pages. James Lyon received "a total of 427 pages" from the FBI and was simultaneously informed that the file contained "about 1000" pages. (James Lyon, "Das FBI als Literaturhistoriker," *Akzente* 4 [1980]: 362). John Fuegi, *Brecht and Company. Sex, Politics, and the Making of the Modern Drama* (New York: Grove P, 1994). Page 426 refers to a "1,100-page Brecht FBI file," though without mentioning a source.
2. References to the main Bertolt Brecht file in the FBI field office in Los Angeles will hereafter be identified with the Zusatz "Los Angeles."
3. All references in the text are from the mostly chronologically ordered file compiled by the FBI office in Los Angeles during the course of Brecht's telephone surveillance.
4. "Was" is the FBI's internal shorthand for "with alias"; "R" stands for "Russian," since Brecht was shadowed as a communist.
5. See Alexander Stephan, *Im Visier des FBI. Deutsche Exilschriftsteller in den Akten amerikanischer Geheimdienste* (Stuttgart: Metzler, 1995, paperback ed. Berlin: Aufbau Taschenbuch Verlag, 1998, English translation New Haven: Yale UP, 2000).
6. See "Exilanten und der CIA," a German TV documentary (2002), and "Thomas Mann und der CIA," a German TV documentary (2002).
7. The legend that says Helene Weigel knew of the telephone surveillance, and that she made a mockery of FBI agents "by occasionally reading recipes out loud over the phone in Polish" (Werner Hecht, *Helene Weigel. Eine große Frau des 20. Jahrhunderts* [Frankfurt: Suhrkamp 2000], p. 307) cannot be confirmed by the files that have been released.
8. The name of the first FBI agent, given in a handwritten note, cannot be determined with certainty.
9. *Im Visier des FBI*, a film by Johannes Eglau und Alexander Stephan, ARD, 1995.

WORK CITED

Fuegi, John. *Brecht and Company. Sex, Politics, and the Making of the Modern Drama.* New York: Grove P, 1994.

Hecht, Werner. *Helene Weigel. Eine große Frau des 20. Jahrhunderts.* Frankfurt: Suhrkamp, 2000.

Lyon, James, "Das FBI als Literaturhistoriker," *Akzente* 4 (1980): 362–83.

Stephan, Alexander. *Im Visier des FBI. Deutsche Exilshriftsteller in den Akten amerikanischer Geheimdienste.* Stuttgart: Metzler, 1995; paperback ed. Berlin: Aufbau Taschenbuch Verlag, 1998; English translation New Haven: Yale UP, 2000.

CHAPTER 10

SOUR NOTES: HANNS EISLER AND THE FBI

JAMES WIERZBICKI

TO JUDGE FROM THE WAVES OF SCHOLARSHIP AND PERFORMANCES THAT marked the 1998 centennial of his birth, in his native Germany the composer Hanns Eisler is fast attaining the status of national hero. But in the United States, where he lived from 1937 until 1948, Eisler remains largely an enigma. Musicological treatment of Eisler throughout the West amounts to a brush-off. When interest in Eisler has been expressed, typically it has centered on the scores he wrote for Hollywood films and a theoretical book about film music that he coauthored with Theodor Adorno.[1] Beyond that, the standard "read" on Eisler is that he was once upon a time an adventurous musical modernist but then consigned himself to the sidelines when, in the mid-1920s, he espoused the idea that music is purposeless if it is directed only toward sophisticated ears. As rapidly as Eisler's music gained in aural simplicity, so it lost status in the minds of Western critics. More than a quarter-century ago, British musicologist David Blake concluded his *Grove Dictionary* article on Eisler with what amounts to an exhortation: "No composer has suffered more from the post-1945 cultural cold war. As the cross-currents between Eastern Europe and the west increase, a proper international assessment of his achievement *must* be made."[2] Blake's revised article for the 2000 *Grove* refers to the founding in 1994 of the International Hanns Eisler Society and the launching, in the same year, of a critical edition of Eisler's collected works. But these German projects, Blake writes, are simply "cause for optimism that a proper international assessment of his significance *can* be made."[3]

Notwithstanding the efforts of Eisler's champions, it likely will be years before American critics afford Eisler's music even a fraction of the attention, let alone respect, it has in Europe. In the meantime, however, Eisler will not suffer posthumously from lack of name recognition. Curiously—and perhaps unfortunately—his claim to fame is based not on his work as a composer but on his reputation as a suspected enemy of the American government.

The first item in the Federal Bureau of Investigation's 686-page file on Eisler is a memorandum (February 27, 1942) in which bureau director J. Edgar Hoover instructs the agent in charge of the New York office to determine if Eisler had ever been an employee of the Works Progress Administration or any other federal agency. Although the New York agent recommended that "no further action [be] contemplated," Hoover nevertheless ordered a six-year investigation that involved not just scrutiny of virtually all of Eisler's published writings but also an elaborate series of wiretaps, tails, and break-ins engineered to uncover incriminating evidence. The investigation was relentless but fruitless, yet Hoover pursued Eisler with what in retrospect seems a passion. Among the last items in the FBI's file is a communication (December 15, 1947) from the acting commissioner of the Immigration and Naturalization Service informing Hoover that Eisler and his wife, in advance of the conclusion of their deportation hearings, had decided to leave the United States of their own free will. Beneath the typed message is a scrawled note, in Hoover's hand, that says: "It certainly would be a travesty of justice to allow them to leave voluntarily."

There is no doubt that Eisler throughout his adult life was a Marxist. More than a mere sympathizer, in Berlin in the mid-1920s he participated enthusiastically in the labor movement, and he devoted considerable energy to the writing of workers' anthems and protest songs. His negative sentiments, however, were only antifascist, never anti-American. Although during the 1940s his brother Gerhardt was indeed an active member of the American Communist party,[4] Hanns Eisler during the same period led a remarkably nonpolitical life. During his California sojourn he associated comfortably with a left-leaning crowd that included Fritz Lang, Bertolt Brecht, Clifford Odets, Harold Clurman, Jean Renoir, Charles Chaplin, and Peter Lorre, but his purpose in Hollywood—as is documented by the FBI's file—was simply to earn a living.[5]

Hoover's FBI turned up not a shred of evidence to suggest that Eisler was a threat to American security, or even that he had ever been a card-carrying Communist. Yet for six years Eisler was the target of intense investigation, and his questioning in 1947 by the House Committee on Un-American Activities—simultaneous with the start of HUAC's purge of the motion picture industry[6]—was unusually prolonged and harsh.

The official reason for the hounding of Hanns Eisler was his alleged but never proven affiliation with the Communist party. Since Eisler was first and foremost a composer, however, one has to wonder if it was somehow his music that made him seem, to Hoover and the FBI, so dangerous. In a statement prepared in advance of his second HUAC hearing (September 24–26, 1947), Eisler summarized his compositional work over the previous seven years.[7] "These, gentlemen, are my activities in the United States," he wrote, "and I must suppose that these are what the Committee considers 'un-American.' Apparently you are not connoisseurs of music."[8] The remark was facetious, intended to suggest that HUAC was, in effect, barking up the wrong tree. But perhaps the remark was more accurate than Eisler realized.

Eisler as Composer

Clearly, Eisler was a busy composer during his American years. Just as clearly, he was a serious composer. The film scores, of course, were works for hire; they abound with craftsmanship but also with cliché, and on the whole their style is in keeping with the generic style of countless other composers who serviced narrative films during Hollywood's so-called classical period. Most of his concert works from the 1940s, however, are staunchly individualistic in expression as well as technique. And like certain passages in the film scores, most of them adhere to a methodology that in the context of the central decades of the twentieth century is fairly synonymous with musical modernism.

Born on July 6, 1898 in Leipzig, Eisler grew up in Vienna, where his father, Rudolf, an Austrian Jew who had earned his doctorate in philosophy in Leipzig, eked out a living as an editor and translator. Both parents were amateur musicians, and from early childhood Eisler immersed himself in music. He composed prolifically, but not until he was 20 years old did he have any formal lessons. After his discharge from the army in November 1918 he took lessons in composition with Karl Weigl at the New Vienna Conservatory.[9] His formative musical education began in the late summer of 1919, when he began private instruction with Arnold Schoenberg.

Schoenberg in 1919 was Vienna's most illustrious practitioner of musical Expressionism, a style that erupted simultaneous with the outbreak of World War I and that was characterized not just by extreme volatility but also by bold rejection of the so-called tonal system that had governed pitch relationships in European music for the previous three centuries. Frustrated with the chaos inherent in the deliberately atonal music he helped create, Schoenberg in the early 1920s invented a method known as serialism. Whereas tonal music involved linear melodic/harmonic movement from stasis to dissonance to resolution, and whereas atonal music favored a stream-of-consciousness flow of whatever pitch combinations might come to a composer's mind, serial music entailed the arrangement of all 12 pitches of the chromatic scale into a germinal row whose permutations—backward, forward, inverted, and so on—formed the substance of an entire work. As is evidenced by the obvious differences in affect between the post-1920 compositions of Schoenberg and his two most famous pupils—Alban Berg and Anton Webern—serialism was not a musical style but simply a means of organizing musical materials. While accommodating all the dynamic and sonic individuality a practitioner might muster, serialism at the same time allowed for abdication of certain subjective thought processes. Logical to the extreme and based to a large extent on precompositional decisions, serialism was an appealing haven for young composers who, like Eisler, might have felt overtaxed by their wartime outpourings of musical emotion.

As might be expected, in the early 1920s Eisler composed music that very much shows the influence of his mentor, which is to say that it is solid in design and dense in content. Quite unlike the consistently sober music of Schoenberg, however, Eisler's first published works[10] feature many moments of levity. Although based on the ordered unfolding of 12-note series, in their harmonic progressions they often allude to traditional syntax, and their rhythmic propulsion typically draws from the vernacular rhythms of jazz and other popular genres. A self-taught Expressionist who vented *Angst* with humor and later a well-trained serialist who referenced tradition in order to temper a rigorous new methodology, Eisler from the start was a composer who valued connection with his immediate audience over an imagined seat in some futuristic pantheon. But however "light" his music might have seemed during his years under Schoenberg's tutelage, it lightened up far more in the autumn of 1925 after Eisler accepted a teaching position at the Klindworth-Scharwenka Conservatory in Berlin.

Almost by definition, the Schoenbergian aesthetic was elitist: to actually hear the relationships between one form or another of a 12-tone series demanded phenomenal listening skills, but simply to appreciate why some composers might find it necessary to create music in the serial vein required a well-educated understanding of the history of nineteenth-century European art music and its relationship to economically fueled societal issues. That Eisler was antielitist at heart is evidenced by his involvement, while still in Vienna, with various workers' singing societies.[11] But after moving to Berlin, where his brother and sister had for several years been active communists, Eisler became a zealot. In 1926 he applied for membership in the German Communist party; that he was denied membership, as is documented by the FBI files, had simply to do with the fact that he failed to pay his dues on time. Also, as is documented by the FBI files, Eisler in 1926 began to write articles on music for the Communist periodical *Die Rote Fahne*. And he fairly threw himself into the creation of the creation of anthems, marching songs, and pieces for unaccompanied men's chorus that were not just overtly supportive of the proletariat in their texts but also self-consciously "accessible" in their musical content.[12]

Not surprisingly, this led to a break with Schoenberg, who accused Eisler of being disloyal to modernist musical ideals. In turn, Eisler accused Schoenberg of being esoteric and bourgeois.[13] In a bitterly rejective letter to his once-revered teacher, he wrote:

> Modern music bores me, it doesn't interest me, some of it I even hate and despise. Actually, I want nothing to do with what is "modern." As far as possible, I avoid hearing or reading it. (Sadly, I must also include my own works of recent years.) . . . Also, I understand nothing (except superficialities) of twelve-note technique and twelve-note music.[14]

Eisler, of course, understood a great deal about 12-note music, and despite his bravado he was not about to abandon either his serialist skills or his awareness of the melodic/harmonic possibilities that serialism afforded. And this led to a dilemma. On the one hand, Eisler had good reason to believe in his own potential as a serious composer in the serialist vein;[15] on the other hand, Eisler was in the throes of rebellion against the very system that allowed him his burgeoning success.

The exile from elitist musical circles and "the bourgeois concert business"[16] that Eisler experienced between 1926 and 1933 was self-imposed. The exile that began in January 1933 was of an entirely different sort. Eisler happened to be in Vienna, supervising the music for a production of Brecht's play *Die Mutter*, on the day that Germany's president assigned to Adolph Hitler the title Chancellor of the Reich. Well aware that his life was now in danger, the outspokenly antifascist Eisler wisely chose not to return to Berlin.

Before Hitler's rise to power, Eisler had twice—in 1930 and 1931—briefly visited the Soviet Union. After Hitler's installation as Chancellor, Eisler moved not east but, for the most part, west. Not until January 1938 would Eisler "settle in" to a teaching position at the New School for Social Research and what he hoped would be permanent residence in the United States. Before that, his odyssey took him to Prague, Paris, Amsterdam, and London (1933); to Copenhagen, Paris, and London (1934); to Strasbourg, London, Moscow, Prague, and—on two occasions—New York (1935);[17] to London, Barcelona, Amsterdam, Brussels, and Copenhagen (1936); and to Madrid, Copenhagen, and Prague (1937).

Even under the duress of traveling almost constantly and without a passport, Eisler managed to compose. His output from these years includes film scores and, as one might expect, music overtly supportive of the proletariat cause.[18] But it also includes concert works that suggest Eisler, now a refugee, was experiencing a change of heart regarding modernist musical techniques that just a few years earlier he had vociferously eschewed.

The op. 29 *Kleine Sinfonie* and the op. 30 *Suite No. 4 for Orchestra* that Eisler completed just before exiting Germany certainly show the hand of a serialist. More self-consciously serial, as is evidenced by the explanatory essay that accompanies it, is Eisler's 1934 *Prelude and Fugue on B-A-C-H*, op. 46, for string trio.[19] The op. 50 *Deutsche Sinfonie*—started in 1935 and completed in 1939—is composed entirely in what Blake calls "Eisler's distinctively tonal type of serialism."[20] Likewise for all nine of the *Chamber Cantatas* for voice and various accompanying ensembles that Eisler produced in 1937 and, from the same year, the *Two Sonnets* set to texts by Brecht; the serial writing in the *Sonnets* is especially rigorous, observes German biographer Jürgen Schebera, yet it is serial writing that "through its 'Eislerian' handling of materials speaks an utterly clear musical message."[21]

Eisler's rapprochement with serialism was hardly limited to his years of travel. It may be that the first major work Eisler composed upon his move to New York, the 1938 *String Quartet* (op. 75), is "fundamentally a linear piece: motivic, melodic, contrapuntal," but its pitch sequences are nonetheless intricately serial.[22] Also intricate in their deployment of serial lines are the 1938 *Five Orchestral Pieces*, the 1940 *Chamber Symphony* (op. 69), and the 1941 quintet titled *Fourteen Ways of Describing Rain* (op. 70); indeed, the quintet stands out as the most strictly organized piece in the entire Eisler catalog,[23] and perhaps this has something to do with the fact that it was a birthday tribute to Schoenberg.

The *Five Orchestral Pieces*, the *Chamber Symphony*, and the op. 70 quintet are works intended for the arguably "elitist" concert hall, yet all of them stem from impulses connected with the "populist" venue of the cinema.[24] Even in his scores for commercial Hollywood films Eisler occasionally used serial techniques, albeit "in an extremely clarified and transparent form."[25] And even in his most serious concert works Eisler managed to fill serialist prescriptions in ways that are likely to strike most listeners as easily comprehensible both aurally and emotionally. Regardless of its genre, the music from Eisler's American period demonstrates what a German writer recently described as "serialism with a human face."[26]

Eisler's willingness to bend the rules of serialism has doubtless contributed to the exclusion of his music from the twentieth-century modernist canon. But Eisler's idiosyncratically "humanistic" use of serialist techniques positions his music at a peculiar ideological cusp. With communication to a nonelitist audience as one of its primary goals, the entire body of Eisler's serial music represents "a mediation of the most heterogeneous elements," a combination of "the most esoteric avant-garde of music . . . and the most exoteric avant-garde of politics."[27] And this persistent dialectic suggests that Eisler was hardly the marginal figure that most American historians of musical modernism make him out to be.

It has convincingly been argued that, with his enduring "search for freedom and balance within well-defined but purposefully limited boundaries of serial organization," Eisler vis-à-vis Schoenberg actually took "quite a progressive stance."[28] Eisler's stance seems even more progressive when his serial music is interpreted through a political filter. Writing in 1958, German musicologist Harry Goldschmidt observed that Eisler rarely identified himself with serialism the way Schoenberg, Berg, and Webern did, and that when Eisler employed serial techniques it was almost always to serve the purpose of social criticism. In the most substantial of Eisler's modernist compositions, Goldschmidt argues, "the extreme tensions of blind subjectivism are objectified, the sparks directed not towards the self but towards the real and bloodily actual enemy—fascism."[29]

THE EARLY INVESTIGATION

As noted, the FBI's file on Eisler begins with a memo from February 1942, but it quickly grows retrospective. After referring to Walter Steele's testimony before "the Dies Committee"[30] to the effect that recordings of Eisler's songs amounted to "subversive propaganda," the memo cites a report from January 1941 in which an unidentified informant claims that "in addition to his radical tie-ups Eisler was known in Germany as having actual Communist connections." Reaching back still further, the memo notes that in June 1940 a different informant alerted the bureau's New York office that Eisler was the brother of someone known as "Edwards," allegedly the American representative of the Communist Party, and that "Eisler came to the United States not primarily to compose music but to conduct G.P.U. activities."[31] Following Hoover's instructions to discover whether or not Eisler had ever been a federal employee, the New York agent answered in the negative and suggested that further investigation was not necessary. By April 1942, however, Hoover was ordering a thorough check, "under an Internal Security Classification," on the status of Eisler's visa.

The first extensive memorandum was filed on December 10, 1942. Among other things, it noted that Eisler "was known in Germany as having active Communistic tendencies," that in 1939 Eisler had been "a member of the Executive Board of [the] Theater Arts Committee of New York, which organization is now extinct but at that time is alleged to have been Communist controlled," and that in 1936 Eisler was "one of the most prominent drawing cards for the Communist inspired musical schools [in New York], . . . the purpose of these schools [being] to instruct revolutionaries musically inclined."[32]

The information Hoover had officially requested did not surface until four months later, in the form of an "Alien Enemy Control" report that begins with details on Eisler's various comings and goings. Significantly, the report includes a memo from the Immigration and Naturalization Service (INS) office in San Antonio explaining that, because the "stateless" Eisler entered the United States from Mexico without a passport, "the subject's presence in the United States after January 28, 1940, was illegal"; in March of 1940, the INS memo states, Eisler and his wife were ordered to leave the United States, and after their request for an extension of their limited visas was denied "the aliens were expected to depart via Miami, Florida on March 29, 1940, by boat to Cuba." Along with that potentially damning information, the Alien Enemy Control report gives Eisler's current address in California, and then offers a detailed synopsis of the Brecht-Dudow play *Die Massnahme* for which Eisler supplied music in 1930. The report notes that Eisler and Brecht were coauthors of the "Song of Solidarity," a march that "was adopted, with the permission of Brecht and Subject, as the song of the Communist youth organization in Germany prior to Hitler's rise to power." In the section labeled "undeveloped leads," the report states that the bureau's Los Angeles office will try to determine "whether Subject has violated provisions of the act requiring enemy aliens to register." Then, in an appendix that demonstrates the FBI's extraordinary industry, the report concludes with a translation of *Die Massnahme* that runs to 20 pages of single-spaced typing.

A memo dated May 5, 1943 reports that during interviews with the INS Eisler declared both that he was not a Communist and that he believed the United States form of government to be superior to that of the Soviet Union. The same memo notes that the INS has in its "very voluminous file" on Eisler a 1936 letter to the Secretary of Labor in which J.E. Wilkie, a representative of the Arizona Peace Officer's Association, argues that the "revolutionary and propagandical nature" of Eisler's concert tour is "sufficiently detrimental to our already steadily menaced peace and tranquility to warrant his expulsion from this country." Referring specifically to a June 10, 1938 interview with INS agents, the memo states:

> In direct answer to the question, "Have any of your compositions been used in connection with political or patriotic songs," he answered "In Germany, I wrote songs which were anti-Nazi in character. I am a refugee." He was asked if those songs were Communistic in character, and he answered "No, in character only against Nazi Germany."

Apropos of the INS's concerns over Eisler's status as an alien, the memo notes that on July 17, 1940 a warrant for Eisler's arrest had indeed been issued and that five months later the warrant was cancelled. "There is no other information on file at Ellis Island," the memo states, "which would explain why the subject and his wife are now legally in the United States."

The first evidence of the FBI's close scrutiny of Eisler's personal activities appears in an Alien Enemy Report dated May 18, 1943. Along with lengthy summaries of previously disclosed information that are typical of FBI memoranda, the report notes that "mail cover discloses Subject in contact with Gerhardt Eisler, . . . known contact of Otto Katz, alleged OGPU Agent in Mexico City."[33] More tellingly, the report states that "a surveillance was placed on the activities of Subject" and it was found that on a particular evening "Subject left his home . . . at about 9:00 p.m., and proceeded in a 1939 Chevrolet sedan, license number 9 × 5100, to the home of Oscar Homalka, 10788 Bellagic Road, Bel Air. At this address the following license numbers were obtained, and a check with the Motor Vehicles Department disclosed that the cars in question are registered to the following persons." In the once-secret file that is now available to the public, the names of the car owners have been deleted, but the license plate numbers remain plainly visible.

Concluding that Gerhardt Eisler was indeed the mysterious "Edwards," Hoover on August 4, 1943 requested that the United States Attorney General "authorize the installation of a technical surveillance on the residence of Hanns Eisler in Santa Monica, California, for the purpose of determining the extent of his activities in connection with the Comintern Apparatus and for the additional purpose of identifying members of the Apparatus, particularly those who are espionage agents."

Like the mail cover, the wiretap yielded nothing. Accordingly, the FBI's Los Angeles office on September 13, 1943 advised Hoover that

> the information presently available against the subject . . ., although undoubtedly indicative of revolutionary tendencies, is about the same as that developed in the case entitled "Bertolt Brecht" . . . . A short time ago, with the Bureau's approval, the Brecht case was presented to the United States Attorney in Los Angeles, who referred it to the Department for an opinion. The Department, at that time, declined authorization of a Presidential warrant for Brecht's arrest as a dangerous alien enemy, and there therefore appears to be no reason for referring a similar set of facts pertaining to Eisler to the United States Attorney at this time.

On the same day, the head of the Los Angeles office reported that "investigation conducted to determine whether the subject should have registered as an alien enemy has failed to disclose a violation of this nature," and that "a review of the file in this case disclosed that all leads set out for other field divisions have been covered." The agent acknowledged that Eisler's alleged subversive activities warranted further attention. As far as the immigration matter was concerned, however, the Los Angeles office informed Hoover that "this case is . . . being closed herewith."

Two weeks later Hoover was informed by a higher authority that Eisler was in no way prosecutable. A memo dated September 28, 1943 reports that "Assistant United States Attorney John M. Gault, having considered the facts in this case, advised that no request would be made for a presidential warrant for subject's arrest as a dangerous alien enemy." According to the memo, Gault considered the case against Eisler to be virtually identical to the case against Brecht. As with Brecht, Gault said, it was determined that Eisler held beliefs that "seem to be anti-Nazi and anti-Fascist and he is therefore not considered a danger to the war effort of this country."

Preparing for HUAC

The files covering the next three years are few and vague. A memorandum from September 1946, however, indicates a seriously renewed interest in Eisler. "This case is being reopened," it states at the outset, "to report information received from Confidential Informant T-1, on May 30 and August 13, 1945, concerning the personal effects maintained by Hanns Eisler in his residence, which was at that time 889 South Amalfi Drive, Pacific Palisades, California." The 78-page memorandum begins with an account of Eisler's birth certificate, various travel documents that Eisler had acquired since 1933, and a letter showing that Eisler had registered with the United States draft board. It continues with summaries of a "rough draft typewritten document" titled "Life History" and an entry on Eisler from the 1942 edition of *Current Biography*. After giving a list of Eisler's compositions, the report focuses on a scrapbook that contains newspaper articles about Eisler, the earliest of which were published in Moscow in July 1935. One, which appeared in English in the *Moscow Daily News*, is simply paraphrased; another, from the journal *Soviet Art*, is represented by extensive quotations from a specially commissioned translation. "This article, together with the following articles," writes the reporting agent, "will be treated in considerable detail herein, inasmuch as they reflect Eisler's revolutionary character and affiliation with Communism."

The other articles treated in detail are from *Pravda, Evening Moscow*, and *Literary Gazette*, all offered in translations from the original Russian. In the FBI memoranda, proper names are generally given entirely in uppercase letters; among the names so transcribed in various of these Russian-language articles are those of Aaron Copland, Henry Cowell, Leopold Stokowski, Wallingford Riegger, and Nicholas Slonimsky, all of whom Eisler has identified as American musicians who are in "a progressive mood" and/or have "a tendency to unite with the labor movement." One of the articles, the reporting agent points out, even quotes Eisler as saying that "the old composer Arnold Schoenberg, an honest, reactionary-thinking master, . . . has now rather naively admitted [that] 'Communism as a method must be tried.'"

In its "undeveloped leads" section, the memorandum notes that some of the letters written in German have yet to be translated. In a memo dated August 29, 1946—a few weeks after the second break-in—an agent reports that "under separate cover there is being transmitted to the Bureau for translation a large number of photographic reproductions of German language letters obtained from a confidential source from the residence of the above captioned individual." The dozen or so pages that come next in the FBI file bear no dates, but they offer summaries and complete translations of the letters that for the most part amount to what the writer of the September memorandum had described as "personal chatter."

Up to this point, the FBI's investigation of Eisler is remarkably free of judgment. The memoranda teem with innuendo, of course, but they contain no definitive statements as to Eisler's complicity in anything resembling criminal behavior. The most solid evidence the FBI had been able to gather concerned apparent irregularities involving Eisler's entrance into the United States from Mexico on a nonquota immigrant visa in 1939, but this matter had been dropped after the INS made it clear that it no longer had a problem with Eisler. That the FBI very much *wanted* to draw conclusions becomes apparent in a series of memoranda that starts early in 1947. A memo to Hoover dated February 27, 1947, from D.K. Ladd, head of the Los Angeles office, summarizes the investigation to date and makes reference to the recent testimony before HUAC of Ruth Fischer, who "identified her brother Gerhardt [Eisler] as a comintern agent in the United States and as a 'dangerous terrorist'" and who also "identified her brother Hanns Eisler as a music composer in Hollywood who is a Communist and whom she also described as 'dangerous.'" Bearing the same date, a shorter memo from Ladd tells Hoover that "the Bureau's investigation has identified Hanns Eisler with many individuals who are known Communists and who are known to be in contact with Soviet Intelligence agents in the United States" and that by means of the examination of documents found in Eisler's home "Eisler's reputation as a composer of Communist songs and as a writer for Russian periodicals [has been] established."

A series of brief memos in late March 1947 review the details of Eisler's activities from 1939–1940 and outline a strategy for interviewing Eisler in light of the Congressional review that his brother was undergoing. A memo dated April 10, 1947 summarizes an interview in which Hedwig Massing, Gerhardt Eisler's first wife, stated that although Hanns Eisler was "very weak politically" and "strongly dominated by his brother," he often seemed "quite anti-Soviet in his opinions." On May 29, 1947 a memo informed Hoover that "Hanns Eisler is believed to be going to Washington, D.C., as a possible witness for his brother, Gerhardt Eisler, whose trial for contempt is scheduled for June 4, 1947, in Washington. Hanns Eisler is also scheduled as a witness before the House Committee on Un-American Activities on June 16, 1947."

In preparation for Eisler's appearances before HUAC, the FBI examined Eisler's account at the Westwood Branch of Bank of America and prepared a list of all the deposits made and checks written between February and April of 1947. The FBI also prepared a list of the license plate numbers of all the cars that had parked outside Eisler's home between February and May of 1947 and a list of all the telephone calls Eisler made from his home between December 11, 1946 and March 10, 1947. According to a memo that bears no date but which apparently was written in April 1947, an agent in the Los Angeles office informed Hoover that Eisler's residence would as soon as possible be subjected to a "trash cover."

Eisler's appearance before HUAC was postponed because its chairman, J. Parnell Thomas (R-New Jersey), was "tied up in court cases," a July 9, 1947 memo notes. On July 10, 1947 the FBI launched "an intensive investigation, including checks of all hotels," in an effort to locate Eisler. The next day, doubtless to the FBI's chagrin, Ruth Fischer told reporters that "it was her opinion that Hanns skipped to Mexico." Later that day, however, a memo informed Hoover that "chairman Thomas had received a long wire from Los Angeles marked at 4:11 a.m., signed Hanns Eisler, in which he indicated he would be available for hearing on September 23." An interoffice memorandum from L.B. Nichols to Clyde Tolson (September 6, 1947) contains a summary of the information the FBI intended to deliver to Thomas in advance of Eisler's HUAC hearing. Presumably referring to surveillance that might have been deemed to be illegal, Nichols writes: "I believe we have deleted all material which might be embarrassing to the Bureau."

EISLER AS WRITER

As the package for HUAC's Thomas was being prepared, the FBI began to express a keen interest in Eisler's literary output. Along with photocopies of various newspaper articles concerning Eisler, the September 6 memorandum contains translations of two articles that Eisler had written for Soviet periodicals in 1935. "Hanns Eisler Narrates" (*Evening Moscow* June 27, 1935) is an autobiographical account of Eisler's travels since leaving Germany early in 1933. Probably more significant in the eyes of the FBI was Eisler's "Annihilation of Art" (*Soviet Art* July 29, 1935), an essay that explores the relationship between fascism and music of all sorts.[34] In a brief passage regarding musical modernism, the essay suggests that Marxist "materialism" is implicit in the rigorous methodology of serialism and that serial music, because of its theoretical underpinnings, is antithetical to fascism.

Its appetite whetted, the FBI searched eagerly for original versions of the Eisler writings whose translated content had been summarized in the memos following the break-ins that had occurred more than two years earlier. On October 7, 1947 the New York office sent an "urgent" telegram to headquarters advising that a copy of the July 18, 1935 issue of the *Moscow Daily News* had been located in the New York Public Library; in regard to certain other publications that were being sought, the wire says, these might be available "under a Russian name" in the "Library's Slavonic Division, which closes at six p.m." The next day another "urgent" telegram from New York to the Washington and Boston offices advised that photocopies of articles from the *Moscow Daily News* and the *Literary Gazette* had been obtained and were being forward to FBI headquarters. The requested copies of *Evening Moscow* and *Soviet Art* could not be located, but the agent offered a plan for finding these sources and reading them without arousing suspicion. He wrote: "Library Harvard Univ. suggested as possible source. Also suggested possible American-Russian Institute Library has these copies which could be viewed under pretext."

A memorandum from New York (October 9, 1947) advises headquarters that the San Francisco and Chicago offices had been asked to join the search. But this is preceded by an "urgent" telegram from Hoover that informs the FBI's entire communications section as to the Russian names of the *Literary Gazette*, *Soviet Art*, and *Evening Moscow* (*Literaturnaia Gazeta*, *Sovyetskoe Iskusstvo*, and *Vechernaia Moskva*); Hoover requests that copies be forwarded immediately, and recommends that searches be conducted at the Harvard Library, the Hoover Memorial Library in San Francisco, and at the Newberry and John Cerar Libraries in Chicago. A subsequent wire from the Chicago office to Hoover (October 10, 1947) reports that after searches at the Newberry and Cerar libraries, the Library of International Relations, the University of Chicago's Harper Memorial Library, and the University of Chicago's Art Library, the July 27, 1935 issue of *Evening Moscow* and the July 20, 1935 issue of *Soviet Art* still could not be found. A follow-up wire from the Boston office adds that a search of Harvard University's Widner Library also yielded nothing.

On November 3, 1947 Hoover informed the executive assistant to the Attorney General that all the material "contained in foreign publications reflecting Eisler's revolutionary and political activity . . . has been located and is presently being translated." Included in the memorandum is a photocopy and translation of a brief biographical entry on Eisler from the 1933 *Great Soviet Encyclopedia* and a photocopy of a lengthy essay by Eisler ("History of the German Workers' Movement from 1848") published in 1935 in a

New York-based journal called *Musical Vanguard: A Critical Review*, a journal that Hoover says "has been identified as a Communist publication."[35] The memorandum also includes a photocopy of Eisler's "Fantasia in G-Men," the statement that Eisler prepared in advance of his September 1947 HUAC appearances and which subsequently appeared as an article in *New Masses*.[36]

Translations of the Russian articles that the FBI worked so hard to obtain finally circulated in a memorandum dated November 12, 1947. Contrary to information supplied earlier by a field agent, the June 30, 1935 piece in the *Literary Gazette* is titled not simply "Hanns Eisler" but "With Hanns Eisler," and it is an interview conducted by a writer identified only as "Delman." The other article, from the June 29, 1935 issue of *Soviet Art*, is titled "Hanns Eisler in Moscow"; in essence it is the same autobiographical account (from the June 27, 1935 issue of *Evening Moscow*) to which the FBI had access when it began its intensive bibliographical research project.

The much sought-after Russian articles, in other words, contained nothing that the FBI did not already know. In what in retrospect seems a frantic search for incriminating evidence, Hoover's agents wasted countless man-hours in pursuit of foreign-language publications whose content in essence had long been in their files. The hunt proved useless in more ways than one, for by the time the articles were located and translated it was too late for their content to matter.

Leaving the United States

Eisler's first HUAC appearance, before a subcommittee in Los Angeles, took place on May 12, 1947; a second appearance, before the full committee in Washington, D.C., took place September 24–26, 1947. While neither hearing yielded incriminating evidence, a memo from the Washington field office (November 19, 1947) notified Hoover that the Attorney General's office was receiving "letters and petitions . . . protesting the deportation proceedings against Eisler." According to the memo, among those who publicly defended Eisler were such prominent musicians as conductor Dimitri Mitropoulos (at the time music director of the Minneapolis Symphony Orchestra) and composers Ernst Toch, Roy Harris, and Aaron Copland.[37]

Hoover advised the FBI's Los Angeles office (November 29, 1947) that an INS hearing for Eisler and his wife was scheduled for January 15, 1948. Acknowledging that "active investigation" was no longer required, on December 3, 1947 Hoover ordered that "spot surveillance" on Eisler should nevertheless be maintained. Twelve days later Hoover was informed by the INS that Eisler—through his attorney, Carol King—was making arrangements to travel to France. At the bottom of this memo Hoover scrawled the "travesty of justice" remark cited earlier in this essay.

It is hard to believe that at this point the FBI still had anything to learn in regard to Eisler, yet a memorandum dated December 6, 1947 includes "facts hitherto unknown to the Bureau" that were disclosed by Eisler in his September 24–26, HUAC hearings. The new information includes details about Eisler's travels in Europe between 1929 and 1936, exact titles of songs Eisler had written over the years, titles for all the films Eisler had scored both in Europe and in Hollywood, and the fact that Eisler had once been "employed by the Department of Agriculture for the purpose of making a short film, the date and title not having been known."[38]

Media coverage of Eisler's hearings was intense, and by early December 1947 it was common knowledge that Eisler intended to leave the United States as soon as possible. Not known to the public was the opinion of the INS, "leaked" to an SAC in New York and communicated to Hoover in a letter dated December 13, 1947, that Eisler "would not attempt to depart illegally" and that "the case against [Eisler] . . . was extremely weak."

In his HUAC hearings, Eisler admitted that in 1926 he applied for membership in the Communist Party but denied that he had ever actually been a member of the party. On February 4, 1948 Hoover was informed by telegram that, according to sources within the INS, "Eisler has indicated willingness to execute stipulation admitting his CP membership for purpose of expediting deportation proceedings." The telegram, from the FBI's New York office, alerted Hoover that the "approval of stipulation by Atty. Gen. will greatly simplify govt.'s case, as other evidence in support of deportation proceedings is not strong." Two days later another telegram notified Hoover that INS authorities had indicated that Eisler would be allowed to leave. A telegram dated February 12, 1947 advised Hoover: "Warrant of deportation issued today by INS for Hanns Eisler, which will permit him to depart voluntarily."

Up to this point the United States Central Intelligence Agency (CIA) had not at all been involved in the Eisler case. On February 19, 1948, however, Hoover wrote to CIA director Roscoe Henry Hillenkoetter and informed him that a warrant of deportation against Eisler had been issued "following allegations that he was a member of an organization advocating the overthrow of this government by force and violence." The letter cites Eisler's plans, as reported in the *New York Times* on February 13, 1948, to fly to Paris to score *Alice in Wonderland* and then to Rome to score *Galileo* and *Christ in Concrete*.[39] Hoover's letter to Hillenkoetter includes a physical description of Eisler and a note that two photographs are enclosed. It ends with the statement: "This information is being furnished should you desire to follow the activities of [Eisler] in Europe."

After this, a series of memos describe various travel arrangements that Eisler and his wife had apparently made but canceled. A teletype dated

March 24, 1948 advises Hoover that Eisler was now scheduled to depart—not for Paris or Rome but for Vienna, via London and Prague—two days hence. On March 26, 1948, Hoover received a teletype confirming that Eisler had indeed left the United States, and on April 2, 1948 Hoover informed the director of the CIA that Eisler had arrived in Prague.[40]

Conclusions

It seems reasonable to assume that at some point during the FBI's investigation agents would have been assigned to attend concerts that featured Eisler's chamber music or orchestral works, to listen to the commercially available recordings of his protest songs, and to watch the films for which Eisler composed scores. Yet the file contains no mention of representatives of the FBI serving as audience members or as music critics. The only passages that might be described as "review-like" deal exclusively with verbal materials (the lyrics of songs, the text of *Die Massnahme*, various essays), and these take the form of studiously nonanalytic summaries. Clearly, an agent's job was to report on a subject's activity, not to interpret it. If Hoover or anyone else in the FBI actually passed aesthetic judgment on Eisler's music, they kept it to themselves. This is not to say, however, that the FBI was indifferent to the fact that Eisler was a composer.

The most curious section of the voluminous file is the part that documents the FBI's all-out search, in the weeks surrounding Eisler's second HUAC hearing, for materials that had appeared in 1935 in specific Soviet publications. The investigation thus far had turned up nothing but innuendo and allegation, and at this point it was almost a certainty that Eisler would soon voluntarily leave the United States. Why, at this late stage of the game, was it so important for the FBI to locate articles that Eisler had written more than a dozen years earlier?

Until it found them and had them translated, of course, the FBI was unaware that the elusive articles contained nothing that in essence was not already in the file. All the FBI knew was that the articles were either by Eisler or about him. Based on its experience with Eisler-related literature from the mid-1930s that had already been examined, the FBI would have been correct to presume that the sought-after material contained strong expressions of opinion. The FBI would have been correct, as well, to presume that Eisler's opinions had to do not just with European politics but also with the relationship between politics and music.

Reference has been made to German musicologist Harry Goldschmidt's view that all of Eisler's serial compositions are in effect exercises in social criticism, the target of which is fascism. If Goldschmidt is on the mark, the political message borne by Eisler's post-1933 modernist works is far more subtle than that carried by his musically conservative Kampflieder and scores for Brechtian theatrical productions.

Eisler never articulated the "modern music as social criticism" theory as clearly as Goldschmidt did, but it is likely that even early in his career he would have subscribed to it. As early as 1935, in the Russian-language "Annihilation of Art" essay mentioned above, Eisler attempted to formulate the idea that certain forms of modernist music—not so much because of the way the music sounds as because of its "materialistic" content and structure—are by definition antifascist. The idea was explored, although not refined, in other Eisler writings from 1935,[41] and to a certain extent it sustained itself well into Eisler's American period. In an unpublished typescript from 1944, Eisler wrote:

> We musicians are apt to consider our art as something a little apart from life and its crises. But on the other hand music is extremely sensitive to all social trends. When fascism first touched German music, German musicians found it difficult to understand this contradiction. If Flaubert for instance could write and publish "L'education sentimentale" under Napoleon III, why couldn't a modern German composer continue to write chamber music under Hitler?
>
> There is a reason: fascism, more organized and brutal than everything Napoleon III could imagine, cannot afford even the slightest dissonance in [its] artificial harmony—or a breath of opposition even in the most abstract and remote arts and sciences. Everything is controlled. Physics, mathematics, even the art of landscape or still-life painting are observed as being potentially dangerous.[42]

Eisler makes the claim that the serialist music of his teacher, Arnold Schoenberg, is especially despised by fascists because it "reflects the complexity and crisis of our times" and because "everything fought for by the Nazis—enthusiasm for their imperialistic goals, devotion to their leader, conformity to their way of life—[is] challenged by the work of Schoenberg." He paraphrases "rules" set out in 1942 by Joseph Goebbels, the Nazi minister for propaganda, to the effect that "no art for art's sake, no individual choice of subject" is acceptable. "According to such standards," Eisler writes, "modern music became the enemy of fascism."[43]

In the early 1940s the United States was engaged in a fight-to-the-finish with Nazi Germany, and it is unlikely that the FBI or any other American agency would have identified itself with fascism. But what if the offensive "f-word" were euphemized, translated into something along the lines of "control of potential subversives" for the patriotic purpose of "maintaining a way of life" that had been predetermined to be unassailably virtuous? If modernist music for the reasons Eisler offers could be the enemy of an overtly fascist regime, could not the same modernist music also be the enemy of a democracy whose attitude toward dissidents was somehow repressive?

If Eisler's modernist compositions are indeed essays in social criticism, doubtless their potent yet ineffable point was sensed by at least some of the listeners who made up Eisler's American audiences in the 1940s. As to whether the point was sensed as well by the professional investigators to whom "secret messages" of any sort were of more than a little interest, one can only wonder. But surely it occurred to Hoover that whatever Eisler had to say about modernist music vis-à-vis Nazi Germany applied as well to modernist music in the United States during and after World War II. And this thought likely would have been bothersome, even if Hoover and the FBI—like the members of HUAC—were "not connoisseurs of music."

Notes

1. *Composing for the Films* (London: Oxford UP, 1947). When the book was first published only Eisler was listed as an author. In a postscript for the 1969 German edition (*Komposition für den Filmen*), Adorno explains that he withdrew his name because he "did not seek to become a martyr" in "the [political] scandal" in which Eisler, in 1947, was involved. See *Composing for the Films*, revised edition (Freeport, NY: Books for Libraries P, 1971), p. 167.
2. David Blake, "Eisler, Hanns," in Stanley Sadie, ed., *The New Grove Dictionary of Music and Musicians Vol. VI* (London: Macmillan, 1980), p. 91. Emphasis added.
3. David Blake, "Eisler, Hanns," in Stanley Sadie, ed., *The New Grove Dictionary of Music and Musicians Vol. VII*, 2nd ed. (London: Macmillan, 2000), p. 39. Emphasis added.
4. Gerhardt Eisler's only imprisonment in the United States, early in 1948, stemmed from charges of contempt of Congress after he refused to cooperate with the House Committee on Un-American Activities; deportation proceedings against him in the same year were based on his allegedly giving contradictory testimony before HUAC. Although charges of espionage were never brought against him, it was nevertheless assumed by many anti-Communists that Gerhardt Eisler was a Soviet agent. Indeed, a character named "Gerhardt Eisler" figures as the chief villain in the 1951 film *I Was a Communist for the FBI.*
5. The Hollywood feature films for which Eisler provided music are *Hangmen Also Die* (1942), *None But the Lonely Heart* (1944), *Jealousy* (1945), *The Spanish Main* (1945), *A Scandal in Paris* (1946), *Deadline at Dawn* (1946), *Woman on the Beach* (1947), and *So Well Remembered* (1947). Most of these are middle-of-the-road genre pieces, but the first two—in keeping with the spirit of the times—feature screenplays strongly supportive of the Allies' war effort.
6. In an attempt to ferret out Hollywood insiders of leftist persuasion, HUAC in 1947 interviewed more than 40 persons involved with filmmaking. Of the 19 persons named as suspected leftists, 10 (Alvah Bessie, Herbert Biberman,

Lester Cole, Edward Dmytryk, Ring Lardner Jr., John Howard Lawson, Albert Maltz, Samuel Ornitz, Adrian Scott, and Dalton Trumbo) famously refused to cooperate with HUAC and served prison sentences for contempt. Under HUAC pressure, the others identified dozens of their colleagues, and the result was the Hollywood "blacklist" that endured well into the 1950s. There is no evidence to suggest that Eisler was ever questioned about the political leanings of his Hollywood colleagues or that any of HUAC's "friendly witnesses" ever pointed an accusatory finger in his direction.

7. Along with the film scores, the works include a chamber symphony (op. 69), a septet (op. 92a), and a quintet titled *Fourteen Ways of Describing Rain* (op. 70) from 1940; a nonet, a set of piano variations, and a group of 20 songs for female or children's chorus (the *Woodbury-Liederbüchlein*) from 1941; a set of 8 songs (the *Hollywood Elegies*), with texts by Brecht and himself, from 1942; the Piano Sonata No. 3 and settings for voice and piano of texts by Mörike (the *Anakreontische Fragmente*), Brecht (*Gedichte im Exil, Die Mutter, Das deutsche Miserere*, and *Vom Sprengen des Gartens*), Eichendorff (*Auf der Heimat hinter den Blitzen rot*), and Hölderlin (the *Hölderlin-Fragmente*) from 1943; incidental music for Brecht's *Furcht und Elend des dritten Reiches* from 1945; settings for voice and orchestra of texts by Brecht (*Die Gesichte der Simone Machard*) and Goethe (*Glückliche Fahrt*) from 1946; and a septet from 1947.
8. Eisler was not allowed to read his statement at the hearing. Under the title "Fantasia in G-Men," the document was published in the October 14, 1947 issue of *New Masses*; one month later it appeared in German translation in Vienna's *Tagebuch*. The statement is available in *Hanns Eisler: A Rebel in Music: Selected Writings*, ed. Manfred Grabs (London: Kahn & Averill, 1978), pp. 150–52, and in *Hanns Eisler: Musik und Politik Schriften: 1924–1948* (Leipzig: Deutscher Verlag für Musik, 1983), pp. 521–23.
9. Eisler spent two years of World War I in a Hungarian regiment. After being injured on the battlefield, he recuperated first in a field hospital and then in a convalescent facility near Vienna.
10. These include the op. 1 Piano Sonata (1923), the op. 2 set of 6 songs with texts by Japanese poets, the op. 3 Piano Pieces, and the op. 4 Divertimento for wind quintet, all from 1923.
11. Specifically, the Karl Liebknecht Gesangverein and the Stahlklang Chorvereinigung.
12. Among the best known of Eisler's proletariat songs, popular not just in Germany but throughout Europe, are "Der heimliche Aufmarsch," "Kominternlied," "Solidaritätslied," and "Stempellied."
13. As late as 1935 Eisler would write, in an article for a New York newspaper, that he considered Schoenberg to be "the greatest modern bourgeois composer. If the bourgeoisie do not like his music that is regrettable, for they have no better composer." Hanns Eisler, "On Schönberg," *The New Masses*, 14 (February 26, 1935). Reprinted in *Hanns Eisler: A Rebel in Music: Selected Writings*, ed. Manfred Grabs (London: Kahn & Averill, 1999), p. 75.

14. Undated letter from Eisler to Schoenberg, presumably written before March 10, 1926. Quoted in Eberhardt Klemm, "'I Don't Give a Damn about this Spring': Hanns Eisler's Move to Berlin," in David Blake, ed., *Hanns Eisler: A Miscellany* (New York: Harwood Academic P, 1995), p. 4. The article, which originally appeared in *Sinn und Form* 39, 3 (1987) is translated by Karin von Abrams.
15. At this time Eisler's music was being published, at Schoenberg's recommendation, by Universal Editions, he was receiving favorable reviews in the prestigious *Musikblätter des Anbruch*, and in April 1925 he had been awarded the Vienna Art Prize.
16. The "bürgerlichen Konzertbetreib." Eisler's article under this title appeared in *Die Rote Fahne* on April 15, 1928; it is reprinted in the original German in *Hanns Eisler: Musik und Politik Schriften*, pp. 74–76, and in English translation (by Karin von Abrams) in *Hanns Eisler: A Miscellany*, pp. 69–71.
17. The first visit to the United States extended from February through May and involved a concert tour whose itinerary included New York, Boston, Chicago, Pittsburgh, Denver, Detroit, St. Louis, San Francisco, and Los Angeles; the second visit, from October 1935 through April 1936, involved lectures at the New School for Social Research in New York.
18. During his years of travel Eisler wrote film scores for Victor Trivas's *Dans le Rues* (1933), Joris Ivens's *Zuiderzee* (also known as *Nieuwe Gronden*, 1933), Jacques Feyder's *La Grand Jeu* (1933), and Karl Grune's *Abdul the Damned* (1934). Theatrical productions for which he provided music are Ernst Toller's *Feuer aus den Kesseln* and *Peace on Earth* (both London, 1934) and Brecht's *Die Rundköpfe und die Spitzköpfe* (Copenhagen, 1936). Eisler composed a large number of politically oriented songs during this period, probably the best known of which are "Das Einheitsfrontlied" and "Das Saarlied" from 1934—written during the 1937 visit to Spain—"The Song for the Seventh of January," the "March of the Fifth Regiment," and "No Pasaran."
19. The essay, reprinted in *Hanns Eisler: Musik und Politik Schriften*, pp. 379–82, is titled "Präludium und Fuge über B-A-C-H (mit 12 Tönen)." The letters B-A-C-H, in German musical nomenclature, refer not just to the name of Bach but also to the pitches B-flat, A, C, and B-natural.
20. Blake, *Grove*, (1980), p. 90. For a detailed analysis of Eisler's use of serialism in the *Deutsche Sinfonie*, see Erik Levi, "Hanns Eisler's 'Deutsche Sinfonie,'" in *Hanns Eisler: A Miscellany*, pp. 181–202.
21. Jürgen Schebera, *Hanns Eisler: Eine Biographie in Texten, Bildern und Dokumenten* (Mainz: Schott, 1998), p. 105. ("Dies trifft auch auf die streng dodekaphonisch geschriebenen *Zwei Sonette* op. 63 zu, bei denen durch die »Eislersche« Behandlung des Materials eine ganz und gar unverwechselbare musikalische Diktion entsteht.") For more on serial techniques in the Sonnet titled "An die Nachgeborenen," see János Maróthy and Márta Batári, "Eisler's 'An die Nachgeborenen': Another Concrete Utopia," in *Hanns Eisler: A Miscellany*, pp. 159–70.

22. Tim Howell, "Eisler's Serialism: Concepts and Methods," in *Hanns Eisler: A Miscellany*, p. 131. The bulk of Howell's essay is devoted to a comparison of the serial techniques of Schoenberg in general and those of Eisler as demonstrated in the op. 75 *String Quartet*. For more discussion on the same subject, see Eberhardt Klemm, "Bemerkungen zur Zwölftontechnik bei Eisler und Schönberg," *Sinn und Form* 4 (1964): 771–84.
23. See Howell, "Eisler's Serialism," pp. 129–30.
24. Like the fairly light *Scherzo* for violin and orchestra, the tautly serial *Five Orchestral Pieces* derive from music Eisler composed for a Joris Ivens documentary film on China titled *The 400 Million*. The 1940 *Chamber Symphony* is based on materials that would surface later that year in the score for the short documentary film *White Flood*, and the 1941 quintet is a set of variations designed to accompany a showing of Ivens's 1929 silent film *Regen* ("Rain").
25. Erik Levi, "Hanns Eisler: Music for the Workers," *BBC Music Magazine*, August 1998. Available at: http://eislermusic.com/eriklevi.htm. Accessed January 17, 2005.
26. See Martin Hufner, "Auf der Suche nach einam 'Serialismus mit menschlichen Antliz'—Vortrag auf dem Ersten Internationalen Hanns-Eisler-Symposium in Berlin an 26. Juni 1998." Available at http:/www.kritische-musick.de/noframes/eisler-adorno.shtml. Accessed January 12, 2005.
27. Albrecht Betz, "Music and Politics: Theme and Variations," in *Hanns Eisler: A Miscellany*, p. 393.
28. Howell, "Eisler's Serialism," p. 132.
29. Harry Goldschmidt, "Thoughts on Hanns Eisler," in *Hanns Eisler: A Miscellany*, pp. 408–09. The article was originally published in 1958 in *Musik und Gesellschaft* (1958): 6.
30. The "Dies Committee" was an unofficial name for the House of Representatives' Special Committee on Un-American Activities, which was established in 1938 with Martin Dies (D-Texas) as its chairman. Walter Steele was chairman of the American Coalition Committee on National Security, and his testimony was given on August 16, 1938.
31. The initials G.P.U. stand for Gosudarstvennoe Politicheskoe Upravlenie (Rосударственное Политическое Yправление), that is, the Soviet Union's State Political Directorate.
32. Eisler's only teaching activity in 1936 was at the New School for Social Research.
33. The acronym OGPU stands for Ob'edinennoe Gosudarstvennoe Politicheskoe Upravlenie (Объединённое Rосударственное Политическое Yправление), that is, the All-Union State Political Directorate.
34. The essay titled "Annihilation of Art" does not appear in either *Hanns Eisler: A Rebel in Music* or *Hanns Eisler: Musik und Politik Schriften*. The latter collection, however, includes two previously unpublished essays that deal more extensively with the material than does the Russian article; these are "Einiges über das Verhalten der Arbeitersänger und -musiker in Deutschland," apparently completed in London in January 1935, and "Musik und Musikpolitik im faschistischen Deutschland," apparently completed in

New York in October 1935. See *Hanns Eisler: Musik und Politik Schriften*, pp. 242–65 and 334–57.

35. Translated by someone identified only as "S.O.," Eisler's essay is similar in content but not identical to the essay "Musik und Musikpolitik im faschistischen Deutschland" noted above. The essay appeared in *Musical Vanguard: A Critical Review* 1, 1 (March–April 1935): 33–48. Along with Eisler's essay, the first issue of this short-lived journal included Lawrence Gellert's "Negro Songs of Protest in America," Aaron Copland's "A Note on Young Composers," and Charles Seeger's "Preface to All Linguistic Treatment of Music." Admon Balber, Max Margulis, and Charles Seeger are listed as the journal's editors; identified as contributing editors are Lan Adomian, Henry Cowell, and Elie Siegmeister.
36. See note 8.
37. Copland, who was summoned for HUAC hearings in 1953, served as national chairman of the Committee for Justice for Hanns Eisler that was formed in February 1948. The committee's cochairmen were composer Roger Sessions and composer-conductor Leonard Bernstein; membership in the committee included such luminaries as Albert Einstein, Thomas Mann, Pablo Picasso, and Henri Matisse.
38. Most probably this was *Soil*, a documentary produced by the United States Department of Agriculture in 1939.
39. At least for Eisler, none of these film projects materialized.
40. After living for a short time in Vienna, Eisler settled in the Soviet-controlled sector of Berlin. He served as a professor at the Berlin Hochschule für Musik, which after his death in 1962 was renamed the Hanns Eisler Conservatory. The German Democratic Republic (i.e., East Germany) used Eisler's 1949 setting of Johannes Becher's poem "Auferstanded aus Ruinen" as its national anthem.
41. See notes 34 and 35.
42. Eisler, "Contemporary Music and Fascism," in *Musik und Politik Schriften*, p. 490. The annotations by editor Günter Mayer suggest only that the typescript was intended for publication ("wahrscheinlich für einen Vortrag"); there is no indication as to where Eisler hoped to publish the essay.
43. Eisler, "Contemporary Music and Fascism," pp. 490–91.

Works Cited

Betz, Albrecht. "Music and Politics: Theme and Variations." *Hanns Eisler: A Miscellany*, David Blake, ed., New York: Harwood Academic, 1995.

Blake, David. "Eisler, Hanns," *The New Grove Dictionary of Music and Musicians, Vol. VI*, Stanley Sadie, ed., London: Macmillan, 1980.

———. "Eisler, Hanns," in *The New Grove Dictionary ofMusic and Musicians, Vol. VIII*, second edition, Stanley Sadie. ed., London: Macmillan, 2001.

———. ed. *Hanns Eisler: A Miscellany.* New York: Harwood Academic P, 1995.

Eisler, Hanns. "Vom bürgerlichen Konzertbetreib." *Die Rote Fahn*, April 15, 1928. Reprinted in *Hanns Eisler: Musik und Politik Schriften: 1924–1948.* Leipzig: Deutscher Verlag für Musik, 1983.

———. "Fantasia in G-Men." *New Masses* (October 14, 1947). Reprinted in *Hanns Eisler: A Rebel in Music: Selected Writings*, Manfred Grabs, ed., London: Kahn & Averill, 1978; and Hanns Eisler, *Hanns Eisler: Musik und Politik Schriften: 1924–1948.* Leipzig: Deutscher Verlag für Musik, 1983.

———. *Hanns Eisler: Musik und Politik Schriften: 1924–1948.* Leipzig: Deutscher Verlag für Musik, 1983.

———. "On Schonberg." *New Masses* (February 26, 1935). Reprinted in *Hanns Eisler: A Rebel in Music: Selected Writings*, Manfred Grabs, ed., London: Kahn & Averill, 1999.

———. [and Theodor Adorno]. *Composing for the Films.* London: Oxford UP, 1947.

Goldschmidt, Harry. "Thoughts on Hanns Eisler." *Hanns Eisler: A Miscellany*, David Blake. ed., New York: Harwood Academic Publishers, 1995.

Grabs, Manfred, ed. *Hanns Eisler: A Reber in Music: Selected Writings.* London: Kahn & Averill, 1978.

Howell, Tim. "Eisler's Serialism: Concepts and Methods." *Hanns Eisler: A Miscellany*, David Blake, ed., New York: Harwood Academic P, 1995.

Hufner, Martin. "Auf der Suche nach einam 'Serialismus mit menschlichen Antliz'—Vortrag auf dem Ersten Internationalen Hanns-Eisler-Symposium in Berlin an 26. Juni 1998." Available at: http:/www.kritische-musick.de/noframes/eisler-adorno.shtml (accessed January 12, 2005).

Klemm, Eberhardt Klemm. "Bemerkungen zur Zwölftontechnik bei Eisler and Schönberg." *Sinn und Form* 4 (1964): 771–84.

———. "'I Don't Give a Damn about this Spring': Hanns Eisler's Move to Berlin." Trans. Karin von Abrams. *Hanns Eisler: A Miscellany*, David Blake, ed., New York: Harwood Academic P, 1995.

Levi, Erik. "Hanns Eisler: Music for the Workers." *BBC Music Magazine*, August 1998. Available at: http://eislermusic.com/eriklevi.htm (accessed January 17, 2005).

———. "Hanns Eisler's 'Deutsche Sinfonie.'" *Hanns Eisler: A Miscellany*, David Blake, ed., New York: Harwood Academic P, 1995.

Maróthy, János, and Márta Batári. "Eisler's 'An die Nachgeborenen': Another Concrete Utopia." *Hanns Eisler: A Miscellany*, David Blake, ed., New York: Harwood Academic P, 1995.

Schebera, Jürgen. *Hanns Eisler: Eine Biographie in Texten, Bildern and Dokumenten.* Mainz: Schott, 1998.

CHAPTER 11

Communism, Perversion, and Other Crimes against the State: The FBI Files of Klaus and Erika Mann

Andrea Weiss

> Of course, I am not in a position to know the exact contents of the adverse information [collected by the FBI]. Yet I am eager to contribute whatever I can to the speedy clarification of my pending case. In doing so, I take it for granted that the suspicions against me are of a primarily political nature. [. . .] I am aware of certain rumors according to which my political views are extremely "left"—practically those of a so-called "fellow traveler" of the Communist Party. These rumors—spread against me by ignorant or malignant people (maybe by Nazi sympathizers or by jealous fellow-refugees)—are entirely untrue. (Klaus Mann, memorandum to the U.S. Attorney General Biddle, 1943. Erika and Klaus Mann Archive, Literaturarchiv. Monacensia, Munich)

Only a man at the end of his rope would write to the U.S. government to defend himself without knowing what the charges were. In 1943 Klaus Mann wrote a seven-page, single spaced memorandum in which he gave Attorney General Francis Biddle ample information about both his political and sexual past—just in case it was the information the government already had. Eloquent and impassioned as his letter is, it would seem an exercise in futility, though he could not have done otherwise. Mann was desperate to be sent overseas as a member of the United States Armed Forces, and had devoted the previous 10 years to railing against the Nazi regime when few were prepared to listen; now he longed to be part of the Allied fight against tyranny and fascism in his former homeland.

When Klaus wrote this memorandum, he was also desperate for personal reasons. His sister Erika, who was his closest friend and lifelong artistic collaborator, was stationed at the front as a war correspondent for the British Broadcasting Corporation (BBC), and he was desolate without her. His lover, Thomas Quinn Curtiss ("Tomski"), had joined the National Guard and was showing signs of losing interest in him. His antifascist literary journal, *Decision*, had folded the previous year. Moreover, his heroin addiction, which had been "under control" after a brief cure in a Budapest sanatorium a few years earlier, was slipping out of control again. He was acutely lonely and ached to be part of a group, to belong somewhere. The army seemed like the perfect solution to all of these problems. After a seemingly interminable wait, Klaus had been inducted into the army at the end of 1942, but he was now stuck in boot camp and with the rest of his unit already overseas, he was still waiting to be shipped out.

Klaus's problems were further compounded by external forces about which he knew very little. Though he correctly suspected that the FBI was investigating him, he could not be sure, and would never know the reasons behind the investigation. Nor did he link his personal difficulties to the FBI probe, or realize the extent of the bureau surveillance and interference in his life. Yet hundreds of FBI documents released through the Freedom of Information Act (FOIA) reveal that his increasing paranoia was wholly legitimate. By considering these government documents in relation to Klaus's own private documents, it is possible to rewrite his personal history in a way that he himself, the author of three autobiographies and copious diaries, never was able to.

For example, the source of the following unsigned letter was someone who personally had known Erika and Klaus during the1920s, when they were involved in avant-garde theater and participated in the wild gay nightlife of Weimar Berlin with virtually no interest in politics.

> I would also draw your attention upon the activities in the United States of Klaus MANN and his sister Erika MANN. They are the son and daughter of the well-known writer Thomas Mann (Heinrich Mann, another internationally reputed writer and essayist, is their uncle). Klaus and Erika Mann are very active agents of the Comintern. They were very active in Berlin before Hitler seized power. Klaus Mann was an active agent of Stalin in Paris, for many years. We hear that he is now editing an English publication, "Decision," in the United States. (Anonymous letter in Klaus Mann's FBI file, undated. Cover

letter from the FBI states it was received from the American Embassy in London and "it is not possible to determine who the writer was.")

The letter makes clear that the information contained in it was being offered in exchange for some visas from the State Department for several German friends residing in southern France. The letter writer's claims were taken seriously: the FBI embarked on an investigation of Klaus and Erika and did not let up until he died in 1949 and she collapsed under the pressure and left the United States for good in 1951.

While fascism swept across Europe, the FBI expended considerable time and resources harassing two of the strongest and most dedicated advocates for liberal democracy, both of whom had great respect for the government of the United States. The FBI surveillance of German émigrés was hardly an outgrowth of an anti-Nazi stance; rather, it was an expression of American xenophobia toward all foreigners, and part of the well-documented campaign against liberalism and socialism. The FBI was not a renegade operation in this regard, out of step with the rest of government policy. The House Committee on Un-American Activities (HUAC), for instance, was founded in 1934 to investigate both Nazis and Fascists but in 1938, incredibly, HUAC seemed to lose interest in fascists altogether and focused instead on the Left as the more dangerous threat.

Though the FBI was unable to link either Erika or Klaus to the Communist Party, because of the Mann siblings' "premature" antifascism, as well as their candid admission of homosexuality, the FBI continued to treat them as dangerous suspects. In the FBI's convoluted moral code, "premature antifascists"—people who opposed fascism in Germany, Italy, and Spain before the onset of World War II officially established these countries to be the enemy—had less credibility than patriotic Nazis during the early and mid-1930, and homosexuals had no credibility at all—an ironic twist given what we now know about J. Edgar Hoover.

Soon after the FBI opened its files on Erika and Klaus, a statement regarding their "more than sibling" relationship appeared in an undated report originating from the bureau:

> Confidential Informant [name blacked out] . . . stated that people are horribly shocked over the sexual perversions of a group of four: KLAUS MANN, his sister ERICA [*sic*] MANN, and the latter's husband, the Englishman AUDAN [*sic*], and his collaborator, CHRISTOPHER ISHERWOOD. [Blacked out] stated that KLAUS and ERICA MANN were having affairs together; that there was reference to it in one of the books of their father, THOMAS MANN. [. . .] Informant further stated that KLAUS MANN is willingly and knowingly a tool of the [Communist] Party [. . .] (Klaus Mann FBI file, December 15, 1941, p. 3)

The FBI apparently was unbothered by the contradiction between the homosexuality of Erika and Klaus Mann and the charge that they had a sexual relationship; both were evidence of their perversion and immorality. To the bureau, Erika's depravity was polymorphically perverse: bisexual, yet married to W.H. Auden and in love with Klaus, she occasionally invited another man to spend the night, a doctor whose office, the FBI file tells us, was on the corner of Park Ave and 86th Street. The FBI's "Confidential Informant T5" informed his superiors on May 29, 1942 that, "[Name blacked out] stated that he thought KLAUS MANN was a psychopathic case and that to all who knew him, it is general knowledge that the subject is a sexual pervert (Klaus Mann FBI file, October 24, 1941, p.11)." Erika's marriage to W.H. Auden was also under suspicion; even evaluating Auden's poetry was not thought to be overstepping the FBI's mission: "Marriage of ERICA [*sic*] MANN to Englishman Auden was one of convenience and [. . .] neither KLAUS nor ERICA believe in marriage. [. . .] Informant advised that he did not think AUDEN was a Communist, but advised that he is an excellent poet, although very eccentric [. . .]" (Klaus Mann FBI file, October 24, 1941, p.13).

The political motivation behind Klaus's literary journal, *Decision*, was also of great concern to the FBI. Klaus established *Decision* in order to support "independent creative work and intellectual liberty," as he stated in its initial subscription drive; this English-language journal quickly became one of the most important, if short-lived, little magazines of the 1940s.

> This periodical is presented as a neutral anti-Nazi publication and belongs to the specific camouflaged Communist propaganda-instruments known as the "Innocents' Clubs". The first thing these Soviet propagandists do, is to secure highly unsuspected international personalities, who sign their appeals and declarations [. . .] (From the undated, unsigned letter that led to opening Klaus Mann's FBI file)

Primarily a literary journal, *Decision* held no political line beyond a commitment to democracy and an abhorrence of fascism. On the editorial page of the first issue, Klaus revealed his own relentless idealism, his high hopes for the future, his love of America, and the inseparability of culture and politics that was behind all of his undertakings. This impassioned editorial was circulated among various FBI offices, with several words underlined and circled:

> All of us feel and know that more is at stake in the present war than political systems or imperialist interests. . . . Ideas and values of supreme magnitude are involved—conceptions are threatened that form the very basis of our civilization. What we are witnessing is nothing more or less than a decisive struggle over the spiritual destiny of the planet.

> ... Another literary magazine? Just now, in the midst of a terrific ordeal—while the planet is convulsed in a paroxysm of agony?
>
> Yes! A new forum for the creative spirit—*now*, at precisely this moment of fatal decisions; and precisely here.
>
> ... Where else is the creative spirit to continue its play and work, if not in this last haven of free thought and free expression? Where else is the seriousness of our plight to be recognized and discussed, if not in this country—the last bulwark of liberty, focus of our hopes? (Klaus Mann, "Editorial")

Decision attracted both German émigré authors and well-known British and American writers, ranging from Aldous Huxley to Stephen Spender to Stephen Vincent Benét. Klaus could hardly believe its success; he was astonished when Sherwood Anderson came through with a story and was amazed that "Decision, Inc." had managed to open a bank account, rent an office, and even hire a secretary who "looks exactly the way a real secretary should look . . . and apparently fails to notice that I don't look like a boss" (Mann, *The Turning Point* 338, 139). So respectable did Klaus make the magazine, to attract public attention and financing, that he grew dissatisfied with it; he felt that the big names dominated to the exclusion of newcomers and more experimental approaches, and he intended to remedy the problem once the journal became more solvent.

It never did. Securing the financing was an unbearable struggle for Klaus. Wealthy patrons would not deliver on their promises—"How cruel and capricious are the rich!" he wrote in his diary—and with each issue the magazine went deeper and deeper in the hole (Klaus Mann, diary entry dated June 2, 1941, qtd. in *The Turning Point* 344, 139). These "failures" were duly noted in Mann's bureau file:

> Informant T4 . . . further advised that the account at X bank maintained by the *Decision* magazine has been closed because KLAUS MANN had made out a check on this account for $4. payable to the informant and the check bounced because the account had been formerly closed. . . . (Klaus Mann FBI file, no date)

A secret informant was sent to report on a financial meeting for Decision, Inc. According to an FBI document, the meeting:

> . . . turned out to be nothing more than a drinking party. Informant stated that at this meeting were VINCENT SHEEAN [*sic*] and his wife, MORRIS SAMUELS and his daughter, STRELSIN and ERICA MANN [*sic*] and KLAUS MANN. Informant stated that VINCENT SHEEAN seems to be pre-occupied sexually and that there was little doubt in his mind but that ERICA MANN and VINCENT SHEEAN had separated themselves from

> the group that night to indulge in sexual pastimes. (Klaus Mann FBI file, October 26, 1941, pp. 13–14)

After such extensive investigation the only criminal act the FBI could find was that Klaus edited *Decision* in violation of the employment restrictions on his INS entry visa. The FBI turned its attention back to the "decadent culture behind the magazine which was obvious from its contents" (Klaus Mann FBI file, December 15, 1941, p. 12). Klaus's lifestyle, more than the actual contents, served to confirm the magazine's decadence.

The Mann file reports that Klaus was "frequently in arrears in his rent" and "many queer looking people" could be seen going into his Hotel Bedford room, which was carefully pinpointed in the file: hotel room 1403, which faces the front of the building, fifth window in from the east side. The doorman of the Hotel Bedford moonlighted as one of the main FBI informants in Klaus's case (Erika suspected as much and tried, unsuccessfully, to have him fired from the hotel). He reported that a soldier spent several nights each week in Klaus's room.

> Informant T3 [. . .] further stated that unquestionably KLAUS MANN is a sexual pervert and that two or three times a week, a soldier by the name of [blacked out] from Governor's Island spends the night with MANN in his room. [. . .] Informant further stated that the soldier, known as [blacked out], is a large 6 foot heavy set individual with fair complexion and dirty-blond hair. He advised that [. . .] the only suitable sleeping place in MANN's room is a single bed. (Klaus Mann FBI file, December 15, 1941, p. 9)

The FBI followed with perverse fascination Klaus's "decadent" lifestyle. Klaus admittedly was drawn rather indiscriminately to the "very gratifying young proletarian types . . . I fancy almost all of them, porters, waiters, liftboys, and so on, white or black. Almost all are agreeable to me. I could sleep with all of them," he wrote in his diary (Mann, *Tagebücher 1938–1939* 139). His close friend, author Sybille Bedford, recalled that at this time "what attracted Klaus were the professional louts, I mean truck drivers and rough trade, as he would say, the 'quick and dangerous.' That was when he began to speak English in America. He used to come back beaten up by them and so on" (private interview recorded on July 31, 1999).

Klaus's poor condition was also due at least in part to the distance he felt from Erika. It seems that what he wanted or needed from her was more than she could give, and he felt her pulling away. He wrote in his diary on February 18, 1940:

> Sadness, without end. Deathwish as physical desire. The feeling of loneliness like frost. Everything dissolves and goes to pieces. [. . .] Erika distracted by

> her successes, travels, activities, and her relationship with G [Dr. Martin Gumpert]. How long ago is *Anja and Esther* [their first play, from the 1920s]—how she has grown. Never totally estranged, but still, step by step, she is receding—Often I think I'm Pygmalion: what would she be without me—what am I without her? (Mann, *Tagebücher 1940–1943* 21–22).

That year, with Europe besieged by war, Erika received an invitation from Duff Cooper, British Minister for Information under Churchill, to become a correspondent for the BBC. Although the job was a dangerous one, Erika jumped at the offer. She simply could not stand by and watch one European country after another fall to the Nazis. England could well be next. In a 1963 radio interview, Erika recalled,

> After the fall of France I felt compelled to leave behind my beautiful, cozy American lifestyle and go to England. I was convinced, in spite of all the evidence, that England would resist. And my reasons for this conviction were purely moral ones. ("Musik für einen Gast," host Roswitha Schmalenbach, 1963)

With "much envy and anxiety," Klaus wrote in a diary entry dated August 23, 1940 (*Tagebücher 1940–1943* 51), he witnessed Erika's departure for London. He could not make sense of the feelings that were tangled up in his heart: fear, envy, pride, sadness, and the feeling of being left behind.

Erika's job with the BBC took her to the war's battlegrounds, which is exactly where she wanted to be. It was a case of her strong sense of moral obligation synchronizing with her craving for adventure. In one of her BBC broadcasts, also published in *Liberty* magazine, a popular American weekly, offering national and international news commentary, she tells of how she managed to put herself right in the line of danger by boarding a rescue boat in the straits of Dover. The rescue boats were standing by, ready to fish out any airmen who had to make parachute landings in the rough, cold English channel. It was a typical morning in that part of the world: rainy and foggy. In one pocket Erika had her "nice neat Air Ministry permit" which entitled her to board a rescue boat, and in the other a small bottle of brandy to keep her warm at sea. However, the British naval officers resolutely refused to let her to board a rescue boat, and she was almost ready to cave in and accept their verdict—until she discovered the real reason for the resistance: "I realized that the whole thing was not a question of civilians, of reporters, not being admitted, but of women being refused. 'There's nothing for females out there—and we've never taken one.' That was what I couldn't possibly stand" (Mann, BBC broadcast, October 25, 1941, London). Erika, who had never been held back from anything on account of her gender, recoiled at such paternalism. She put up a huge fight and did not back down until she had won. She did not have much time to savor her victory, however. She took off on a Naval boat with a 22-year-old college student at the command when suddenly, she told the BBC interviewer, "Out of the Calais air, the Messerschmitts [World War II fighter planes] leaped at us. There were two of them. Their crosses and swastikas could be easily distinguished." The gunner on the rescue boat, a young man named George, sat behind his huge machine gun, held his breath, and took aim as the planes dived, climbed, and circled. He was just about to shoot when the 22-year-old captain shouted; she recounts:

> "You are not to open fire." The captain's voice was hoarse. "Do you hear me? This is an order!" There—the devil knows where they came from—suddenly there they were: two more Messerschmitts at our back, at George's back, rushing toward us, the air full of that buzzing crescendo which the screen has made so familiar to all of us. (BBC broadcast, October 25, 1941, London)

After the four fighter planes departed and everyone breathed a huge sigh of relief, the young captain explained that this was a "good old decoy performance." Rescue boats were supposed to be off-limits as targets; they could not be attacked without provocation. The Nazis wanted the boat to shoot at the first two planes, so that the second two could justify opening fire. Then, the captain explained, the second set of Messerschmitts "'would have finished us up from the rear like that.' He snapped his fingers," she told her radio listeners.

With Erika's new position at the BBC, she found she had little time for Klaus back in New York. Her cables to him were infrequent and brief—one read only "safe so far" (qtd. in Klaus Mann, *The Turning Point* 334)—which did little to quell either his loneliness or his anxiety about her wellbeing. Klaus wrote in his diary on August 10, 1941:

> I suppose this is the most lonely summer I've ever experienced. The city seems to be deserted by everybody I know. Erika is in England. . . . The only person I see is Muriel Rukeyser, who recently joined the staff of the magazine. She is a great help in these trying days. . . . But even she, the only comrade in this arid solitude, escapes to the country from Saturday until Monday: while I have to stay—paralyzed, as it were, by the demon of this fierce and relentless summer. At times I actually fear suffocation in the stifling hole that's my room. The only comfort on those painful Sundays are the calls from Savannah [Georgia, where "Tomski" was stationed in the National Guard]. (*The Turning Point* 346)

Despite his despondency, Klaus fought for the journal's survival "like two mother lions," Erika wrote on May 1, 1942 (unpublished letter to Annemarie Schwarzenbach, Erika and Klaus Mann Archive, Literaturarchiv Monacensia, Munich); but she believed that the sooner it folded, the better for all concerned, especially Klaus. Her patience with his depressed state of mind was wearing thin just when he needed her most. She did not realize that Klaus at one point was near suicide. In the autumn of 1942, Klaus wrote in his diary:

> Tomski called and asked how things were going. I told him, miserably, that I had nothing to eat and no money for a haircut and just absolutely nothing. He replied it was awful, and why didn't we eat together? He had arranged to have a few drinks at 6 o'clock with someone from Camp Stewart, but . . . promised to call me at seven. So I said okay, and postponed the suicide. (*Tagebücher, 1940–1943* 116, Diary entry dated October 24, 1942)

As a British citizen (through her marriage to W.H. Auden), Erika did not require American citizenship for her assignments and therefore was in a very different position from Klaus, who had, after four years of total statelessness, only a temporary visitor's visa in a Czech passport (granted by the Czech government as a gift to Thomas Mann). He longed to enlist in the United States Army, driven by his genuine desire to fight the Nazis in every way possible but also by his desperate need to be part of something. "I *want* to go into the Army. I *want* to wear the same uniform as the others. I don't want to be an outsider or an exception any longer. Finally, for once, I'll feel in solidarity with the majority," he wrote in his diary (*Der Wendepunkt* 461).

It is possible that Klaus could have been admitted as a regular soldier without American citizenship. But he knew he was not cut out for combat, and was hoping for a post in counterintelligence or propaganda, where his German background and his polyglot talents could be best utilized. For such a sensitive job, American citizenship was required. He applied for it, but it was just one more thing on which he seemed to be waiting. Finally, when he could bear it no longer, he asked to be allowed to enlist without citizenship. Reflecting on his lifelong dread of isolation, Klaus wrote in his diary,

> The obsession that haunted me when I was a child—the paralyzing fear of moral and physical isolation—never ceased to perturb me [. . .] To be an outsider is the one unbearable humiliation [. . .] And so I conclude my reply to the Selective Service Board with these words: I want to notify you of my willingness, indeed, my eagerness to join the U.S. forces, even before my naturalization has actually taken place. (*The Turning Point* 362–63)

The U.S. Army and the FBI both had their doubts about Klaus. The FBI stepped up its surveillance when an SAC received a letter from Hoover himself. Hoover called the New York and Philadelphia FBI offices "delinquent" in the case of Klaus Mann, and demanded "this matter be given prompt attention." The New York office started to tail Klaus around the clock, and recorded such mundane activities as his eating pastry and buying stationery.

> KLAUS MANN entered [blacked out] Street at 12:32 P.M. at which time he was wearing a gray suit, no hat, horn-rimmed glasses and brown shoes. He left the doctor's office at 12:47 and took a Lexington Avenue subway to 86th Street. At this point, he left the subway and walked over to Geiger's Restaurant at 206 East 86th Street and made a purchase of some pastry. It was 1:06 P.M. at this time. He thereafter returned to the Lexington Avenue subway and took an express train to Grand Central Station. Leaving Grand Central Station, he stopped and made a purchase at "Filing Equipment and Office Supplies," on the south side of 42nd Street off Lexington Avenue. He thereafter returned directly to the Hotel Bedford at 1:30 P.M. (Klaus Mann FBI file, June 18, 1942, p. 5–6)

Klaus's first physical exam revealed (according to this FBI report) a "syphilitic condition" and "13 arsenical and 39 heavy metal injections," likely injections of heavy metal chelators used to treat heavy metal poisoning to which he could not possibly have been exposed to. Klaus's diary indicates that he received 48 injections from Dr. Gumpert, 36 of bismuth (a metal once used to treat stomach ulcers, before it was deemed too dangerous) and 12 of salvavsan (for syphilis). Gumpert was known to give Klaus a variety of prescription drugs that he took without knowing what they were. Results from his first physical led Klaus to be classified by the U.S. Army as 4-F. The FBI informant's report stated,

> . . . now that "Decision" had folded up he had staked everything, "including his self-respect" on joining the American Army. [Klaus believed] that the Army had rejected him "because the F.B.I. had told them that I was a homo-sexual." KLAUS MANN alleged that he admitted to the Army people that he was a homo-sexual "because that is nothing to be ashamed of." (FBI internal memo, NY field office to Washington DC headquarters, August 16, 1932)

Though utterly unashamed of his homosexuality, Klaus *was* ashamed of the 4-F classification he earned because he complained it put him in the same grouping as criminals and insane men. But when the Army interviewed him at length after the physical exam, Klaus backtracked on his avowal of his homosexuality. He insisted that syphilis test result was "a dubious plus-minus reaction," not a clear positive. And even if it were positive, he would have contracted it "from a prostitute in New York" rather than from "any form of perversion." Clearly he had no indication that his admissions to the U.S. Army doctors would be passed on to the FBI.

When Klaus was called back for another Army examination on June 4, his syphilis had been cured but the military doctor was again dissatisfied with him: "Provisional Rejection" was the verdict. Klaus proposed yet another exam and retreated to his room in the Bedford where he lived increasingly like a hermit. He wrote in his diary on July 1, 1943, "But if my application were straightaway *rejected*, SUICIDE actually would be the only logical response, would be almost inevitable." On September 7, after standing naked all day in a line with other recruits, he was rejected once more. His disappointment was immeasurable, and he spent the next few months in a deep depression. Daily he wrote in his diary that he wished to die, nothing else. In these dark times, many had experienced far worse than Klaus, and he knew it—his own brother Golo, for example, had been held in an internment camp in Nîmes. But the awareness of his relatively privileged condition could do little to release Klaus from the clutches of his death wish, something rarely amenable to rational thought. In September 1942, his autobiography *The Turning Point* was published to overwhelmingly favorable reviews in the *Sunday Times*, the *Herald Tribune*, and elsewhere; but his depression did not lift until December 14 when he took a boat to Governor's Island once more for his physical exam.

This time, several friends had given him "lessons" on how to appear heterosexual—not that he really needed them. The American Army was so eager by then for additional able-bodied men that the military doctor was willing to overlook his homosexuality, as well as the huge scar which remained from his six childhood appendicitis operations. The Army psychiatrist merely asked him if he had a girlfriend (he answered he had several), and pointed to a woman out the window, commenting, "She must have a nice bosom!" According to Curt Riess, one of Klaus's friends who gave him the lessons in "normality," "Klaus, who never in his whole life was interested in any woman's breasts, nodded enthusiastically: 'Yes! Nice bosom!' And with that he passed the test and was in the American Army." (Reiss, *Meine Berühmte Freunde* [Freiburg, 1987] 92)

Klaus was instructed to report for active duty at Fort Dix, New Jersey two weeks later, more than a year after he had first tried to enlist. The following day, the FBI was notified, and his case was supposedly closed.

> On December 29, 1942 [blacked out] Clerk, Local Board 15, 570 Lexington Avenue, New York City, advised that the subject had been inducted into the United States Army on December 28, 1942. [. . .] In view of the subject's induction into the United States Army as noted above the investigation in this matter is being discontinued and this case is being closed.
>
> CLOSED (Klaus Mann FBI file, February 9, 1943 for the period ending December 29, 1941)

From Fort Dix, Klaus was shipped off for eight weeks of basic training at Camp Robinson in Arkansas, and then transferred to Camp Ritchie in

Maryland. At the age of 36, he was for the first time financially independent of his parents, he was a soldier in the United States Army, and his father finally had reason to be proud of him.

Despite Klaus's deepest wish to belong, he remained an outsider in the Army—certainly it was not the job he was born for. His fellow soldiers in basic training had little in common with him. He was a good 15 years older than they were, obviously homosexual, physically weak from over a decade of drug abuse, exceptionally poor at sports and other physical activity (as he had been since childhood), and to make matters worse, probably spoke better English than they did, but with a thick German accent at a time when Germany was the enemy.

When his unit was shipped off to Europe in the spring of 1943, Klaus was left behind—his citizenship, which finally was to be granted the very day before departure, was held up at the last minute. Klaus did not know the reason, but suspected it had to do with either his left-wing political views or his homosexuality. Though stamped "CLOSED" in December 1942, Klaus's FBI file shows further FBI activity in the file after that date. Stuck in boot camp, he wrote his desperate memorandum to the attorney general, answering the unspecified charges against him. After denying his affiliation with the Communist Party he moved on to defend himself against the other probable cause, his sexuality:

> It may be, however, that the adverse "special information" in question includes also rumours or denouncements of a very different kind . . . Since I do not know what has been said against me, I take the liberty to state . . . nobody has yet dared to doubt or to deny into my face: that my character and "sex moral" are "excellent." (Klaus Mann, Memorandum to U.S. Attorney General Biddle, 1943. Erika and Klaus Mann Archive)

Klaus stagnated in Camp Crowder, Missouri, where he had been assigned to the 825th Signal Repair Service Company, "clearly a mistake, as I am not a technician and can not be of any use in a repair service unit." To do something constructive and keep himself busy, he took over editing the army camp newsletter, *The Camp Crowder Message*. Finally he humbled himself to appeal to his father. Thomas Mann, disturbed by Klaus's anxious mental condition, intervened on his son's behalf and wrote a letter to the U.S. government vouching for Klaus's integrity.

On June 4, 1943, the FBI showed up to interview Thomas Mann at his home in Pacific Palisades regarding his views on his son. The father insisted that he had few if any disagreements with his son, about politics or anything else. Both were moderate and pro-democratic in their political views. Klaus's mother, Katia (called Mrs. Catherine Mann in bureau files) was interviewed two days later, and she confirmed that Klaus was "quite like his father" (qtd. in Stephan, *Communazis* 95).

It is not clear whether the testimony from his parents was the deciding factor that turned his case around, but on August 30, 1943, Klaus faced one final interrogation, this time by a Special Agent for Military Intelligence, and his report was most favorable: "Subject is highly intelligent and possesses a wonderful command of the English language [. . .] This Agent is of the opinion that Subject would be very useful in combat propaganda and [. . .] citizenship should be allowed Subject" (qtd. in Stephan 547). In September 1943, nine months after he was admitted into the Army, Klaus was finally approved for citizenship. His naturalization took place immediately.

Klaus shipped out on an overcrowded transport carrying 8,000 men. Eventually it reached Casablanca, and after stops in Algiers and Tunis he crossed the Mediterranean to meet his former comrades from Camp Ritchie in Naples, where he became part of the Psychological Warfare Branch of the United States Army. Within two days of his arrival, the very street he was traveling down was bombarded, not far from his jeep. It was not the only time he would come under enemy fire. Yet Erika commented that when Klaus finally joined up with his unit overseas, it was the only time in his life, since their childhood, that he was "almost happy" (Bayerische Rundfunk radio interview).

Klaus described his elation in a broadcast over Swedish radio in 1947: "We German refugees, the first victims and most inexorable enemies of Nazism, were eager to contribute our bit to the fight against the Brown Plague. I was happy and proud therefore, to join the army of my new country, the United States of America, and to be sent overseas—first to North Africa, then to Italy, where I served with General Clark's Fifth Army" (*Turning Point* 368).

Despite his uniform and the military ideology behind it, Klaus remained an intellectual pacifist. He justified his participation in the war by saying that his goal was to end it as quickly as possible. His high-security-clearance job was to produce propaganda leaflets to be dropped over the Nazi-occupied territories for the purpose of demoralizing German soldiers and convincing them to go AWOL. When Germany finally did surrender, however, Klaus and Erika both were left in a kind of limbo. They had devoted all their energies during the past 12 years to fighting fascism, and now that they had reached their goal, they found themselves suddenly without one.

EPILOGUE

Fulfilling a deep life-long yearning, Klaus committed suicide by way of a sleeping pill overdose in 1949. Erika lived a full 20 years without him, but she was never the same again: her spirit was broken. She became embittered and her health deteriorated. She was physically and emotionally depleted, first by the loss of her brother, and then by the animosity she faced in McCarthy's America.

As if Klaus's death were not enough, Erika was forced the following year to withdraw her application for U.S. citizenship, which had seemed within her grasp. The Treasury Department and the War Department had awarded her citations, commending her for her "patriotic services during the War," and she felt her actions entitled her to citizenship. She wrote to the Director of Immigration and Naturalization:

> Immeasurable are the times I endangered my life while . . . covering the war as a correspondent accredited to the U.S. Forces . . . Had I been an American citizen [during the War] I could not possibly have tried harder to be helpful. In fact, I felt like an American, lived like an American, and to all practical purposes was an American . . . I lived and worked in the United States, and since I wished to go on doing so I deemed it only fair to add myself legally to the good people of this country. (Mann to Edward J. Shaughnessy; December 11, 1950. Mann Archive)

But as soon as the war was over, the FBI renewed its investigation of Erika like a dog finding its favorite bone. Erika was in their files dating back from spring 1940, when she, somewhat naivëly it turns out, had actually offered information to the FBI. An internal FBI memo indicated that Erika approached the FBI office in New York and "indicated a desire to be of assistance." Her motivation: to prevent Nazis from slipping into the United States. One German refugee, she reported to the FBI, was traveling on a passport with a "J" on his German passport although he was definitely not Jewish (usually it was Nazis who had access to these passports, stolen from Jews, alive or dead). Erika assumed that the FBI was interested in tracking Nazis, when in actuality they were far more preoccupied with tracking suspected Communists, Erika included. Because she was so strategically placed in the German exile community, the FBI was eager to make use of her. By way of thanks she became a subject for surveillance.

To the INS, Erika described the damaging effects the investigation by the FBI had on her life, especially after the War:

> Ever since then an investigation has been going on that could not help casting doubts upon my character, gradually ruining my career, robbing me of my livelihood and, in short, changing me from a happy, busy and fairly useful member of society into a humiliated suspect. Friends of mine have been questioned for two and three hours at a stretch until they all but collapsed. When it became obvious that I was neither a Communist, nor a "fellow traveler" . . . the authorities took to digging into my personal life in a way most

> shocking to those questioned . . . Small wonder, prospective employers felt ardently disinclined to engage my services . . . (Erika Mann to Mr. Edward J. Shaughnessey. Director of Immigration and Naturalization, New York District office, December 11, 1950. Erika and Klaus Mann Archive)

And this, according to declassified FBI files, is how Erika herself came under such intense scrutiny, although she never had any inkling of it herself. The FBI discovered that she had socialized with the wrong person, Englishman Guy Burgess, someone with whom she was barely acquainted, and the investigation spread like an invisible deadly virus from him to her. The upper class Englishman Burgess was a graduate of Trinity College, Cambridge, who worked for the BBC. He had developed pro-Communist sympathies during his college days, became a Soviet spy after the War, and eventually defected to the Soviet Union in May 1951. Erika met the man through W.H. Auden, during a wild homosexual party in England during the War, and he was too drunk to carry on a conversation. She saw him again on one or two occasions, always as part of a group. Asked directly about Guy Burgess by the two surly FBI agents who dropped in on her in October 1951, she could hardly remember him and, when pressed, recalled only that she did not like the man, and had not bothered to learn his last name. She never discovered that this remote acquaintance was the key to her current misery.

To the INS director she went on to report her bafflement at her current predicament, "ruined—through no fault of my own":

> Personally, I am at a complete loss as to what may have prompted the investigation to take on such disastrous proportions. I have never been granted a hearing . . . Yet I—and only I—could have supplied whatever information was required . . .
>
> I [have] had to witness the gradual destruction of all I had built up in more than a decade. This spectacle was all the more painful since it involved the third existence I had made for myself. Nazism drove me from my native Germany where I had been quite a success; Hitler's growing influence in Europe caused me to leave the continent which I had been touring with my own show for more than a thousand performances; and now I find myself ruined—through no fault of my own—in a country I love and whose citizen I had hoped to become. (Erika Mann to Edward Shaughnessey)

Despite such moving rhetoric, in 1950, the INS asked the FBI for assistance in building a case to deport Erika from the United States. According to FBI documents, "INS has . . . expressed an interest in the subject and has not as yet obtained sufficient evidence upon which to base the issuance of a warrant of arrest in deportation proceeding." The FBI tried to comply with the request for evidence, and although they were unable to uncover any, they harassed Erika to the point that she felt forced into exile yet again.

Erika was still in her 40s when she unpacked her belongings in her final home in Switzerland, but between Klaus's death and the FBI ordeal, she had aged visibly in just a few years. The move did not signal an attempt to start over: she insisted she was not strong enough, nor did she have the will, to undergo the tremendous efforts of building a new life in a new place all over again.

Works Cited

Bedford, Sybille. Interview by the author, July 31, 1999.

Erika and Klaus Mann Archive. Literaturarchiv Monacensia, Munich. FBI Files of Klaus Mann, no. 65-8483, and Erika Mann, nos. 6549395 and 100-6368, were obtained under the Freedom of Information Act and are in possession of the author.

Mann, Erika. "Die Schrift an der Wand" (Radio Interview). Bayerische Rundfunk. October 20, 1952. Tape housed in the Munich Stadtbibliothek.

———. Letter to Mr. Edward J. Shaughnessy, Director of Immigration and Naturalization, New York District Office, dated December 11, 1950. Housed in the Erika and Klaus Mann Archive, Literaturarchiv Monacensia, Munich.

———. "Musik für einen Gast" (Radio interview by Roswitha Schmalenbach). Sendung des Radio Studios Basel, 1963. Tape housed in the Munich Stadtbibliothek.

———. "Out of the Calais Air," BBC broadcast, October 25, 1941. Transcript housed in The Erika and Klaus Mann Archive, Literaturarchiv Monacensia, Munich.

———. Unpublished letter to Annemarie Schwarzenbach, May 1, 1942. Erika and Klaus Mann Archive, Literaturarchiv Monacensia, Munich.

Mann, Klaus. *Der Wendepunkt.* Reibek bei Hamburg: Rowohlt, 1999.

———. "Editorial." *Decision: A Review of Free Culture* 1.1 (January 1941).

———. *Tagebücher 1938–39.* Munich: Spangenberg, 1989.

———. *Tagebücher 1940–43.* Munich: Spangenberg, 1989.

———. *The Turning Point: Thirty-five Years in This Century.* London: Oswald Wolff, 1984.

———. Unpublished letter to U.S. Attorney General Francis Biddle, [dated?] housed in the Erika and Klaus Mann Archive, Literaturarchiv Monacensia, Munich.

Reiss, Curt. *Meine Berühmte Freunde.* Freiburg: Herder, 1987.

Stephan, Alexander. *Communazis: FBI Surveillance of German Émigré Writers.* New Haven: Yale University Press, 2000.

CHAPTER 12

EXTORTING HENRY HOLT & CO.: J. EDGAR HOOVER AND THE PUBLISHING INDUSTRY

CLAIRE A. CULLETON

AT AMERICAN PUBLISHER HENRY HOLT'S DEATH IN 1926, the *New York Times* declared "New York has lost one of its most distinguished citizens and the American publishing trade has lost its dean." Founder of the important publishing house Henry Holt & Co. in 1866, Holt developed a reputation in the industry that would lead Donald Sheehan to note in *This Was Publishing* that when men like Henry Holt and Charles Scribner "commented on conditions in the industry, they spoke for the regular book trade from coast to coast." Foreseeing calamitous changes in the industry, Henry Holt vigorously campaigned against Big Business's takeover of the book trade; but he probably never anticipated Big Brother's superintendent interventions. This chapter follows J. Edgar Hoover's custodial relationship with the Holt firm at mid-century, and describes a situation that would have Holt, I imagine, rolling in his grave.

Inspired by research completed for my two recent books on the topic of Hoover's FBI and the bureau's involvement in American arts in the twentieth century, this project began when I received the FBI file of publisher Henry Holt too late to discuss its extraordinary contents in my *Joyce and the G-Men*, a book that details the bureau's engagement in the publishing industry, examines J. Edgar Hoover's role in manipulating the contours of literary Modernism, describes the ongoing politics that framed continuing debate in the American intellectual community over the meaning of *modernism* during the years between and beyond the two world wars, and analyzes the substantial influence of J. Edgar Hoover on the nature and direction of the debate. Though the Holt FBI material arrived just after my book had gone into production, the file substantiated the remarkable hunch that led me to request it in the first place: Henry Holt & Co. had been running manuscripts by Hoover for decades, seeking his explicit approval on authors and his advanced sanction on works and topics under consideration by the press. Once he approved a book for production, Hoover insisted on getting advanced copies of page proofs or galleys, and orchestrated the details of Holt's advertising and marketing campaigns. The Henry Holt FBI File numbers 234 pages, and although the file was opened by FBI agents in May 1949, after the octogenarian book publisher who founded Henry Holt & Co. had been dead for more than 20 years, and after his sons Roland, Henry Jr., and Elliot had already quit the business and gone on to other work, the file stands out as the single most astonishing bureau file I have read among the thousands of pages of documents I have received under Freedom of Information Act (FOIA) provisions in the past 15 years.

More a scrutinizing record, then, of the "loyalty" of the Holt firm than a bureau dossier on the publisher, evidence in the file reveals that over the course of at least 36 years, roughly from 1936 until J. Edgar Hoover's death in 1972, the FBI director held considerable sway over the firm, reviewed sets of advanced galleys, and approved the contracting or publication of most books dealing with the FBI, Communism, or anti-Communism. By the 1950s, remarkably, he was manipulating the firm, gouging its marketing and production resources, and extorting thousands of dollars from the company by ordering hundreds (and hundreds) of copies at a time of his books *Masters of Deceit* (1958) and *A Study of Communism* (1962) at a generous author's discount of 46 percent, a higher rate usually offered only to authors of textbooks marketed through the firm's School Division.[1] He insisted in letters to the firm that the company respond favorably to organizations requesting permission to reproduce full or partial chapters of his work, with no apparent concern over what those cost-free arrangements would do to the company's proprietary rights or revenues.

In matters regarding his own books, Hoover continually questioned the validity of the firm's billing, kept his accounts in arrears, bullied the firm into translating his work into "such little-known languages as Assamese, Bengali, Burmese, Gujarati, Kannaba [*sic*], Laotian, Marathi, Punjabi, Pushtu, and many others" (letter to Tolson, November 28, 1966), and strong-armed reluctant Holt executives into discussing uncomfortable "special price arrangements" with reprint publishers such as Pocket Books, Inc., on his behalf. Even the simplest mention from a bureau higher-up of one of

Hoover's requests would send Holt & Co. into a production frenzy, as Clyde Tolson's coercive letter to Holt president Edgar T. Rigg suggests: "Dear Ed: When [name blacked out] visited Mr. Hoover this morning, he expressed an intense interest in seeing that a paperback edition of 'Masters of Deceit' printed in the Spanish language is published in Latin American countries, and he plans to get in touch with you soon regarding this matter. We naturally are grateful for his interest, and I trust you will give serious consideration to his desires" (February 4, 1959). Before the year was through, within a matter of months, in fact, Holt & Co. published *Maestros del engaño: revelaciones del director de la FBI*, a Spanish edition of the bureau director's book.

J. Edgar Hoover and his associate and deputy directors Clyde Tolson and "Deke" DeLoach (Hoover's publicity chief and later head of Crime Records) used other maneuvers to keep Rigg's attention squarely focused on Hoover's books, and sometimes invented reasons for the publication of new editions of his work, running these ideas by Rigg and the firm's trade department. One particular memo in the Holt file outlines the idea of a contest for American high school seniors who would submit essays inspired by *Masters of Deceit.* The winners, the memo suggests, could receive special editions of Hoover's book. Other memos in the file allude to even more editions. One memo shows that Hoover approved a special edition of *Masters of Deceit* for use by Young Americans for Freedom Inc., and that their edition differed significantly from "the very special edition" prepared for Constructive Action Inc.[2] One wonders how Holt & Co. could support these requests from Hoover and his aides, and how the firm kept up with their unremitting "suggestions" about foreign language translations, paperback editions, reprints, special editions, and so forth? How did it manage these requests fiscally, and how did the firm accommodate Hoover in the face of its usually tight production schedules?

The extensive Henry Holt file also reveals that Holt & Co. employees kept in personal contact with Hoover and communicated with the director on a first-name basis. Rigg, for example, wrote Hoover on October 21, 1959 to importune, "Please keep up the good work. Please keep showing us the way" (Holt FBI file). Another employee insider wrote at the end of one letter to Hoover, "I am beginning to feel like a member of the FBI myself," presumably on account of all the information she had supplied him (name blacked out; Holt FBI file; November 6, 1961). Another assured Hoover in a letter, "As to the policy of our publishing house, we have only one, and that is that we will not publish books that we consider detrimental to the best interests of this country. . . . Year by year so many of this nation's ideals and aims are being chopped away by anti-Americans or non-thinking Americans that it is frightening" (name blacked out; Holt FBI file; February 1, 1962). Employees also sent Hoover tips about people "who should be closely watched" (name blacked out; Holt FBI file; November 22, 1950). One message to Hoover typed on letterhead from the trade department, for example, ended with the writer's conviction, "I have no hesitancy in bringing [this] to your attention" (name blacked out; Holt FBI file; April 20, 1951). The firm continually had to assure the bureau of its loyalty and patriotism, making sure to contract and publish only works that trounced Communism, or equally important to Hoover, dealt positively with the FBI. At a time when American book publishers and publications were under the careful observation of sanctioned or self-appointed government censors, and were subject to the unrelenting scrutiny of bureau functionaries working day and night reviewing manuscripts and books in the FBI Reading Room, or clipping articles from some 625 newspapers daily, Hoover was busy, too, manipulating publishers, editors, and other staff associated with the industry, and was instrumental in "showing them the way."

As the firm's relationship with Hoover developed, letters from Rigg and his company employees grew more obsequious. One worker wrote Hoover asking whether he would consider writing "a factual book of the magnificent activities of the extremely important bureau of which you are the Director" (name blacked out; likely William E. Buckley; Holt FBI file; April 20, 1951). Even Holt president Edgar T. Rigg resorted to overstatement in his letters. One of his letters to Hoover described a book project on juvenile delinquency, a topic, he knew, was "close to [Hoover's] heart." Rigg wrote "Please believe me, this is not a request, an asking for a favor. This I will never do, and I know you know that. It is merely an exposure at the request of the author . . ." (Holt FBI file, November 3, 1958). These "exposures" were somewhat frequent, the file reveals. Rigg wrote to Clyde Tolson using a similar expression: "Please believe me, Clyde, this is not a request, but more in the nature of an exposure to you" (Holt FBI file; November 14, 1958). These exposures provided the bureau with timely information about forthcoming projects, prospective authors, and apropos topics under consideration by the firm. Other forms of exposure are evident in the Holt file, as well, such as descriptions of phone calls between the firm and the bureau to discuss prospective authors. A year later, bureau memos about the Holt firm would indicate that "The Bureau has excellent relations with this publishing house. The Director addresses Rigg as 'Dear Ed'" (Holt FBI file; December 16, 1959). Other reports identify Rigg as being on the "Special Correspondents List," one of Hoover's lists of "friendlies," and indicate "we enjoy very cordial relations with Holt and Co." While president of Holt & Co., Edgar Rigg was careful to maintain cordiality; nonetheless, it was a complicated relationship whose most interesting particulars have been redacted, expunged from bureau files, or lost to the recesses of time.

As early as 1936, the FBI file shows, editors at Holt & Co. ran book ideas by Hoover, seeking his explicit approval on projects and their proposed authors. Hoover and his men followed these projects carefully, and monitored the books from pre- to postproduction. Holt employees sent Hoover everything from proposals and galleys, to page proofs and advance copies of books. In addition to what the Holt FBI File discloses about this practice, a set of 1937 letters in the Holt Archive at Princeton University's Firestone Library demonstrates the convention, as well. Hoover's letters thank the firm for advance page proofs of *In 1936*, a book that contained a chapter titled "Crime and the G-Men." Pleased with "the commendatory manner in which the work of the Federal Bureau of Investigation [was] described" in the book, Hoover wrote to Holt's Harmon Tupper that it was "indeed a good resume of our activities during the past year," and added that he was sure the book would give "a better understanding of our efforts to improve the existing crime conditions" (Princeton University, C0100 Holt Archive, Box 57 folder 17). Already 15 years in the position of Director and not yet half the autocrat he would become—or as former bureau agent William W. Turner described him, "the most dangerously ambitious bureaucrat in modern American history" (328)—Hoover was eager to control and regulate what was published about the FBI, and he made his pronouncements about books and their authors in writing, giving the thumbs up or the thumbs down to Holt editors seeking his opinion on Holt & Co. projects.

Letters in the FBI file reveal Hoover's custodianship at the firm, as well. In December 1959, for example, Rigg sent Tolson proofs of a forthcoming Holt book titled *The Hidden Russia*, and wrote that the proofs were being sent "at the urgent request of [name blacked out] who feels that perhaps you and Mr. Hoover might like to get an advance look at it because of its anticommunistic slant. I have not read it myself," Rigg added (Holt FBI file; December 4, 1959). FOIA redactions in the Holt file make it impossible to know who made the "urgent request" to send proofs to the bureau director—a federal agent, an editor, or the book's author. Because Hoover and his ghostwriters often wrote prefaces or provided dust jacket commentary for books that critiqued Communism, the "urgent request" to send Hoover the proofs may have had something to do with seizing upon an opportunity to maintain Hoover's stance as America's "top cop," upon whose words and blurbs hung the nation's security;[3] but the urgent request may also be linked to the director's maniacal obsession to control and manage whatever he could in American culture, including what got published. In this case, "proofs [of the Krasnov book] were reviewed in the Crime Research Section . . . and there was no mention of the FBI," one memo notes. Rigg's interesting disclaimer about the book, "I have not read it myself," lets him avoid blame, should Hoover doom the project or its author. Hoover doomed some projects at Holt, the file reveals, or caused the agency to second-guess contracting certain works or working with certain authors.

To reinforce and reiterate the bureau's "lean" on Holt & Co., Hoover sent president Edgar T. Rigg newspaper clippings and articles about publishing houses, organizations, or associations that he felt had turned in a wrong direction. "Dear Ed: I thought you might be interested in the attached copy of an article which appeared in today's Washington Post and Times-Herald entitled 'Legion Unit Now Backs Red Studies.' With kind regards, Sincerely, Edgar" (Holt FBI file; November 22, 1957). The clipping describes a reversal of the long-standing American Legion policy against teaching anything about Communism in public schools. Rigg responded to Hoover two weeks later, thanking him not only for his letter with the American Legion clipping but for a previous letter and clipping, as well. Rigg added some brief information about a book project and wrote, "I have also heard from [entire line blacked out] who wants to see proofs when available. You can be sure this will all be followed carefully. My best, Ed" (Holt FBI file; December 10, 1957).

The publishing company's relationship with the bureau and with J. Edgar Hoover in particular likely troubles today's readers. We do not want to think of a publisher so driven and compelled by Hoover that he would follow his instructions carefully. But Rigg did, and we cannot help but wonder what other publishing firms Hoover and his men may have been leaning on at this time, and to what end. We know that Hoover avidly began to "develop" informants in the publishing industry after the 1950 publication of Max Lowenthal's *The Federal Bureau of Investigation*, an "unauthorized" book published by ex-Holt & Co. editor William M. Sloane. Hoover had not seen Lowenthal's book coming, and not only was caught by what he considered a surprise attack but was furious at his agents' oversight. As Curt Gentry reports in *J. Edgar Hoover: The Man and the Secrets*, although Lowenthal had been working on the project for 10 years, the director only learned about it after seeing an advance notice of the book in *Publishers Weekly*, and he knew the book would highlight and critique certain aspects of his FBI. "That Hoover knew what the book contained and was able to order the preparation of a detailed rebuttal in September 1950, two months before the book was published, was interesting. Perhaps coincidentally, perhaps not, about this same time the page proofs of the book vanished from the motorcycle sidecar of a messenger en route from the printer to the publisher" (Gentry 386). Quickly, anti-Lowenthal editorials were planted in newspapers across the nation, and "the press favorites Walter Winchell, Fulton Lewis, Jr., George Sokolsky, Rex Collier, and Walter Trohan were unleashed, as were all of the [bureau's] special agents in charge, who were instructed to discourage booksellers from stocking the book. One SAC suggested agents steal copies from libraries," but his suggestion was rejected after someone pointed out that the libraries would likely replace the stolen copies, and thus drive up sales of the book (Gentry 386–87). William C. Sullivan, who rose to become one of the bureau's assistant directors in the 1960s, noted that after the Lowenthal debacle, "'we developed informants in the publishing houses.' These were not necessarily lower-level employees. They included at least two publishers, Henry Holt [*sic*, already dead] and Bennett Cerf" (Gentry 387). William W. Turner adds that "in 1962 when the manuscript of Fred Cook's critical *The FBI Nobody Knows* was submitted to Random House, Cerf grievously breached publishing ethics by dispatching a copy to Hoover" (124). Subsequently, Random House passed on Cook's *The FBI Nobody Knows*, which he published two years later with Macmillan. Bennett Cerf's relationship with the bureau has been difficult to trace. Obtaining a copy of Cerf's FBI file has proven impossible, for example;[4] but I expect that the same sort of information that trafficked back and forth between Holt & Co. insiders and the bureau was trafficked back and forth between Random House insiders and the bureau.

To be sure, other publishers and publishing houses fell under bureau scrutiny. The bureau investigated Benjamin W. Huebsch, for example, whose B.W. Huebsch publishing firm had done so well that it was able to merge with Viking Press in 1925. Huebsch attracted the attention of the bureau in 1912 after publishing the controversial and anonymously authored *Philip Dru: Administrator: A Story of Tomorrow, 1920–1935*, a novel that went into several subsequent printings. One of Hoover's "friendly" journalists, Westbrook Pegler of the *New York Journal American*, called the novel "[a] cabal against the Constitution" (Huebsch FBI file; October 15, 1954). Huebsch's FBI file numbers only 25 pages, but glosses indicate that he was a member of the advisory council of Book Union, an organization described in the file as "A Communist 'Book-of-the-month' club" (Huebsch FBI file; December 14, 1954). Huebsch's file, like so many others, teems with a richness of private information, and registers, for example, petitions and letters signed by the publisher over the course of his life. Keeping a watchful eye on men holding the reins in the book publishing industry, and noting their involvement in "radical" or dissident activities, bureau SACs worked up files on publishers by auditing their activities and scrutinizing their alignment with industry or political associations. For example, as editor in chief of G.P. Putnam's Sons, Henry Hart's involvement on the preplanning committee of the First American Writers Congress rendered bureau suspicion, and quickly earned him a bureau file, making his professional association with Benjamin Huebsch an added problem. Similarly, a report in the Holt file includes a tidbit about the sighting of then Holt Vice President William Sloane at New York's Henry Hudson Hotel for a meeting of the Independent Citizens' Committee of the Arts, Sciences, and Professions, Inc., an organization "cited as a Communist front by the House Committee on Un-American Activities," a postscript reads. In a culture such as this, it is no wonder that publishers like Rigg worked to cultivate good standing with the bureau, and made sure to engage the bureau's "opinion" on projects. In August 1950, for example, someone from Holt & Co. telephoned Lou Nichols to advise that the company was "considering doing a book with [name blacked out]. He wanted to know if the Bureau could give any guidance as to whether Jordan could be trusted (Holt FBI file; August 29, 1952)." Nichols's response was "no comment." Not incidentally, Holt & Co. got cold feet and passed on the project. The Jordan referenced here is USAF Major George Racey Jordan, whose important diaries described covert collaborations between the USA and the USSR in building atomic bombs. After getting "no comment" from the bureau, Holt grew cold, and Jordan went on to publish his work with Harcourt, Brace & Company, instead. Other examples abound. In *Hoover's FBI*, William W. Turner also describes the bureau's involvement with G.P. Putnam's Sons, and traces through bureau documents Cartha DeLoach's notes on his interventions with "Random House, Holt Co., Harpers, et al." (124). DeLoach's "et al." is most troubling, since it indicates an exponentially unknown list of publishing firms he regularly interviewed and likely bullied.

In order to get fuller and timelier information on the industry, the bureau also had in-house sources in magazine and newspaper offices, people who would supply Hoover's agents with notes from editorial board meetings at magazines such as *Time, Life, Collier's, Fortune, Newsweek, Look*, and *Reader's Digest* (Gentry 388), or with copies of minutes taken during Advisory Council meetings at newspapers such as the *Daily Worker*, published by the CPUSA. Louis Budenz, for example, managing editor of the *Daily Worker*, was a bureau informant; Quentin Reynolds, an editor at *Collier's*, also would "cooperate" with the bureau, and became not only a close friend of Hoover's but "a Bureau friend," as well, Natalie Robins notes in *Alien Ink* (134). With such a large network of sources connected to American print culture, Hoover was able to know what articles and book reviews were as yet unassigned and thereby up for grabs, which were forthcoming, and what stories were proposed for future issues (and by whom). His insiders also supplied him with lists of office numbers and telephone extensions for employees at these publications.

Importantly, not only publishers but authors, too, described or discussed future projects with the bureau, and sought clearance from J. Edgar Hoover and his top aides. An August 29, 1952, memorandum in the Holt file notes that Milt Hill, an editor of the 1950 Holt title *Smersh*, wrote to Louis Nichols in 1952 about a book project proposed to him by Joseph McCarthy *on* Joseph McCarthy. Hill asked Nichols's "advice as to whether he should do the book or not." According to an August 29, 1952, memo from M.A. Jones, Nichols "commented that although [he] did not think we should become involved in this matter [he] could see no objection to telling Hill to go ahead as it would be a friendly book from the Bureau standpoint." Friendly press, in fact, mattered most to Hoover and his bureau aides. One memo to Hoover reports on Charles Carver's proposed book with Holt on the German Saboteur case, and notes that "Mr. Nichols thought the Saboteur case would make a good medium of showing excellent work on the part of the Bureau." Though Carver's project approached bureau endorsement, Jones's memorandum concludes, "I am having a name check made on [Carver]" (April 21, 1958). Hoover commented across the bottom, "Right."

Hoover was involved in Holt & Co. decision making even after the firm merged with the Rinehart and Winston companies in 1959, and continued to manipulate the publishing house long after Rigg's departure. When a *New York Times* article described a forthcoming book in Holt, Rinehart and Winston's catalog, a book that was likely to be unfriendly to the bureau, Hoover immediately went into full bullying mode, reading deputy director "Deke" DeLoach the proverbial riot act. DeLoach consequently shot off a memo to Tolson that indicates the bureau's mad dash to block the publication:

> The Director approved a recommendation that I discuss with [name blacked out] of Holt, Rinehart & Winston publishing firm in New York City, an indication in a New York Times article of 6/5/66 that his publishing firm planned to publish the captioned book [caption blacked out]. [Name blacked out] was out of the city until today, 6/15/66. Upon mentioning the reference in the New York Times article he admitted that his company had contracted to publish this book. The contract was arranged by Al Edwards, Editor in Chief, who has taken over most of the old duties of Ed Rigg. Edwards approved the manuscript and later had [name blacked out] also read the manuscript. [Name blacked out] told me that neither he nor Edwards knew of [name blacked out's] background . . . . I told [name blacked out] that we, of course, had no doubts concerning [name blacked out's] feelings toward the FBI, and it would indeed be surprising if he praised us at any time. [Name blacked out] told me he would definitely bring our opinion to the attention of Al Edwards, and Edwards would no doubt call us in the next day or two . . . . It would seem that Holt, Rinehart & Winston would have checked on the author prior to signing a contract. (Holt FBI file; June 15, 1966)

This memo begs the question, "Checked with whom?" and exposes the bureau's insistence that publishers seek license on any and all projects related to the FBI.

While he was manipulating and controlling Holt & Co, Hoover also went after the man who would become one of Holt's future partners, Rinehart's President and Chairman of the Board Stanley Rinehart. Like the Holt firm, Rinehart and Company regularly sent Hoover advanced copies of books, proof copies, or prepublication information about projects in the pipeline. In fact, I would guess from reading the Holt file that Holt & Co. was expanding the FBI Reading Room library at the rate of five or more books every season. Rinehart and Company obviously participated at the same rate. In 1950, according to one report, based on nothing more than "a rumor received at the Bureau in August that Rinehart and Company planned to publish a book around the first of the year (1951) that would be critical of the Bureau," agents interrogated Stanley Rinehart (Holt FBI file; December 16, 1959), who reported that while he had discussed the project with author Dave Jacobson, who wanted to do a book on the bureau, "nothing ever came of it." By constantly checking up on American publishers, by red-flagging their titles, by bullying and harassing them about who could and could not write about the FBI, Hoover and his men cultivated an industry atmosphere grounded in anxiety and rank with panic and dread. This culture allowed them to pull the strings of some of the most important and influential publishers, editors, and writers of the twentieth century. Richard Hack's 2004 biography of J. Edgar Hoover titled *Puppetmaster* certainly acknowledges the sort of string pulling symptomatic of Hoover's reign.

Yet even while wielding such formidable control, Hoover was marionetted by his own paranoia, which grew by leaps and bounds as his tenure in the bureau matured. An episode detailed in the Holt file substantiates the extent of his obsession. A February 20, 1958, letter from Rigg to Clyde Tolson delicately reminds Tolson that Hoover said he would be glad to autograph copies of *Masters of Deceit* for some Holt employees. Rigg wrote,

> Needless to say, everyone would like to have one, but I have listed below those who worked very closely on the book and who would certainly be proud to have such a personalized copy. [A list of nine employees follows; names blacked out]. I certainly appreciate Mr. Hoover's offer and hope that this is not too much of a bother for him.

Paperwork in the Holt file indicates that signed copies were mailed to the firm five days later, but not before the bureau ran background checks on those nine lucky Holt employees, and opened bureau files on every last one of them. They, too, would fall under bureau scrutiny, and the simple notation that they held autographed copies of Hoover's book would follow them for decades. One such employee, for example, wrote to the bureau some years later to ask whether he and his family could have a tour of bureau headquarters, since they planned to visit the nation's capital. The request is duly noted in the Holt file, as are descriptions of the man's wife, his nine-year-old son, and that autographed 1958 edition of *Masters of Deceit* (Holt FBI file; May 10, 1966). Such was Hoover's desire to maintain records on everything, even on matters that seem to us now incidental.

While agents and bureau higher-ups were busy managing the Hoover image and countervailing unfriendly representations of the director and the bureau, who was protecting the nation? Bennett Cerf, in *At Random*, a memoir of his days as Random House's publishing giant, recounts an anecdote that asks the same question. When Random House published Donald Whitehead's *The FBI Story* in 1956 (Hoover provided the book's preface), more than 50,000 copies were sold in the first two weeks of its release. The public was mad for copies of the book. Cerf noted that sales of the book were so swift that booksellers actually took copies out of store window displays to sell, and replaced the display books with impostors dressed with dummy book jackets. Copies of the book sold after Christmas and well into the next year, he noted; it was one of those books that would not stay put on the shelves. The book's immense popularity gave rise to an amusing telephone conversation between Cerf and assistant director Lou Nichols. Cerf explains:

> One morning in January the phone rang just as I arrived at my office and it was Lou Nichols calling from Washington. "Bennett," he said, "what's wrong with the book?" I said "What do you mean, what's wrong? It's selling as fast as we can print it." Then he said "As of this morning, I must tell you there are no copies of *The FBI Story* in Brentano's or Scribner's and none in the Doubleday Shops, or for that matter in any shop or department store in mid-Manhattan. None in Penn Station; none in the Wall Street area. So I ask you: what's wrong?" I tried to explain that this wasn't bad, that the book was selling faster than the stores could reorder or we could deliver them, and I guess I convinced him.
>
> I was so amused by this switch on the usual report about the author's aunt who couldn't find a single copy of his book in any shop in Schenectady, I couldn't wait to tell somebody. So I went to the office next to mine where Jim Michener, just back from the Austrian-Hungarian border, was putting the final touches on *The Bridge at Andau*, which we were rushing for March publication though he had finished it after our spring catalogue was already printed. When I told Jim about my phone conversation, he said "Well, with all those agents checking bookshops, this would have been a great day for somebody to rob a bank in New York." (247–48)

Hoover reportedly kept fastidious track of who did, and did not, purchase copies of *The FBI Story*. Athan Theoharis notes that "FBI officials not only reviewed proposed publicity plans but actively promoted *The FBI Story*, including purchasing thousands of copies through FBI recreation association funds and ensuring favorable book reviews, notably by Harry Overstreet" (309). Two years later, with the publication of Hoover's *Masters of Deceit*, these practices not only continued but evolved.

Clearly warehousing *Masters of Deceit*, the bureau ordered 500 or 1,000 copies at a time from Holt, Rinehart and Winston, and placed coterminous orders even before invoices reflecting previous shipments had arrived. The following special note to Hoover's secretary Miss Gandy was typed across the bottom of the office copy of a November 18, 1960, letter to the publishing company requesting another 1,000 copies of the book, and certainly indicates the outlandish extent of the bureau's reserve:

> NOTE: Regardless of the fact that we have at this time 1,200 copies of "Masters of Deceit" on hand, it is felt we should place this additional order immediately. SAC [Frank] Price in a letter received today requested that 175 copies be sent to him for the city and county schools of San Diego, as well as 69 books for employees in his office. It was felt better to have them shipped from New York than to use our supply at Headquarters.

The stockpile of discounted books was managed and paid for by funds from the FBI Recreation Association, and copies were sold at full price to bureau employees, to new agents in training, and to "good friends of the Bureau." In 1960, three of these "good friends" purchased copies of Hoover's book but made out their checks to Henry Holt and Company instead of to the FBI Recreation Association. A December 14, 1960, memo from M.A. Jones indicates that because one of the men was considering buying 500 or 600 additional copies of *Masters of Deceit*, he did not want to ask him or the others to redo their checks. "The only way we can use these checks," Jones wrote in a memo to DeLoach, "is to deduct the total of the 6 checks, which amounts to $138.65, from the total amount of the 3 invoices set forth in the letter and make out a check for the difference from the FBI Recreation Association" (December 14, 1960). By 1962, the bureau had the ordering and reordering of books down to a science, and incredibly micromanaged every aspect of the Holt, Rinehart and Winston shipments. Clyde Tolson wrote on May 28, 1962, "At this time I would like to order 1,000 additional copies of 'Masters of Deceit' with the usual six-months' extended billing. Please bill these to us in lots of 500 books to each invoice. I would appreciate your advising me from which city the books will be sent, the method of transportation and the name of the transportation company." I picture a roomful of agents scrupulously mapping out the route of Hoover's books as the cartons make their way to Bureau Headquarters, applying the same punctiliousness to this task that they would use to track the movements of Public Enemy #1.

With the publication later that year of Hoover's *A Study of Communism*, the bureau's accounts at Holt, Rinehart and Winston grew more complicated and delinquent. A February 19, 1968 interoffice memo from M.A. Jones to Mr. Bishop alludes to a recently received "FORM LETTER FROM CREDIT DEPARTMENT HOLT, RINEHART AND WINSTON," and grumbles about "contemplated Christmas sales which were not as heavy as anticipated," and the temporary suspension of the bureau's "sure thing," its steady sales clientele, the new agents:

> Elimination of New Agents' classes from 11/13/67 to the present time has had a big effect on the sale of books. At the present moment we have an inventory of more than 400 books on hand but as soon as the New Agents' classes start again on March 4, 1968, the sale of these books will decrease our inventory drastically. It is felt that the payment of this September invoice in the amount of $575.52 will satisfy Holt, Rinehart and Winston until we can sell additional copies of these two books.

Jones explains that from the beginning "there was a mutual understanding between the publisher and the Bureau that the books would be paid for as they were sold to Bureau employees," and he takes exception with the firm's request for payment in the amount of $1,730.36, a figure Jones describes as "alleged to be past due." Refusing to square up, the bureau only settled one-third of the February past-due bill.

Stubborn, headstrong, persistent, J. Edgar Hoover had the kind of personality he despised in other people. Until his death in 1972, he created a culture that thrived on bullying, harassment, and intimidation, and he used his power to micromanage intellectual life in the United States by working effectively with publishing companies such as Holt & Co. Hoover's efforts yielded him clout and advantage when dealing with Rigg, Sloane, and Edwards at Holt & Co., since they relied on him to sanction authors, vet proposals, preview galleys, and comment on page proofs or advanced copies. Though we are only beginning to understand his manipulation of the book industry and his efforts to finagle and process American readers, through FBI files and documents we have a better understanding of Hoover's racketeering and his extortion of the Holt & Co. firm, when he used personal might, bureau manpower, and institutional money to ensure that his books were printed, translated, reprinted, marketed, bought, sold, and otherwise disseminated to an international reading public. Moreover, he was obsessively prophylactic about warding off negative critiques about him and his bureau.

The so-called "HENRY HOLT" file has little to do with the publisher who founded the company more than 140 years ago. Often described as one of the "gentleman publishers" of the early twentieth century whose integrity evinced his ideals and principles, Henry Holt was known for his straightforwardness, and he did not hesitate to critique the changes being wrought on the industry in the early decades of the century. Holt grew increasingly intolerant, for example, of changes in the book trade, and wrote nostalgically of the days when "custodial" relationships built on loyalty and friendship emerged between publishers and authors. In her important work *The House of Holt: 1866–1946, An Editorial History* (1993), Ellen Gilbert examines the founding and growth of the Holt company from its beginnings through 1946, and details the company's various management and editorial shifts. Paying special attention to the ways "key figures in the company's history influenced its editorial direction" (246), Gilbert identifies Lincoln MacVeagh, Alfred Harcourt, and William Sloane as essential figures contributing to the history of Holt as well as the publishing industry, and traces each man's hand in acquiring for the firm some of its most important writers. Gilbert also notes Holt's and Sloane's constant battles with "big business at the controls of Holt & Co.," something that caused Sloane to leave in 1946 and start his own publishing house (3). Though Gilbert adds that neither of the men loosened his "resistance to outside influences dictating the way in which they conducted the business of publishing books" (4), it is now clear that others following in their footsteps at the firm certainly did loosen their resistance to outside influences, and by yielding to Hoover and the FBI, they surrendered to the bureau the power associated with what Holt & Co. acquired, what it published, and how it was marketed. More than that, they conceded freedom of expression. Perversely, though Holt worried about Big Business's interventions into the book trade, it would be Big Brother and not Big Business that would compromise the firm.

In closing, it is important to note that it was not only the FBI who manipulated the Holt firm; the State Department also became involved especially in relation to textbooks published out of Holt's School Division. In late 1941, Holt Executive Vice President Gilbert Loveland wrote to Professor Donnal Smith about the textbook *Story of Nations*, which he believed was being interdicted by the State Department or by "some people in it" who were "recommending instead a book which drags tenth-graders back and forth across the ages sixteen times in one year" (Princeton Holt Archive, C0100, Box 118, folder 9). In a climate where government agencies select and critique texts, exercise State authority to suppress or promote books, and sanction or prohibit authors from expressing themselves, agencies like the FBI and the State Department acted as custodians of American culture, and by limiting cultural texts they circumscribed twentieth-century historiography.

Notes

1. Correspondence in the Holt Archive at Princeton University's Firestone Library indicate that authors publishing textbooks through the firm's School Division received author's discounts up to 50 percent. For trade books, though, an author's discount was rarely as high as Hoover's 46 percent. Former bureau assistant director William C. Sullivan says he was "one of six Bureau

employees who 'put together' *Masters of Deceit*, the book [that] made the Director very rich, though most people thought he had given away his royalties to charity. . . . Hoover was annoyed when he found himself in a higher tax bracket because of those royalties" (Robins, *Alien Ink* 278).

2. Several nationwide programs were based on Hoover's book, too. On February 26, 1960, for example, Rigg learned in a letter from Tolson that "Kay Clancy Metz, Director of Women's Activities, The Quaker Oats Company, [was] awarded a George Washington Honor Medal by the Freedoms Foundation of Valley Forge for her program based on 'Masters of Deceit.'" Tolson continued, "We, of course, are certainly pleased with her success, and I know you will be glad to receive this news" (Holt FBI file).
3. For a fuller discussion of Hoover's obsession with remaining in the public eye, see Chapter 3 of *Joyce and the G-Men*. Part of his self-promotion campaign included constantly circulating articles that he or his various ghostwriters had written. He also exerted some control over what would be published concerning him, the bureau, or anti-Communism in popular magazines. For instance, he often sent *Reader's Digest* publisher DeWitt Wallace pieces he had written himself or he had ghostwritten. One count has it that *Reader's Digest* printed more than a dozen of the ghostwritten articles under the Hoover byline—a figure bettered only by *American Magazine*, which published 18, and *U.S. News and World Report*, which published 25. What he did not write himself he asked others to pen on behalf of the bureau. Prominent ACLU legal counsel Morris Ernst's legendary *Reader's Digest* defense of the bureau in 1950, titled "Why I No Longer Fear the FBI," was "reprinted and distributed for years" (Gentry 387), and Hoover always kept on hand for quick dissemination reprints of his speeches and pamphlets.
4. Attempts to get information from the bureau on Bennett Cerf have been frustrating. As I explain in *Joyce and the G-Men*,

    Several years after I requested the Bennett Cerf file, I got a letter from J. Kevin O'Brien, Chief of FOIPA Section in the Information Resources Division, informing me that the file I requested on Cerf was processed and ready for mailing. It comprised 183 pages, the letter said, but pursuant to Title 28, Code of Federal Regulations, Sections 16.10 and 16.47, I would be asked to pay copying costs at the rate of ten cents per page after the first 100 pages. The letter continued, "upon receipt of your check or money order, payable to the Federal Bureau of Investigation, these documents will be forwarded to you" (July 14, 1997). Immediately I sent off a check for $8.30 but got a letter back from one James Meyen saying that my request for Cerf's file had been denied and that I might be able to appeal his decision by writing to Judge Advocate General Code 34, Department of the Navy. I was floored. So I drafted an appeal letter, but within days I learned that my appeal to JAG #34 was denied.

    I have not heard again from the FBI about those 183 pages of Bennett Cerf materials that were processed for me and made available for release . . . . Some weeks after my appeal to JAG #34 had been

> denied, I received an unaccounted-for 12-page document from the Criminal Investigation Service of the U.S. Department of the Navy about Cerf's "loyalty." The report had been prepared under Hoover's orders, who had the report made when he learned that Random House was preparing to publish Quentin Reynolds's children's book *The F.B.I.* Hoover wound up writing the foreword to Reynolds's book and asked Cerf to discount the book to all FBI employees. "Cerf complied," Robins reports, "and according to [Quentin Reynolds's] file, the FBI kept track of every single copy bought. Reynolds later wrote Louis Nichols that it was [his] . . . 'most popular book'" (137). A few years later, Cerf would get the chance to work with Hoover and the bureau again in bringing out a book on the FBI, Don Whitehead's 1956 *The FBI Story*. (81–82)

Hoover was careful, in fact, to remain up-to-date on leaders in the fast-changing world of publishing. A 1956 memo dashed off to Lou Nichols in late February responds to one of Hoover's exacting and demanding questions. It begins, The Director inquired, "*Who is now President of Henry Holt and Co.?*" The short memo identifies Edgar T. Rigg as president, and lists the addresses of his Baltimore birthplace, his New York City office, and his Bronxville home. Another memo responds to Clyde Tolson's question of January 15, 1958, "What do we know re [name blacked out] now with Henry Holt & Co? Nichols used to contact him." The statement sent in reply is almost entirely redacted except for the opener, "Mr. Tolson asked if we knew anything about [name and several lines blacked out]."

WORKS CITED

Cerf, Bennett. *At Random: Reminiscences of Bennett Cerf.* New York: Random House, 1977.

Culleton, Claire A. *Joyce and the G-Men: J. Edgar Hoover's Manipulation of Modernism.* New York: Palgrave Macmillan, 2004.

Gentry, Curt. *J. Edgar Hoover: The Man and the Secrets.* New York: Norton, 1991.

Gilbert, Ellen D. *The House of Holt 1866–1946: An Editorial History.* Metuchen, N.J.: Scarecrow Press Inc., 1993.

———. *The House of Holt, 1866–1946: A Documentary Volume.* Dictionary of Literary Biography; vol. 284. Farmington Hills: Gale, 2003.

Holt & Co. Archive, Princeton University Firestone Library, Collection C0100.

Holt, Henry. FBI file. 1 Section. 234 pages.

Huebsch, Benjamin W. FBI file. 1 Section. 25 pages.

Robins, Natalie. *Alien Ink: The FBI's War on Freedom of Expression.* New Brunswick: Rutgers U P, 1992.

Sheehan, Donald. *This Was Publishing.* Bloomington: Indiana U P, 1952.

Theoharis, Athan G. Ed. *From the Secret Files of J. Edgar Hoover.* Chicago: Ivan Dee, 1993.

Turner, William W. *Hoover's FBI.* New York: Thunder's Mouth Press, 1993.

List of Contributors

Emily Banwell has translated several nonfiction books for Hunter House Publishers and Berkeley Hills Books. She is currently employed as a German lecturer at the University of California, Berkeley. Her most recent translation project is a 3-part series of books on children's games.

Claire A. Culleton is Professor of Modern British and Irish literature at Kent State University. Her books include *Joyce and the G-Men: J. Edgar Hoover's Manipulation of Modernism* (Palgrave Macmillan, 2004); *Working-Class Culture, Women, and Britain, 1914–1921* (Palgrave Macmillan, 2000), and *Names and Naming in Joyce* (U of Wisconsin P, 1994); and she has coedited a collection of essays focused on Irish modernism and the global primitive. Culleton has published articles on twentieth-century literature and culture in the *James Joyce Quarterly, Eire-Ireland, the Imperial War Museum Review*, and *Women's Studies International Forum.*

Christopher Faulkner is Professor of Film studies and Director of the Institute of Comparative Studies in Literature, Art and Culture at Carleton University, Ottawa, Canada. The Institute is home to the Ph.D. in Cultural Mediations, an interdisciplinary degree that involves film, literature, music and art history. Faulkner has written a number of books and articles on various aspects of French cinema. His most recent book is *Jean Renoir: A Conversation with His Films*, 1894–1979 (Taschen 2007). His current project is a production and reception history of Renoir's "La Règle du jeu."

Josh Gosciak is the author of *Shadowed Country: Claude Mckay and the Romance of the Victorians* (Rutgers UP 2006). He had been active for many years as an independent publisher in New York City. He teaches literature and media studies.

Steven G. Kellman is Professor of Comparative Literature at The University of Texas at San Antonio. His books include*:* *Redemption: The Life of Henry Roth* (New York: Norton, 2005); *The Translingual Imagination*

(Lincoln, NE: University of Nebraska Press, 2000); *The Plague: Fiction and Resistance* (Boston: Twayne, 1993); *Loving Reading: Erotics of the Text* (Hamden, CT: Archon Books, 1985); *The Self Begetting Novel* (New York: Columbia University Press, 1980).

Karen Leick is Assistant Professor of English at The Ohio State University at Lima, where she teaches twentieth-century literature and culture, American modernism, and poetry. She is the author of articles on the popular reception of "little magazines," Ezra Pound, and H.L. Mencken. She has recently completed a book about Gertrude Stein's mainstream American reception.

William J. Maxwell is Associate Professor of English and Interpretive Theory at the University of Illinois, Urbana-Champaign, where he teaches modern American and African American literature. He is the author of *New Negro, Old Left: African-American Writing and Communism Between the Wars* (Columbia UP, 1999) and the editor of Claude McKay's *Complete Poems* (U of Illinois P, 2004). He is now at work on a book manuscript for Princeton UP entitled *FB Eyes: How J. Edgar Hoover's Ghostreaders Framed African-American Modernism.*

Debra A. Moddelmog is Associate Dean of Humanities, Professor of English, and coordinator of the Sexuality Studies program at The Ohio State University. She is the author of *Reading Desire: In Pursuit of Ernest Hemingway and Readers and Mythic Signs: The Oedipus Myth in Twentieth-Century Fiction.* In addition, she has published articles on various American writers, critical multiculturalism, and coming-out pedagogy.

Jeanne Perreault is Professor of English at the University of Calgary, (Alberta, Canada). Her most recent publication includes a coedited collection of essays on contemporary life writing, *Tracing the Autobiographical* (2005). She continues to work on subjectivity, feminism, and social change. Current projects include an investigation into women photojournalists in World War II and coediting a collection of essays on photography and social justice.

Alexander Stephan is Professor and Ohio Eminent Scholar in the Department of Germanic Languages and Literatures and Senior Fellow at the Mershon Center for International Security Studies at The Ohio State University. His books include: *Im Visier des FBI. Deutsche Exilschriftsteller in den Akten amerikanischer Geheimdienste* (Metzler, 1995)-English translation: "*Communazis.*" *FBI Surveillance of German Emigré Writers* (Yale, 2000); *Anna Seghers: "Das siebte Kreuz." Welt und Wirkung eines Romans* (Aufbau, 1997); *Anna Seghers im Exil* (Bouvier, 1993); *Max Frisch* (Beck, 1983*); Die deutsche Exilliteratur* (Beck, 1979); *Christa Wolf* (Beck, 1976, 4th, enl. and rev. ed. 1991).

Andrew Strombeck is Assistant Professor of American Literature at Wright State University. His work has appeared in *Cultural Critique*, *African American Review*, and *Postmodern Culture*. He is currently completing a project on postwar American masculinity and conspiracy theory.

Andrea Weiss is a documentary filmmaker, nonfiction author, and Associate Professor in the Film/Video Program at The City College New York. Her many films include *Escape to Life: The Erika and Klaus Mann Story*, *Paris Was a Woman*, *International Sweethearts of Rhythm*, and *Before Stonewall* (for which she won an Emmy Award). Her book, *In the Shadow of the Magic Mountain: The Erika and Klaus Mann Story*, will be published by the University of Chicago Press in 2008.

James Wierzbicki, who specializes in twentieth-century American music and film music in particular, teaches musicology at the University of Michigan.

Index